State of Conflict and Democratic Movement in Nepal

State of Conflict and Democratic Movement in Nepal

by

Uddhab Pd. Pyakurel

Indra Adhikari

Vij Books india Pvt Ltd
New Delhi (India)

Published by

Vij Books India Pvt Ltd
(Publishers, Distributors & Importers)
2/19, Ansari Road
Delhi – 110 002
Phones: 91-11-43596460, 91-11-47340674
Fax: 91-11-47340674
e-mail: vijbooks@rediffmail.com

Paperback Edition 2015

The views expressed in the book are of authors and not necessarily those of the publishers.

Contents

Preface

The politics in Nepal has reached a crucial phase. After the failure of the elected Constituent Assembly (CA) to bring new constitution, new date of the second CA election has been announced. Each and every section of Nepalese society have a great hope that the country, along with the new constitution, would enter into a new phase of democracy along with a number of structural changes.

During the last two decades many a significant issue has emerged on the scene of Nepali society and polity. The process of political transition has unfolded many dimensions of considerable importance. The questions of stabilization of democracy, federalism, ethnicity, regionalism, gender, etc., are becoming the core issues. The issues like causes and consequences of conflict, peace process, and negotiation are gaining rapid currency demanding immediate attention. The internal and external political players have started acquiring a relevant role in this context. Likewise, the civil society finds itself assuming new shape and role accordingly. On the whole, the 'State of Conflict and Democratic Movement in Nepal' is beset with a host of fresh and burning issues. The present volume is an attempt at understanding and analyzing some of these issues.

We would like to acknowledge the inputs provided by Amol Acharya, and express our sincere gratitude to him. In fact, this venture would not have been complete without his timely effort and co-operation. We would also like to thank Brig. P K Vij of Vij Books (India) Pvt. Ltd, for taking interest in bringing out this humble work. Further, we tender our sincere thanks to South Asian Dialogues on Ecological Democracy (SADED), Prof. Lok Raj Baral, and Hem Raj Kafle for their generous help.

While compiling this work, the authors are well aware of their limitations. Therefore, this is never an exercise claiming to be comprehensive and exhaustive. But, nevertheless, it can be said with confidence that this effort, so far, is the only one of its kind that seeks to pave the way for further studies and researches in this field. Hence, it is hoped that readers and scholars interested in Nepal's society, history, polity and the current political transition would find it particularly useful.

Some of the Chapters written by us, that appear in the book may have appeared in some of our earlier works/publications. These have been suitably modified with latest inputs and reproduced in this book. The details of such publications is acknowledged at the end of the book.

June 10, 2013   Uddhab Pd. Pyakurel
& Indra Adhikari

Chapter I

Introduction

Nepal has been in a political transition from as early as 1940 when, for the first time, people started to organize against the Rana oligarchy. Since then, various successful revolutions have been staged, but each one has proved futile in ensuring stability within the nation. That is why Nepali scholars, i.e. senior political scientist Prof. Lok Raj Baral, started saying that Nepal is in "permanent political transition". According to them, continuous interplay between authoritarian (monarchy) and democratic forces for power has been the main reason behind Nepal's prolonged transition (Baral 2012; Upreti 2010). Other than the perennial confrontation between democratic and authoritarian forces, centralized system of governance can also be attributed as a reason behind the political instability in Nepal. The centralized system of governance one-sidedly forced peoples of Nepal with plural identity to accept Sanskritization and Nepalization (Pyakurel 2007), which out-rightly excluded marginalized section of the society from the mainstream of development. However, the concept of Sanskritization and Nepalization gave undue advantage to Brahmin, Chhetri, Newars, etc. to be in the helm of power throughout the course of modern history.

Apart from the class inequality, extreme form of socio-cultural inequality also existed in Nepal among numerous linguistic, ethnic, religious, racial, caste and regional groups. The 'high castes' such as Bahun, Chhetri, Newar and Tarai 'high caste' had better access to material resources, while Dalits, indigenous nationalities, mid-level Madhesis, and Muslims are generally worse off (Lawoti, 2010a). Due to the marginalization, the question of ethnic representation became equally important in Nepal. Strong discontent among ethnic groups can be often witnessed regarding upper-caste domination in representative bodies (Upreti, 2010). Therefore, ethnic organizations started demanding their adequate representation in political institutions along with the political change of 1950. But it was only after the restoration of democracy followed by Jana Andolan I in 1990 some change was visible in this regard. However, even after the dawn of democracy in 1950s and 1990s the minorities and the marginalized were not main streamed to the extent it should have been.

The Maoist Insurgency which began in February 1996 found support from the same oppressed lower castes. The reason is they were successful in portraying the long legacy of oppression based on caste and ethnicity as the main reason behind the initiation of the conflict (Tiwari, 2010; Pyakurel 2007). The Maoists mobilized the ethnic groups, Dalits, Madhesis and women, who had cherished a feeling of discrimination and segregation for a long time. The Maoist attracted them by raising the slogans of "people's democracy", "equality" and "autonomy". On the other hand, failure of the democratic governments in the post- 1990 to bring adequate political and economic reforms also fuelled the growth. In fact, political instability, corruption, unemployment and bad governance fostered a wider dissatisfaction leading to the growth of the movement (Pandey 2005; Pyakurel 2007; Tiwari 2010; Baral 2012). This way, greed and grievances were the two major motivations behind the rise of conflict. However, the theory of grievances best describes the initiation and growth of Maoist movement in Nepal (Tiwari, 2010).

In the meantime, overthrowing of Sher Bahadhur Deuba's government in October 2002 followed by royal coup of February 1, 2005 by King Gyanendra, gradually induced political change in Nepal. On the one hand, the political parties which were for parliamentary democracy with the existence of ceremonial monarchy started realizing the limitation of the system. On the other hand, Maoists also began to realize that the political dynamics of the country was quite complex, and the tactics they were applying to capture the state were becoming doubtful (Upreti 2008). Within this background, both the agitating forces (the then Seven Party Alliance and the Maoists) reached an agreement in November 2005. In other words, King's confrontationist attitude towards the political parties and the Maoists brought them together resulting into the 12-point agreement. The 12-point agreement led to Jana Andolan II and thus King was forced to reinstate democracy in Nepal. The Comprehensive Peace Accord (CPA) signed between the Maoists and the government on 21 November 2006; Madhesh uprising of 2007; election for Constitution Assembly (CA), etc. were the major political steps witnessed after the CPA was signed. However, differing opinions on the issues like restructuring the state ultimately became instrumental reasons for the demise of CA in May 2012 without promulgation of the constitution. The CA's failure not only deepened the conflict among the major political parties, but also pushed the country toward further uncertainty and instability. That is why everyone – either a Nepali or a sympathizer of Nepal-- is worried to find a way out to overcome the present state of instability..

However, we cannot deny that many significant issues have emerged in Nepali society and polity during the last two decades. Though Nepal and Nepalese are compelled to face many more problems in day-to-day life due to the prolonged political transition, it has unfolded many dimensions of considerable importance. The questions of stabilization of democracy, federalism, ethnicity, regionalism, social inclusion, gender, etc., are becoming the core issues. The demography, migration and health issues are gaining rapid currency demanding immediate attention. The media have started acquiring a relevant role in this context. Likewise, the civil society finds itself assuming new shape and role accordingly. These are very significant developments we have ever seen in Nepal. If these assertions are properly discussed and sorted out (that is called institutionalization) in a comprehensive manner, Nepal can achieve a remarkable transformation. In other words, if everything goes well, Nepal will enter into a new phase of democracy along with a number of structural changes. However, the institutionalization process seems to be very discouraging in Nepal, and Nepal has once again missed the opportunity along with failure of the Constitutional Assembly (CA) to bring a new constitution. In fact, the political transition in Nepal has reached a critical phase.

Why? What are the reasons for such a prolonged transition Nepal has been facing? Why political parties are fond of introducing new issues each day, but are not serious in sorting out those issues through the proper mechanism? Where does the major problem lie? Are there external factors as well inducing political actors to prolong transition? These seem to be the prominent issues to be dealt in order to understand Nepal's political situation today. The book, which is a compilation of published articles, attempts to provide answers to the issues raised above. A couple of articles included in this book, were prepared and published before Jana Andolan II (2006); some of them were during the negotiation period and the rest written recently. However, this book does not contain any article that deals with the social and political scenario following the dissolution of CA. Though the titles are different, basically the book deals with the concept of the State of Conflict and Democratic Struggle.

The most important feature of the book is its collection of different articles from varying fields of Nepal's social and political life so as to present a comprehensive picture to the readers about how Nepal has reached the present state. Though the topics discussed in the book are recent ones, each topic also includes the historical part of the subject being dealt with. For example, the chapter about the genesis and growth of Maoist movement in Nepal, besides explaining the core issue, also explains the origin and development of communist movements and parties in Nepal. Similarly, the other chapters also follow the same trend. Except the first and the third chapter which deals, at large, with the political transition and democracy of Nepal respectively, all the other chapters representing the political phenomenon that came into the scene after Jana Andolan- *I* of 1990. The most dominant discussion present in all the chapter is about the Maoist movement. In fact, in one way or the other, the book's one of the important ingredients is the Maoist movement. This is not unusual given the pervasiveness of the movement after the Jana Andolan – I till the present time.

The chapter that follows, titled '**Political Transition in Nepal: An Overview**' by Uddhab Prasad Pyakurel states that Nepal has been in a 'state of permanent transition' all the way since 1940 to the 2011. It explains that 'weak, vision-less and inefficient delivery systems of the governments formed after the revolutions, "unnecessary" dependence on external powers, and lack of clarity of political parties about how to deal with the issues of minorities and deprivations' are the major factors that have directly and indirectly kept Nepal in the vicious cycle of transition. However, the basic focus of the chapter is to explain the political transition that Nepal is going through; generally, after the Jana Andolan II and particularly, after the CA election. Explaining the constitution making process in Nepal by the CA, the chapter first points out and explains the differences of opinion among the political parties over different features of the to-be-promulgated constitution. According to the chapter, political parties of Nepal have differing opinions on the issues like judiciary, land reform and property rights, form of governance, electoral system, federal structure, etc. While in the second part, reasons that helped in delaying the constitution-making process have been explained. Lack of conceptual clarity, political parties' concern about uncertain future, dilemma of the Maoist Party and increased suspicion among other political parties, India - centric Nepali polity, etc. are some of the reasons provided. The chapter concludes by explaining the important of consensus among the major political parties of Nepal for the drafting and promulgation of constitution in time.

The third chapter, entitled '**Conflict transformation: A Nepali Experience**' by Indra Adhikari, opens with a theoretical background of conflict and conflict transformation and, based on the background provided, evaluates Nepal's experience with Maoist conflict and the conflict transformation that started after the 12-point agreement was reached. The chapter explains the contradictory characteristic of Nepali society and state and presents Nepali conflict as a conflict between society and regime. Starting from violent war of Nepali Congress (NC) against the Rana Oligarchy to the recent conflict between state and the Maoist, the chapter explains the failure of state to adopt the policy of inclusiveness and empowerment in the country with such diverse language, culture, social traditions. Claiming the Comprehensive Peace Accord (CPA) along with the peace process between state and the Maoist as a fully indigenous process, the chapter elucidates the formalization of conflict transformation in Nepal. It points out integration of Maoist combatants into Nepal Army (NA) as the main hurdle in the process of conflict transformation. Further, indecisiveness of political parties about the State Restructuring Commission the State Reconciliation Commission as dictated by CPA and the Interim Constitution of Nepal have been described as the weaknesses of the conflict-resolution process in Nepal. Finally, the chapter explains the horizontal spread of conflict from a vertical mode all over the nation. It blames the exponential growth of expectation among the people and algebraic growth of nation's capacity as reasons behind the scattering conflict. In particular, it blames Maoists for bringing-in arm culture in Nepal and predicts the culture to continue for years to come.

The **forth** chapter entitled **'Democracy and Problems of Democratization in Nepal'** by Adhikari explains that 'democratizing democracy' has been difficult in semi-traditional countries. Taking Nepal as a case of semi-traditional countries, it explains the different aspects of government/state that has positively and negatively affected the process of democratization. The article has basically kept its focus over the period after 1990 till the period when the 8-Point agreement was signed between SPA and Maoist on 16 June 2006. According to the chapter, active monarchy, ideological aberrations and inter and intra conflict among the political parties, sporadic election, excessive militarization, inconsistent judiciary are some of the negative factors that have still affected the democratization process of Nepal. However, though very few, the chapter has identified media, civil society and human rights organizations, the 12-point agreement between Seven Party Alliance (SPA) & Maoist and finally the curtailed power of the monarch as some of the positive factors that have been the silver-lining in the dark clouds. Finally,the chapter raises concerns over the environment of mistrust growing between the SPA and Maoist, and also hints towards the breakdown of peace process and finally devaluation of the spirit of the *Jana Andolan II.*

All the other remaining chapters of the book, as mentioned earlier, concern the Maoist movement in one way or the other. For example, completely focused on Maoist movement, the **fifth** chapter entitled **'Genesis and Growth of the Maoist Movement in Nepal'** by Pyakurel explains the origin and growth of Maoist movement in Nepal. In the first part, the chapter elucidates the history of communist parties in Nepal and explains the formation and disintegration of communist parties in Nepal. The first part ends explaining the declaration of "people's war". The second part of the chapter then explains the Maoist movement referring to environment, ideology, organization, and strategy as four dimensions. It argues that the Maoists used all the four dimensions to capitalize the sentiment of the suppressed groups of people like Dalits, women, ethnic/ native groups, regionally backward groups like Terai people and people of Karnali area, to strengthen the movement. The third and the final part discusses the origin, growth and expansion of the Maoist movement. The main argument of the essay is: For the expansion of the movement, the Maoists exploited the multi-ethnic, multi-lingual and multi-cultural status of Nepal in the backdrop of non-functional state and constitution which could not address demands of ethnic and marginalized communities of Nepal.

Taking note of the role of ethnic and marginalized communities with respect to Maoist war, chapter six titled **'Changing Patterns of Nepali Ethnic Movement and Consequences'** by Pyakurel explains how the ethnic communities have been used and then left out (marginalized) in different political eras *viz.* pre-unification, Shah Regime 1769-1846, Rana Regime 1846-1951, Pseudo-Democratic Period 1951-60, Panchayat regime 1960-1990, and Democratic System after 1990. There are seven parts in the chapter. The first part provides an overview on the demography of ethnic communities based on 2001 census and the following six parts focus on the ethnic groups and their access to power and other social domains in different political eras. The chapter views that every ruler from different political eras has either exploited and/or marginalized ethnic communities in order to either ascend or sustain their power. The notion of exploitation and/or marginalization is applicable to all the rulers of Nepal, from Amsuvarma to the present day Maoists. The Shahs seem to have done both – exploited and marginalized the ethnic communities. For example, Prithvi Narayan Shah first exploited ethnic communities by using them in the unification campaign, but later disregarded them in favour of Brahmin and Kshatriyas – a high-class people in Hindu Varna system. However, the Ranas were the ones who out-rightly kept the ethnic communities at bay. Hinduisation, Nepalisation and Ranaisation were the dominant tools used by the Shahs and Ranas to marginalize ethnic communities. According to the chapter, even after the dawn of democracy in 1950s and 1990s, the ethnic communities were not main streamed to the extent it should have been. Except for opening the high posts of army to other castes/ethnicities, giving national status to languages like Newari, Hindi and Maithali and broadcasting news in languages other than Nepali, even the B. P. Koirala government of 1950s could not bring any substantial changes in favour of ethnic communities. The failure of Koirala government, however, can be attributed to its short tenure. Similarly, none of the governments formed after the restoration of democracy in 1990s could do anything substantial to erase the past grievances of the non-democratic governments towards ethnic communities except for the constitution of Nepal recognising Nepal as a multi-ethnic and multilingual nation. The Supreme Court's verdict of 1999 against the use of local language as the official language along with Nepali has been explained as a continuation of Nepalization process where marginalization of ethnic communities continued. Thus, the domination of Brahmin and Kshatriyas in the various state apparatuses continued in the post-democratic era after 1990. Likewise, the Maoists also cleverly used the dissatisfaction of ethnic communities to broaden the base of their party during the insurgency and also to ascended to power through the first Constitutional Assembly (CA) election held in 2008. However, though the ethnic communities have been exploited many times by rulers of different eras to serve their own purposes, ethnic issues are at the centre of politics at present. Towards the end, expressing its dissatisfaction over the modus operandi used by the state to handle the aspiring ethnic movement, the chapter hints towards the problems of ethnic federalism and explains that only a pro-active and matured government can handle the complex issue of federalism.

With the **seventh** chapter entitled '**Women in Conflict: The Gender Perspective in Maoist Insurgency'**, by Adhikari, the book shifts its focus towards analyzing the Maoist insurgency from the gender perspectives. The chapter starts describing the patriarchal characteristic of Nepali society and goes on to explain that women in Nepal have been marginalized socially, economically, politically as well as religiously. It further claims that there is continued discrimination against women legally and practically, even by the state. So, the failure of the governments even after the restoration of democracy in 1990, to uplift the socio-economic conditions of women has been recognized as a reason behind the participation of women in Maoist insurgency.

The chapter states that there are 40 per cent women in the Maoist guerrilla, most of whom are Kiratis from western Nepal. Further, it explains women's participation in Maoist movement as a result of the revolutionary slogans of the Maoists which promised all kinds of emancipation for women. Likewise, social reform activities of the Maoists against alcoholism, polygamy, gambling, sexual exploitation, etc. also attracted women towards the broader cause of insurgency. Atrocities by security forces equally prompted young girls to join the militia either for their security or for taking revenge. Some of the women interviewed, claim to have participated in the insurgency to end class struggle in Nepal; particularly, to end discrimination against women. In addition, some women assert to have joined the movement - 'to see the world', for simplified love and marriage, etc which otherwise was impossible in the traditional society they come from. However, the women guerrillas who say they have taken up arms for women's liberation cannot give logical and analytical views except ready made, stereo typically ideological statements.

Additionally, the chapter notes that women have become double victims due to the insurgency. First, they are direct victims of the security forces as relatives, wife, daughter and mother of the rebels. Second, the Maoists also demanded lodging, food, money and sex from women any time and any day. Finally, acknowledging the empowerment of women brought about by the Maoist movement, knowingly and unknowingly, the article criticizes the under-representation of women in the central and politburo level of the Maoist party as compared to 40% representation of women in the war-field.

Chapter **eight** entitled **'Women in Armed Conflict: Lessons to be Learnt from Telangana People's Struggle'** by Pyakurel extends the study of women in conflict. It is also related to Maoist movement because it is a comparative study of the role of women in two political movements - the Maoist movement in Nepal and the Telangana people's struggle in India. Studying scenario, aspiration and compulsion of women involved in Telangana people's struggle, the chapter compares both the struggles in terms of their objectives, goals and achievements. Finally, the chapter suggests the Maoist leadership to think about the successful landing of their struggle taking lessons from the unsuccessful struggle of Telangana people, which left women who participated in the struggle to suffer without actually emancipating them. The chapter explains that women who participated in the Telangana struggle were not forced into the struggle. However, in case of women participating in the Maoist struggle, both voluntary and forceful involvement has been noticed. After explaining the reasons for the participation of women in Telangana and Maoist struggles, the chapter endorses that both Telangana struggle and Maoist war have sensitized the gender issues and brought the women's agenda in the mainstream politics. After describing the frustrations and dissatisfactions of women involved in Telangana struggle, the chapter concludes that radical agendas would be harmful for society if the agendas were raised just to woo the people. It will not only be harmful to the organizer, but also to the individual participants by causing frustration. Such frustration may possibly direct another revolt.

The **ninth** chapter entitled **'The Vision of the Jana Andolan-II for the Future of Nepal'** by Pyakurel explains the development of politics in Nepal since 1950's to the success of Jana Andolan – II. However, the chapter is mainly focused to explain different reasons of Jana Andolan – II. High hope for peace, democracy and prosperity in the country which came after the SPA and the Maoist signed the 12-point agreements for the purpose, and popular discontent caused by the repeated failure of the king's direct and indirect rules have been explained as the two basic reasons for the success of Jana Andolan – II. Quoting the report of International Crisis Group (ICG), the chapter claims that the Jana Andolan – II was a victory of Nepali on four fronts viz. king, political parties, Maoists and international community. Furthermore, the chapter explains declaration of Nepal as a secular as well as a republic state overthrowing the monarchy as the success that Nepali politics had achieved after the election of Constitution Assembly (CA). Also, under-representation of ethnic minorities and socially excluded groups in the cabinet of Prachanda-led government have been pointed out as being against the spirit of Jana Andolan – II and the interim constitution. At last, the chapter highlights the problems faced by CA in its aim to write a new constitution, and pleads for consensus between the political parties of Nepal for its bright future.

Then the **tenth** chapter entitled **'Internal Conflict in Nepal after the Comprehensive Peace Agreement (CPA)'** by both Adhikari and Pyakurel presents different issues related to the CPA: what is CPA, the tasks opened up by CPA, prohibited actions according to the CPA, major movements after the CPA, internal conflict in Nepal today, causes behind the mushrooming militant conflicts after the CPA, internal conflict and external consequences. After providing the background information related to CPA, the chapter, in general, shifts its focus into the armed conflict seen by the country after CPA while, in particular, the armed conflict seen in the Terai after CPA has been the prime focus of the chapter. The authors report 109 armed, semi-armed, and criminal groups in Nepal, most of them active in Tarai-Madhesh. Unfulfilled hope of people, weak conflict management practice, use of vague, ambiguous and ambivalent terms in each and every agreement between the conflicting parties, unresponsive governments towards the demands of general people until the protest turns violent, and non-adversarial civil society and media have been identified as some of the major factors behind the prolonged state of violence in Nepal. In addition to the above reasons, the vacuum created in Tarai-Madhesh after the Madhesh Movement, criminals from UP and Bihar taking shelter in Nepal, geographical proximity of Tarai-Madhesh with India which can be exploited to weaken Indian influence in Nepal, have been described as some of the reasons behind the armed conflict in Tarai-Madhesh after CPA. The chapter asserts that conflict never remains internal as it spills over to the neighbouring areas and has hinted that the Nepalese conflict would be affecting India more than China; on the part of China, the effect is negligible. Similarly, the chapter expresses its disappointment towards the blame-game that India and Nepal have put on the open-border for the conflict in the plains bordering Nepal and India. Finally, negotiation and dialogue have been described as the only way to ensure peace and make the internal social transformation easy.

The **eleventh** chapter entitled '**Nepal Constituent Assembly Election 2008: An Observer's Account**' by Pyakurel elucidates why the pre-poll surveys and guesses which predicted the win of NC and CPN (UML) in the CA election went wrong and how the CPN (Maoist) came victorious. The article written on the basis of field observation during CA election elucidates that the prime reason behind Maoist victory in the CA election was the terror tactics used by the party. Maoists frightened people and stopped them from uniting for the political campaigns of other parties. Likewise, people were asked/ordered to cast their vote for them. Shedding light on the differences between context and environment of previous elections and that of the CA election, the article concludes that ineffective security agency and the threat tactics used by Maoists had been determinant to the CA election results. However, the article also mentions the inclusive character of candidates, fresh and attractive slogans, radical agenda, spirit of the cadres, dynamic strategy etc. as the strengths of the Maoists over other political parties to reap benefits. In the end, the article has also criticized the international election observers during CA election for not having enough background information about election environment in Nepal and for not travelling the rural parts of Nepal to see how the election was actually being carried out.

The final chapter, '**Relevance of Lohia in Nepali Political Crisis**

Today' Pyakurel acknowledges the permanent political transition and the issues of minorities and socially excluded groups that Nepal is facing at present, and explains the relevance of Lohiya's views (regarding the issues) in case of Nepal. The author argues that the reasons for Nepal being in permanent political transition in spite of several successful revolution are the weak, vision-less and inefficient delivery systems of the subsequent governments formed after the revolutions. In this background, the chapter opines that the Lohiya's idea to quickly implement socio-economic reforms just after the end of revolution would have settled and systematized the political transition of Nepal. Nepali leaders procrastination in implementation of people-oriented socio-economic programs has been described as the missing link between successful revolution and the stabilized democratic process. Similarly, the chapter has presented Lohiya's idea of affirmative action and eradicating the evils of caste system as the first and foremost step to address the demands of minorities and socially excluded groups of Nepal. Similarly, inter-marriage and inter-dining are observed as the best ways to deal with the tribulations posed by the caste system. Likewise, Lohiya's appeal to the Nepalese leaders to maintain good relationship with all the political parties of India and to stop being confined to the Indian government once they ascend to the government has also been suggested as a key way to tackle the turbulent India-Nepal relationship. According to Lohiya, bureaucracy has its own limitations and, unlike political parties and their leaders, it has nothing to do with any radical/progressive agenda that Nepal pursues.

To conclude, this book is successful in taking account of a lot of issues that happened in Nepal, especially after the advent of democracy in 1950s. The book, foremost, has tried to link the past of Nepal with its present; it tries to analyse the present with the lens of historical realities. For example, the permanent nature of transition in Nepal has been attributed to power-greedy rulers of the past who always tried to play India or China card to remain in power. Similarly, marginalization of ethnic communities, Dalits, women, etc. by the King, political parties like Nepal Congress and CPN (UML) has been described as the prime reason behind the growth and rise of Maoist movement in Nepal.

References

Baral, L.R. (2012). *Nepal - Nation-State in the Wilderness: Managing State, Democracy and Geopolitics*. New Delhi, Sage Publications.

Lawoti, Mahendra. (2010a). 'Evolution and growth of the Maoist insurgency in Nepal' in Mahendra Lawoti and Anup K. Pahari (eds.), *The Maoist Insurgency in Nepal: Revolution in the twenty-first Century*. New York: Routledge.

Lawoti, Mahendra. (2010b). 'Maoist Electoral Victory', in Mahendra Lawoti and Anup K. Pahari (eds.), *The Maoist Insurgency in Nepal: Revolution in the twenty-first Century*. New York: Routledge.

Pyakurel, U. P. (2007). *Maoist Movement in Nepal: A Sociological Perspective*. Delhi: Adroit Publishers.

Tiwari, Bishwa Nath. (2010). 'An Assessment of the Causes of Conflict in Nepal', in Mahendra Lawoti and Anup K. Pahari (eds.), *The Maoist Insurgency in Nepal: Revolution in the twenty-first Century*. New York: Routledge.

Upreti, B.C. (2008). *Maoists in Nepal: From Insurgency to Political Mainstream*. New Delhi: Kalpaz Publications.

Upreti, B.C. (2010). *Nepal: Transition to Democratic Republican State*. New Delhi: Kalpaz Publications.

Chapter II

Political Transition in Nepal: An Overview

Uddhab Pyakurel

Overview of Nepal's Struggle for Democracy

Nepal has been struggling to set up a democratic system since 1940s, but it is yet to come up with a stable democratic set up. As the political situation in Nepal has been in turmoil for a long time, some scholars used to say that Nepal is in a "state of permanent transition". Even sixty years after the end of the Rana hereditary 'prime ministerial system' in 1951, the political situation has neither been stable nor has improved. In fact, the struggle for democracy in Nepal gathered momentum after 1940s, especially after four Nepali youths were sentenced to death by hanging, by the government in 1942, as they were involved in protesting against the Ranas. It can be said that the movement in Nepal was inspired by the anti-British movement in India. The Nepalese, especially those who were in India as students, led the anti-Rana movement. Formation of Nepali Congress (NC) and adoption of a strategy of armed revolution to overthrow the Rana regime at its Bairgania (India) Conference of September 26-27, 1950 were two bold decisions which helped and inspired the Nepalese to strengthen the movement. Later, the revolution was supported not only by the then King Tribhuvan, but also by Indian and Burmese socialists, as the former put the throne to risk and went into exile in India; the latter actually fought as comrades-in-arms physically .

The anti-Rana revolution ended successfully on February 18, 1951. It was followed by a tripartite agreement that led Nepal to the path of democratization. But after two years of the successful movement, the then King Tribhuvan amended the interim constitution and started involving himself in day-to-day politics by violating the mandate of the movement, agreements and constitutional provisions. It prolonged the transition for almost a decade. Later in 1959, his son King Mahendra agreed to hold general elections for parliament only after strong pressure exerted by the political parties. The election had paved the way for formation of the first elected government in the country. However, the king dismissed the old one-and-a-half year's government on December 15, 1960, and imposed party-less political system — *Panchayat* - claiming that he (the king) is the source of the constitution, and sovereignty vested in him. Nepali people once again threw out the authoritarian Panchayat regime through their continued struggle followed by successful *Janaandolan* in 1990, and restored the democratic set-up. However, this struggle could not be sustained for long as it was challenged by both extremists viz., the extreme left (the Maoist), and the extreme right (the royalists). Again, in 2006 people came out on the streets to protest against the violent and authoritarian activities of both the extremists, and succeeded in a democracy struggle by overcoming all the threats posed by the institution of monarchy, the political parties, the Maoist, and the international community. In spit of the fact that Nepal witnessed a historical political transformation after 2006, it is yet to overcome the political crisis. In fact, there are still challenges ahead before ending the ongoing political transition by drafting a new constitution. Nepal failed to institutionalize the achievements of the various successful and historical movements. Weak, vision-less and inefficient delivery systems of the governments formed after the revolutions, "unnecessary" dependence on external powers, and lack of clarity of political parties about how to deal with the issues of minorities and deprivations, are the major factors that directly and indirectly have weakened political parties .

In fact, *Janaandolan-II* in 2006 was a path breaking example for democracy struggles in the world. For, in spite of shoot-on-sight curfew imposed by the government, more than one-sixth of the total population of Nepal came in the street to support democracy struggle. And the participants were not only the lawyers, journalists, doctors, poets, writers, teachers and other politically conscious section of people but also the generally apolitical people from every walk of life such as the labourers, farmers, rickshaw pullers, footpath traders, small hoteliers and others participated the movement. Even taxi drivers and transport workers, normally the first to complain about a shutdown which affects their earnings, were supportive. The movement gained further momentum when government employees, and local administration officers, families of security forces and some palace-appointed administrators also supported the *Janaandolan*. The numbers of participants increased when the Maoist facilitated people from the villages to join the movement. It may be recalled that prior to the 12-point understanding, the Maoist used to bar people from taking part in activities announced by other political parties, especially the Seven Party Alliance (SPA).

Why did so many ordinary people join the movement? The answer was simple: they hoped the movement would end the conflict which had adversely impacted their day to day life for a decade. In rural areas, people were victimized by both the security forces and the Maoists during the "people's war". People were forced to provide food and shelter to both sides, but were then victimized by each side for helping their enemies. The security forces killed, raped, arrested, and tortured the villagers blaming them of feeding and sheltering the Maoists, and the Maoists killed, extorted, kidnapped and compelled the people to leave their homes for the same charge. Villagers lost confidence to speak with strangers about polity and society due to the fear created by both sides. On the other hand, people residing in the urban areas had relatively low impact from the Maoist conflict but especially transport workers, hoteliers and petty businessmen in the highway also faced hindrances due to the frequent and indefinite blockades, bandhs, extortion, coercion etc. during the conflict.

No doubt, Nepal has achieved a lot after the successful *Janaandolan-II* in 2006. The election of the Constituent Assembly (CA) held in 2008 made a significant gain in making democracy inclusive. . The CA which has been also functioning as parliament is the most inclusive elected body in South Asia with the representation of almost 33% women, 34% Janajatis, 35% Madhesis and 9% Dalits[1]. Also, peaceful end of the institution of monarchy and entry of the rebel Maoists into the mainstream politics peacefully should be seen as a positive indicator of the democratic innovations in Nepal. However, in the post -CA period, Nepali democracy faces several challenges from various fronts. Though process of constitution making through the CA is a great opportunity for Nepal to consolidate democracy, it seems that every major party wanted to derail the process. On the one hand, the CA could not meet its deadline for promulgating the constitution even after an extension of its tenure for a year in May 28, 2010, there are also dozens of unresolved issues concerning the constitution on the other.

An atmosphere of uncertainties prevail across the country despite the extension of CA tenure for another three months following a 5-point deal signed by heads of three major political parties (UCPN-Maoist, Nepali Congress and CPN-UML) in the country on May 28, 2011. The agreement states that the basic tasks related to the peace process will be concluded within three months. The first draft of the constitution will be submitted

---

1 Of Nepal's population, 37.8 per cent are Janajatis, but 33.39 per cent of CA members are Janajati. On the other hand, Madhesis make up 31.2 per cent of the population but have 34.9 per cent representation in the CA. Dalits make up 13 per cent of the population but have only 8.17 per cent representation. Similarly, 51 per cent of Nepalis are women, but they have only 33.22 per cent representation in the CA (for details, see http://www. nepalitimes.com/issue/2009/03/13/ConstitutionSupplement/15753).

to the CA within three months; various agreements reached previously with the Madhesi Front, including the one to make the Nepal Army (NA) inclusive will be effectively implemented, and the prime minister will resign to pave the way for the formation of national unity government based on consensus.

This is the second extension of the CA after its term (defined in the constitution) was over last year on May 28, 2011. Last year, it was the Maoist Party which did hard bargaining with the then government and its coalition partners. This time, the NC along with the major Madhes based parties put forward conditions for the extension of the CA. Finally, the three major political parties signed a 3-point pact and extended the term of CA for a period of one year. But not a single point of the agreement was implemented by political parties after the extension of the CA last year. It was primarily due to the vagueness of the agreement. Interestingly, a similar ambiguity has existed in 5-point deal signed on May 28, 2011. As the clauses of the deal are ambiguous and lack clarity and detail, the concerned parties have started interpreting the clauses of the agreement in their own ways. For instance, Clause 1 of the agreement states, "basic tasks related to the peace process will be concluded." There is no precision about what "basic tasks" means. According to the Maoist, Clause 1 is related only to the issues of management of its combatants, removing the dual security provision of its leadership, and reaching an agreement on the modality of integration. Clause 1, as per the Maoist, deals with the number of combatants to be integrated, the ranks of the combatants after integration, the rehabilitation package, and the regrouping of combatants. But, the NC and other non-Maoist parties link this clause with other issues such as surrendering of arms to the state, returning the seized property to the owners, dismantling the Maoist's paramilitary force (the Youth Communist League). Also, there is party-wise and individual-wise interpretation about when the Prime Minister must resign, and who would lead the country after his resignation.

The presentation of the first draft of the constitution within three months seems impossible unless the parties intensify parleys to resolve the 99 unsettled crucial issues. 78 of the total 99 these issues are related to state structuring. The three major parties have agreed to form State Restructuring Commission (SRC) to recommend the model of federation. However, the decision has not materialized as yet. There is speculation that the Maoist, the NC and the-UML may agree to promulgate a new constitution without declaring the form of the federal set-up. Rather, they would agree to have a federation only after the recommendation of the

SRC. On the contrary, Madhesi parties and ethnic organizations, doubting the intention of the three major parties, have said that they will not allow promulgation of the new constitution without a clear-cut provision on federation.

Further, the issue of mass integration or at least ten thousands Madhesi youth into the Nepal Army seems to have complicated Nepal's political transition. Though no figures are mentioned in the recent agreement, Madhesi parties are demanding that 10,000 Madhesi youth to be given a chance to join the Nepal Army. This agenda will be initially backed by those who oppose Maoist combatants' integration, thus complicating the integration issue. Eventually, all hill people including the Maoist, are likely to oppose the proposal to integrate Madhesis in the army, in spite of the fact that the move will help the army become an inclusive institution. Consequently, Madhesi parties are likely to launch protests demanding the implementation of that demand

As all other non-Maoist parties seem to be reluctant about further extension of the term of the CA and as common people also seem to be tired of its repeated extensions, unless there is substantial progress in the peace process, the CA may become defunct by August 28, 2011. Once the tenure of the CA will be over without any progress in the integration process of Maoist combatants, they are likely to take a decision to prepare for a "people's revolt" once again[2].

Constitution making Process

In spite of the fact that the CA, which has been simultaneously working as parliament in Nepal, was able to endorse and institutionalize the decision of the Interim Parliament to replace 210-year old Hindu Monarchical Nepal to a secular and federal republic by the election of Nepal's first President and Vice-President, it had not done much work on statute drafting within its tenure. However, the CA members across the country were mobilized from February 27, 2009 by dividing them into 40 separate teams to collect public opinion. Around 3.5 million copies of 300 semi-structured -- close-ended and open-ended – questions were circulated. The CA secretariat tabulated the public opinion and incorporated them into the preliminary concept papers to be drafted by the Constitutional Committee (CC) and

---

2 See, Uddhab Pyakurel, Nepal After Three Months, IDSA Web Commentary, June 17, 2011, available at http://www.idsa.in/idsacomments/NepalafterThreeMonths upyakurel_ 170611.

other 10 thematic committees[3]. Most of the CA's thematic committees submitted their drafts to the CA. However, differences of opinion were found in 210 issues while collecting from various thematic committees in order to make a list. Along with them, there were 78 unresolved issues related only to State Restructuring Committee.

Regarding the progress about statute writing, only seven meetings of the CA were held during the time of the extension period from May 29 2010 to May 28, 2011. The CA has formed a high level task force of political parties under the leadership of the Maoist supremo in order to achieve a consensus on these 210 contentious issues. The task force was able to narrow down the contentious issues from 210 to 73. There was consensus on 127 issues by the end of December 20, 2010. In the meantime the task force became defunct after the Maoist decided not to extend that term. Interestingly, the decision came just before the Palungtar Plenum of the party through which the Maoist party had adopted a political line to prepare for 'people's revolt'. However, the Maoist party agreed to form and lead the Difference Resolution Sub-Committee (DRSC), under the CC in order to deal with disputed issues related to constitution writing on February 24, 2011. The Maoist party again decided not to extend the term of sub-committee, once its term was over in March 14, 2011, though the sub-committee had already settled other 40 issues within a short period and brought down the number of dispute to 35. Again, the Maoist supremo Pushpa Kamal Dahal expressed his willingness to resign from the post of the convener of the sub-committee. It is said that Dahal's decision to quit was due to the continued pressure from Maoist hardliners, who held the view that the party "had to compromise a lot and go back on its position on various issues" for the sake of consensus. However, Dahal again agreed on April 7, 2011 to continue in leading sub-committee following the mounting pressure from other political parties and civil society. Till May 28, 2011, there were only 21 issues that (along with the separate 78 issues which are directly related to state restructuring) remained as disputed.

A perusal of the main reports of all the 10 thematic committees and

---

3   The names of thematic committees are: (1) Committee for Restructuring the State and Sharing of State Power (2) Committee on Judiciary (3) Committee on Natural Resources, Economics Rights and Sharing of Revenues (4) Committee for Determining the Structure of Legislative Bodies (5) Committee for Determining the Structure of Governance of State (6) Fundamental rights and Directive Principle Committee (7) Committee for the protection of the Rights of Minority and Marginalized Community (8) Committee for Determining the Structure of Constitutional Bodies (9) Committee for Preserving National Interest (10) Committee for Determining the Basis of Cultural and Social Solidarity (11) Constitutional Committee

various decisions taken by the DRSC through a range of meetings, show differences of opinions on the following issues:

1. Nepal as a Republic, Federal and Secular State: Though all major parties are working together on these issues, and all these themes have been adopted as part of the Interim Constitution 2007, these issues are yet to be a unanimous national agenda due to the voices of dissent from some smaller parties in the CA viz., Rastriya Prajatantra Party (RPP-Nepal) has been proposing to revive the constitutional monarchy and declare Nepal once again as a Hindu State; and Rastriya Janamorcha Nepal (RJN) has been advocating against any kind of federal set-up in Nepal. The RJN is of the opinion that federalism brings about division and disintegration in the country. The RPP Nepal had advocated for a national referendum to decide Hindu state, monarchy, and federalism before the constitution is finally drafted.

2. Nepal as a Multi-national State based on Pluralism: The Maoist have proposed to remove the word "pluralism" from the preamble of the constitution. They argue that after having followed the competitive multi-party system, it is unscientific to adopt the provision of 'pluralism' in the constitution. Taking this stand of the Maoist, NC and UML have expressed their doubt over the intention of Maoist. They hold the view that Maoists have not yet accepted democracy from their heart. Pluralism and plural thoughts, for them, are the corner stone of democracy. That is why, they want to enlist basic or fundamental principles of democracy such as freedom of press, rule of law, human rights, adult franchise, periodic election, free and accountable judiciary, supremacy of constitution, social justice, etc., in the constitution, and uphold or endorse them by making these principles unamendable . When the Maoist opposed the addition of all these points to the list of unamendable provisions of the constitution, other parties have accused the Maoist party of nurturing authoritarian thought and character by denying pluralism and the competitive multi-party system.

3. Right to Self-Determination: The debate is about preferential rights on natural resources, economic sector and prior rights (*Agradhikar*) on politics should be given to oppressed community, Janajatis, indigenous people and Madhesis. Though the NC and the UML and other parties are in favour of the rights and identities of the oppressed community, Janajatis, indigenous people and Madhesis, they are not inclined to consent to the right to self-determination. The Maoist holds that the oppressed community, Janajatis or indigenous people and Madhesis should be given the right to self-determination, autonomy and self-governance.

4. Inclusive Polity and Proportional Representation System: The debate on this issue is whether or not there should be freedom to form political parties, or should there be some preconditions to form a political party. This issue emerged when political parties had differences over the conditions for opening up political parties. The Maoist has forwarded a new condition in this regard, according to which, "It will not be considered prohibitive to formulate a law on banning political parties that encourage formation of mechanism or structure working toward treason and betrayal of the nation, working as stooges of the foreign powers, plotting against the nation, and regressive work." The NC and UML have expressed doubt about this the in new constitution stating that this provision is a ploy of the Maoist to ban the political parties that hold different philosophies and ideas.

5. Land Reforms and Property Rights: Three major political parties have reached an understanding to impose land ceiling. But a fundamental difference among them is whether land beyond the fixed ceiling which an individual can own, can be seized by compensation. Maoist party is against the compensation, whereas others want to seize the excess portion of land only after providing compensation. Also, the Madhes based parties are not in favour of ceiling on land, but they want ceiling on property as per the market value.

6. On Judiciary: Major differences regarding the following points have been observed: (I) separate constitutional court to interpret the constitution; (II) Such interpretation should be made by the Supreme Court, and (III) whether the judiciary should be a separate constitutional body or it should be under the parliament. The Maoist had proposed that the Chief Justice of the Supreme Court could also be appointed from outside. The NC and UML had objected to this provision. For them, the system of appointing judges from outside of the courts can lead to the politicization of the courts. They also did not agree to the appointment of judges. For the Maoist, a special judicial committee of federal legislature should appoint the judges. The NC, UML and other parties were in favour of appointing judges from the judicial council. Over the issue of whether the constitution is to be interpreted by the federal Supreme Court or the parliament, the Maoist stand was for the system of interpreting constitutional issues by the parliament. On the other hand, the UML, the NC and other parties argued that the right to interpret the constitution should be given to the Supreme Court on the principle of check and balance of power. Eventually, an agreement was made on the proposal of 'Madhesi Janadhikar Forum (MJF) that recommends a Constitutional Court for dealing with the issues of interpretation of the constitution, issues of national concern and importance, human rights and citizens' concerns, and issues related to policies of the country.

7. System/Form of Governance: On the issue of form of government, the parties are debating whether to have 'Westminster" system, or go in for Presidential system, or to have a different one. The Maoist party proposed the Presidential system with the executive power. In fact, the Maoist advocated that the executive president be directly elected by the people. NC and UML are in favour of the Westminster model parliamentary system, though UML's formal proposal advocates for popularly elected Prime Minister. The NC and UML are of the view that if the president is directly elected from the people there is a probability for him "to be powerful and even authoritarian." They further state that in a country where there is diversity of culture, language and race, president with executive power directly elected by the people will not appropriately symbolize national unity. They argue that if the prime minister is elected from the parliament and executive power is vested in him, and if the president is elected from the parliament and is given constitutional status, the president can represent the diversity of the country, and the president can also be elected from the minority, marginalized, and other communities. In the question of stable governance, the NC and UML proposed that a no-confidence motion can be registered against the prime minister within one year of assumption of office, and in case of doing so, the opposition has to suggest the name of the future prime ministerial candidate. NC and UML believe that this provision will contribute to minimizing political instability and frequent over throwing the government. Terai Madhes Loktantrik Party (TMLP) wants that the president be elected from the Lower House of parliament as the head of the State and Head of the Government. For the TMLP, if the head of the state and head of the government is the same person, it can contribute to ending political instability.

Also, a proposal of Maoist party states there should be a provision to recall the popularly elected president, and the matter should be decided by two-thirds majority of a political party to which he belongs. Again, the Maoist party is for an all-party cabinet, based on their strength in the parliament. However, non-Maoist parties unanimously oppose these ideas on the grounds that these proposals are against the spirit of democracy. About the proposal of Madhes-based parties, the MJF is in harmony with the Maoist's proposal to have a popularly elected executive head, but the

TMLP is for executive President elected by the parliament.

8. Electoral System: Political parties are divided over the issues of electoral system also. The NC and UML favour mixed electoral system with compensation. The Maoists favour multi-member Direct Full Proportional Election system in which people have to vote for a party's symbol, and all the candidates of that single political party (under that symbol) would be declared elected once the party bagged majority of votes in a particular constituency. In between, the CA committee on determining the form of legislature bodies finalized its preliminary concept and report on July 29, 2009 through majority. According to the report, there will be 151-member Federal House of Representatives elected through mixed electoral systems (76 - will be elected under a first-past-the-post electoral system, and the rest 75 - through a proportional electoral system). It has been decided that there would be a 51-member National Parliament Assembly, out of which 38 members would represent states, and 13 would be nominated by the House of Representatives. The draft has recommended 35-member unicameral legislatures in the states which would also be elected through a mixed electoral system. Also the committee has recommended giving the right to vote to all Nepali citizens aged 18 years and above. The proposal was supported by the NC and UML. However, the Maoist party has written a note of dissent on various issues of the report. According to the Maoist party's stand, there should be a multi-member constituency system with a 245-member unicameral people's representative, similar to the system practiced in China. The party also proposed forming a standing committee with 21 members at the most, under the people's representatives with an authority to carry out legislative work when the people's representatives are not in session. Regarding the issue on universal franchise, the Maoist proposal is to allow the franchise for all above 16 years of age.

9. Federal Structure: If we go through the debate about restructuring the state, it is clear that   there is no single voice within and between various parties. The NC and UML leaders have put forward their idea of state restructuring individually. The NC has not officially submitted its outline for state restructuring in the CA. Though UML has submitted its copy, it is hard to tell which one is officially approved by the party. However, a very important fact is that the NC and UML are against making caste and ethnicity the basis of state restructuring, and argue that promoting caste distinction gives rise to the communalism, and finally leads to communal violence.

According to the report submitted to the CC, the country shall be restructured into 14 Provinces based on 'identity' as the primary basis for determination of provinces, whereas 'capability' would be the secondary basis. The Committee has proposed 23 autonomous regions. According to the report, indigenous people and Madhesi people shall be entitled to right to self-determination with regard to politics, culture, religion, language, education, etc. The NC[4] and the UML[5] have been claiming that the division of provinces on the basis of caste and ethnicity might disintegrate the nation, while Madhes-based political parties have been demanding the 'entire Madhes (Terai) as a single province'.

Though the Maoist has been backing the proposed 14 provinces passed by majority votes in the Committee. The UML lawmakers defied the party decision and supported it. The UML lawmakers' decision to support Maoist's proposal was possible as most of the lawmakers in the committee were from ethnic group background and Madhesi community. In fact, the preliminary report with 78 contentious points is yet to be settled. Earlier, the political parties decided to withhold the report of the State Restructuring Committee as they agreed to form a high-level State Restructuring Commission to suggest the model of federalism and number of provinces prior to finalizing the committee's report. But an all-party meeting decided to forward the report to the CC, after they agreed to send it to the drafting committee at the all-party meeting, on the condition that the government would form the commission soon. This was not sent to the CC because the leaders of the major parties have agreed to form a SRC, which is expected to be formed (as per Article 138 (2) of the Interim Constitution) as soon as the new government is in place[6].

The Maoist and Madhes-based parties, however, are against forming the commission. They have argued that further delaying the issue of state restructuring, under the pretext of forming the body, was not wise.

---

4   The NC has concluded that a maximum of seven federal states will be viable for Nepal. According to the NC decision, the federal structure will be divided as following: one province in the far-western region, two provinces in Madhes, one in Kathmandu Valley and it's surrounding areas, one in eastern hill districts, and two states in the central region (http://www.reviewnepal.com/detail_news.php?id=2324).

5   In fact, the UML has proposed 15 states—five in the Tarai (Bhojpura, Mithila, Birat and Lumbini) and 10 in the Hills and Mountains (Limbuwan, Kirat, Sunkoshi, Tamsaling, Newa, Magarat, Tamuwan, Gandaki, Karnali and Khaptad states) (for details, see http://www.ekantipur.com/2009/11/17/0/State-Restructuring-UML-proposes-15-states/303035/).

6   For details, browse http://www.ccd.org.np/new/index.php?newsletter_detail_id=45, accessed by author on June 27, 2011

Though there are twenty-nine parties in the CA, most of the contentions in the committee discussions were specific to UML, NC and Maoist. As these three parties did not move from their respective stands, committee discussions ended inconclusively. Other parties also expressed their diverse opinions in the course of discussions, but they waited for the big parties to come to the meeting and take their consensus for the solution to many key contentious issues. They seemed to have succumbed themselves to the notion that the big parties' decisions would finally overpower and dominate the political setting. The following section deals about the reasons that have helped delaying the constitution-making process.

Lack of Conceptual Clarity

The major problem that confronts the constitution-writing process is the lack of conceptual clarity of the CA. The CA could not decide the kind of model -- communist, or social democracy, or liberal democratic constitution. The NC proposed to decide about the model of the constitution on priority before debating on other issues. But the Maoist party suggested not to postpone the decision on the constitutional provisions, saying that the basic model of the constitution would be decided once the draft constitution is in hand. Here, the non-Maoist parties were right, i.e., the constitution-making process would be easier if there was agreement and clarity on the type of constitution they are going to draft.

Political Parties' Concern about Uncertain Future

The transitional phase has been prolonged solely because of the fact that these parties are not sure about their future after the constitution comes into force. The Maoist party, which has emerged as the single largest party with 38 per cent seats in the CA, seems to be reluctant to introduce the new constitution since it has sensed that it cannot impose its views in the constitution. Also, the leadership is not sure whether the party would be able to continue its position once it becomes a 'civilian party' by detaching itself from arms and combatant. Such uncertainty of the Maoist leadership regarding the future seems to be genuine as it would have been impossible for the Maoist party to bag the large number of votes in the last election if it could not have created an atmosphere of intimidation and terror[7] through arms and combatant. And the Maoist leadership is well-known for the impact the combatants, cantonment and Youth Communist League

---

7   For details about the situation in Nepal during the election, please see, Uddhab P. Pyakurel, Nepal Constituent Assembly Election 2008: An Observer's Account, *Mainstream*, Vol XLVI No 29. Available at http://www.mainstreamweekly.net/article804.html.

(YCL) had on the election results. On the contrary, the Maoist leadership seems to have suffered from fear for its combatants cantoned for more than five years. Dahal's statement, which was shared with his "hardliner comrades" just before the Palungtar Plenum and Bhattarai's plea to the party and government against the conspiracy to kill him, can be analyzed in this regard. According to a report[8], Dahal once stated, "I will be finished first if there is no integration. Then you all will not remain safe. That is why we should conclude the matter related to army integration". Also, the Maoist party seems to be more conscious of the "culture of threat" once its Vice-Chairman Baburam Bhattarai had received death threat from its own members. In fact, Bhattarai then informed Home Minister Krishna Bahadur Mahara and party General Secretary Ram Bahadur Thapa about the incident. He also informed Chairman Pushpa Kamal Dahal about the incident saying "people who can threaten me today can also threaten you tomorrow; people with criminal mentality in the party should be punished"[9]. In this very complex situation, Maoist party seems to be in a quandary about where to go and what line to follow. That is why, they often shift party positions regarding the peace and constitution-making process.

Other major parties have also suffered from such uncertain future. The NC, which was badly defeated in the last election, seems to be optimistic about the future. But its leadership is fully aware of the complicated situation; they know that the party has to come up with a visionary proposal in order to address the voices of new aspirant groups for which its leadership is yet to be ready. In this situation, the NC may not improve its last election results. Also, the NC is focusing on ending the peace-process rather than on constitution-writing, as it is aware of the constitutional provision which states that each and every article of the constitution has to be finalised either through consensus or through two-thirds majority, though without the Maoist support this is not possible. For the UML, its leadership has suffered from a similar anxiety about the future as they are vertically divided on each and every major issue. The Madhes-based political parties seem to be going through a similar anxiety crisis as they could not be united but were to split in many groups for power. Such a split has been considered by Madhesi people themselves as betrayal of successful Madhes Andolan 2007. While analyzing all the dynamics, it seems that there is consensus between all the major parties of

---

8   See, Bhojaraj Bhat *"Chalbaji Ki Badhyata? (Strategy or Compulsion?)" Nepal Weekly,* May 13.

9 For details, see http://www.nepalnews.com/archive/2011/may/may17/news02.php._

not completing the mission of writing the constitution on time so that they could remain intact in their present position.

Dilemma of the Maoist Party and Increased Suspicion among Other Political Parties

If we analyze the present situation, the Maoist party, being the single largest party in the CA, is more at fault as it is reluctant to adopt pluralism with multi-party competitive politics. Unwillingness of the Maoist party to dismantle its cantonment and paramilitary forces - the YCL - also creates confusion and suspicion. It is busy in forming a new "volunteer force" instead of implementing its promise to dismantle the existing YCL. More than that, their statements and decisions to retrieve the violent politics have given ground to others to suspect the Maoists' and unwillingness to join the peaceful democratic politics through democratic constitution. On reading a statement of the Maoist leadership, i.e., "Anarchy and instability help Maoist to consolidate power for the further revolution — people's republic," one always has a doubt about Maoist commitment towards peaceful and plural politics. Also, the decision at a party plenum of the Maoist Party held in last November in Gorkha, a revolt and state capture could alone remove people's doubts over the Maoist strategy.

It seems that the recent 7-point agreement signed by the chairpersons of two communist parties — the Maoist and the UML — helped in polarizing the political parties sharply into two blocs — the leftist and non-leftist or democrat. The NC seems to be more conscious of its leftist counterparts after the agreement came into existence. I personally think that this is a genuine concern of the NC party, and past experiences give a lot of indication for the NC to be fearful of others. This is because the NC leadership has given a kind of moderation to the Maoist party in the beginning even if others, including the UML party and international communities, criticized the NC's approach as "unnecessary".

The government led by NC President late G.P. Koirala managed to hold the election of the CA even though the situation was not favourable due to the intimidation and violent activities of the Maoists. It has been acknowledged that the Maoist party could secure 27 per cent vote and emerge as the single largest party, only due to the patience and tolerance shown by the NC party and G.P. Koirala. In fact, the NC was arguing that bringing a Maoist party into mainstream parliamentary politics was more important for the NC as well as the Nepali democracy and was prepared to bear with the adverse electoral prospects within one or two elections. But the Maoist party always considers NC's "wise" decision as its weakness. It is the Maoist party which goes all-out against the interests of the NC when the time comes to reciprocate NC's support. Either it is the advocacy of the left alliance, or the advocacy for the alliance of real nationalists including the ex-monarchists; attempts of the Maoist do not help to implement the agreement entered into with the NC. The Maoist party, on the one hand, appreciated the role of late G.P. Koirala for bringing the then rebellious Maoist into the mainstream politics. At the same time they also decided not to support his efforts to become the first president of the country. Once the Maoist party emerged as the single largest party in the CA and formed a coalition government under the leadership of its Chairperson Dahal, it pushed the NC into the opposition by denying the NC's demand to have Defence portfolio in the cabinet. Instead of negotiating with the NC on its concerns, the Maoist leadership went on saying that "beggar cannot choose." Then onwards, the trust deficit between the two largest parties began.

If we observe the priority of Nepali political parties today, it seems that the non-Maoist parties, especially the NC, have given priority to bring the peace process to the logical end before promulgating the new constitution. In other words, the NC shows its unwillingness to let the constitution be promulgated unless the Maoist take some steps forward on the on-going peace process by implementing the past agreements such as dismantling of paramilitary forces, dismantling of the cantonment by rehabilitating and integrating the Maoist combatants, return of the confiscated properties by the Maoist, etc. All non-Maoist forces by-and-large have an agreement on it. According to them, there should be substantial time gap between the end of the peace process and to promulgate the constitution. Then only the country will save the constitution-writing process from the shadow of Maoists' 'arms and armies', and people's desire to have a democratic constitution will be met. That is why it was mentioned in the Comprehensive Peace Accord (CPA) that the task related to integration and rehabilitation of the Maoist combatants should be complete within six months of the election of the CA, and constitution should be promulgated in two years.

On the contrary, the Maoist party does not seem to be interested in concluding the on-going peace process before writing the new constitution. Rather, the Maoist wants to keep the cantonment intact till the new election so that it can influence the election in the future too. Sometimes the Maoist party advocates for the 'leftist and nationalist alliance' just to avoid the concerns put forward by the NC. Once there is a call from the Maoist party on 'leftist alliance' a faction of the UML party becomes instrumental in helping the Maoist in this regard. However, it eventually helps to absolve Maoist from all past agreements. Though it was the NC which helped to form the UML leader Madhav Nepal-led government just after Maoist-led government resigned, the recent alliance between two leftists became possible because the UML was not happy with the NC leader, late Koirala, when he offered equal seats to the UML and the Maoist in the interim parliament. The move has been considered by UML leaders as an attempt of the NC to weaken the UML.

If we analyze Maoist party's decisions of the last couple of months, we get an impression that it wants to keep intact the cantonment till the new elections so that it helps them not only to influence the election outcome but also to provide large monetary benefit it is receiving from the cantonment as levy. In fact, it has changed its decision thrice either to focus on constitution writing and ending the peace process, or to prepare for "people's revolt" within a year. The Maoist leaders are playing such dual role even after they signed 5-point agreement. Leaders like Dr. Baburam Bhattarai, who has been popularized by media and foreigners as pro-democracy and pro-peace leader inside the Maoist party, also takes the position that integration of the Maoist combatants as well as the writing of the constitution "should take place simultaneously"[10]. Such repeated ideological dilemmas and confusion of the Maoist whether to lead or to withdraw from the sub-committee (formed to settle disputed issues related to constitution-writing) led us to conclude that they have other priorities over the constitution-making process.

Another very important issue is that the Maoist party always shows it vertical division once it has to implement provisions of the agreement signed with other counterparts. According to Lok Raj Baral[11], individualistic thinking and lack of political culture are the leading causes of such a rift inside the Maoist Party. He further argues that there should not be such a rift, and differences if the Maoist party goes through an objective analysis on the idea of extreme Maobad before taking any precipitous decision on their "revolt". Here, I think, it has to be analyzed – whether such internal rift of the Maoist party is genuine or artificial just to avoid implementing their earlier promises. Evidence shows that the entire leadership of the Maoist party (either so-called hardliner or soft) sits with a united version when there is dialogue/negotiation with other

---

10 See an interview of Dr. Bhattarai by Jyoti Malhotra, *Business Standard*, May 29, 2011.

11 See Lok Raj Baral, *Maobadi Bhitra Nirarthak Jhagada* (Meaningless Fight inside the Maoist), *Kantipur*, June 20, 2011.

parties. Surprisingly, however, they show their vertical division after the dialogue gets over, and time comes for implementing it. A political analyst considers the rift of the present Maoist party as an 'acting' or drama[12]. The same thing has been repeated during and after May 28, 2011 too; the entire leadership was together to put forward their agenda while their dialogue was on about how to go for another extension of the CA. Dahal himself not only shared dais with Baidya, but also went on talking in Baidya's line on May 27, 2011. He stated, "they are not surrendering weapons easily which was exchanged with human blood"[13]. As there are many things to be done by the Maoist party based on the 5-point agreement, a "serious" rift has again been developed within the Maoist party. It is said that Dahal and Baidya are at loggerheads ever since the former took the line of peace and constitution on April 30, and decided to accept Nepal Army's proposal on army integration and ending the dual security system of Maoist leaders. The miffed Baidya faction has intensified its campaign countrywide. The Baidya faction has circulated a two-page document to leaders and cadres alleging that Dahal is deviating from the official revolutionary line, putting aside the issue of national independence, heading towards a democratic republic instead of "people's republic", disarming the combatants in the name of integration, accepting Indian investment in hydropower sector, abusing party funds and attempting to maintain relations with the Indian intelligence. The following are the main points of the document entitled "Problems of Deviations in Chairman Comrade", which has charged Dahal with financial irregularities and misuse of resources[14].

- On the issue of financial discipline, Dahal is seen tilted toward corruption.

- Dahal is seen having the tendency of doing anything -- both moral and immoral -- for the sake of power, money and prestige.

- Dahal has deliberately left the party without an accounting system and misused financial means and resources in an individualistic way.

- Dahal is of "self-centric individualistic tendency", intolerance toward those holding dissent and using his power to silence their voices.

---

12 For details, see Bijay Kumar, *Rajnaitik Siddhanta Ra Jibanka Pharak Pharak Ranga* (Political Ideology and Different Dimensions of Life), *Kantipur*, June 18, 2011

13 See *Kantipur*, May 13, 2011

14 For details, see http://www.mastinepal.com/showthread.php?t=52477; http://www.ekantipur.com/np/2068/2/29/full-story/330778.html.

- The chairman has developed a "fascist tendency".

- Dahal is extending relations with the Indian intelligence agencies.

- On the peace process, the hard-line faction has launched criticism campaigns against Dahal for bringing the Maoist combatants under the control of the Special Committee and accused him of disarming the PLA and emptying the cantonments in the name of "regrouping" without forging a national security policy, controlling the open border and setting up a border security force.

- The circular states Dahal deviated from the party's ideological goals by not launching appropriate programs to counter the party's "principal enemy" -- India -- and accused Dahal of extending relations with the sympathizers of "Indian expansionism and its comprador class".

- The Baidya faction has also come down heavily on Dahal's moves on the constitution drafting front as well. "Despite being said that we would go for a federal system with autonomy to ethnicities, the documents states that Dahal has emphasized unitary and centralized system". According to the document, Dahal has agreed to go for bicameral legislature succumbing to the "bourgeois theory of separation of power, and to minimize the participation of people in the judiciary under the pretext of judicial independence, instead of empowering the "People's Assembly".

- The document also criticizes Dahal for agreeing to make appointments of judges by a commission, not by the federal assembly as demanded by the party. The document expresses dissatisfaction over the party's move to go for "federal democratic republic" instead of the party's line of "People's Federal Democratic Republic."

- In a strategic move, the Maoist Chairman Pushpa Kamal Dahal is preparing to shift his focus for the time being to the constitution writing process to ensure that it moves ahead simultaneously[15] with the peace process in the next three months. Party insiders said Dahal took the decision to persuade the disgruntled hardliner faction led by Vice-Chairman Mohan Baidya to accept the party leadership's decision to complete the 'fundamentals' of the peace process as per the five-point deal. Baidya has disowned the five-

---

15 For details, see http://www.ekantipur.com/2011/06/04/top-story/peace-statute-will-go-side-by-side-dahal/335115.html.

point deal that led to the extension of the CA tenure on May 28. He has objected to Dahal's decisions, including the one to send Maoist combatants deployed for security of Maoist leaders to cantonments and handing over their weapons to the Special Committee. In fact, the Baidya faction has lately launched vitriolic polemics against Dahal and has been registering a series of notes of dissent against the party's decision. The relations between the hard-line faction and the moderators have further strained after the party establishment decided to end security being provided by Maoist combatants to the senior party leaders. Over two dozen combatants deployed for the security of the leaders from the hard-line faction have not yet surrendered their weapons and returned to the cantonments, despite the party's official decision to this effect. For the Baidya faction, any move by the party to hand over weapons or combatants to the government would tantamount to a complete "surrender" and dishonour for the combatants. The faction argues that peace process issues can only make headway if they are taken up simultaneously with the statute writing process. The integration of former Maoist combatants, Baidya insists, can start only after contentious issues in the new constitution are resolved. It is likely that the Dahal faction will address the rift by adopting Baidya's idea of making parallel progress in the statute drafting and peace processes which seem to be unacceptable to other non-Maoist forces including the NC. In fact, the NC has said the statute's first draft cannot be introduced without completing the peace process[16].

India - Centric Nepali Polity

There is no doubt about the socio-cultural proximity between the two countries - Nepal-and India. As Nepal being located in the Himalayas and being surrounded by India on three sides, India cannot remain unaffected by any kind of internal matters in Nepal. Hence, the Nepal-India relationship is called "indo-closed" and "indo-opened" with the sharing of not only open border, but also security threats by foreign aggressors in either country. The dual characters— open borders[17] and socio-cultural proximity, have "people flow" between the two neighbours and established

---

16 http://www.ekantipur.com/2011/06/13/top-story/statute-draft-congress-for-revision-of-calendar/335618.html

17 In fact, Indo/Nepal border, which is open, is 1,580 kilometers long with 940 KM land boundary and 640 Km river boundary.

the good people-to-people relation for centuries.[18] However, at the same time, Nepal's India - centric polity becomes a big hurdle, and it affects the internal socio-political matters.

By and large, Nepali political leadership including the Kathmandu elites, are India - centric in many ways. They want to involve India unnecessarily in all internal matters, before resolving their own issues. Due to such mis-reporting of Kathmandu elites, middle ranks of Nepalese all over Nepal have built a negative perception towards India and Indians. Also, political forces helped defaming India inside Nepal as both the right-wing and left-wing Nepali political forces were in connivance to popularize anti-Indianism in Nepal.[19]

In fact, till recently, it was only the NC which was considered as 'India friendly political party' in Nepal. Then, the Madhes-based political parties also joined the camp of 'India friendly political party'. Hence, the NC was defamed as an 'anti-national element' by the monarchy backed party-less Panchayat system till 1990. However, the NC also seems to be divided on the issue of how to deal with India; there were some leaders in NC who used to join the so-called "nationalist camp" and distanced themselves from India. The NC seems to be hesitant to show its unconditional support to India in new context.. So far as the major grievances of the NC are concerned, the NC is willing to be the best friend of India in Nepal, but that sentiment of the NC should not be taken as granted. Rather India should take the NC on board before the former revises or introduces the new policy on Nepal. A similar sentiment seems to be with the Madhesi parties too. Such a sentiment seems to have developed after 2006 once the NC cadres, especially those 'conservatives' who did not like the recent political change, including the ouster of monarchy and bringing of inclusive political system, joined the anti-India camp. Once the Madhes-based parties emerged as the fourth largest force in the CA, most of Nepalese, especially the hill origin people started defaming those parties as political forces 'backed by India'.

---

18 The political and economic implication of such a relation is worth mentioning. Nepalese prefer to go to India which is an emerging economy in South Asia not only for hunting jobs but also for taking shelter or asylum while there is any kind of political crisis in Nepal. It has been witnessed in the past that the migration from Nepal to India was on the increase when there was insecurity in the country due to insurgency and state violence. Similarly, history says that Nepali leaders and students living in India were in jail with their Indian counterparts who were struggling for independence of India. Also, not only the working class but also business classes of Indian people are having job in Nepal.

19 See, Uddhab Pd. Pyakurel, "Nepal-India Relation in the Context of Nepali Nationalism" *Think India Quarterly,* Vol.14, December, 2011.

As Kathmandu elites are well aware about position of the common Nepalese on India, it seems that they have started a new strategy to link India and "Indian interest" in all the domestic matters so that people will react in a different manner. The 'new strategy' has often been used by those elites when they want to sabotage some plan from its implementation. If we follow the recent trend, they bring India in-between so that they could weaken public sentiment and fulfil their own vested interest.

While dialogue was on between major political parties whether to extend the tenure of the CA around May 28, 2011, the Kathmandu elites, especially pro-Maoist columnists, opinion makers and journalists involved India once again in the debate. They basically argued that India, after May 2009, have a one-point agenda, viz., to keep the Maoist in general, and Chairman Dahal in particular, out of power. According to them, India is ready to attack and dismantle the entire political framework established through the successful *Janaandolan-II*. They also tried to link the stand taken by non-Maoist parties including the NC on the issue of the extension of the CA saying that these parties are trying to serve Indian interest. Once there was heavy media coverage on the extension of the CA[20], even the NC could not stand intact and push for those preconditions. Rather, the NC was divided on the issue of whether to continue bargaining with the Maoist till the end, or to support the proposal of the CA's term extension without any commitments and progress on peace process. As a result, the NC had to support the idea to extend the term of the CA without any major achievement in the party's stand.

What is widely accepted is that the preconditions which the NC and Madhes-based parties had set for the extension of the CA before May 28, 2011 were by-and-large related to the democratization Nepali Maoist by detaching the party from its arms and combatants. It is not the issue to be debated about whether there was any link on the very demand of non-Maoist parties and Indian interest, and w hat India would gain or lose as it is primarily Nepal's internal matter. But Nepal could have made a great achievement in concluding the on-going peace process if those parties could take the stand till the last moment. In other words, if Kathmandu

---

20 See, Rajendra Maharjan, *Delhi ko Naya Marga Chitra* (New Roadmap of Delhi), *Kantipur*, May 27, 2011; Puranjan Acharya, *Kangress Le Bujhe Nabhujeko Kura* (Fact Whether the Congress is Known or Unknown), *Nepal*, May 22, 2011; Puranjan Acharya, *Sushil Da Lai Patra* (Letter to Sushil Koirala), *Kantipur*, May 28, 2011. Rajaram Gautam and Dinesh Wagle, *Kasle Jitla Khel?* (Who will Win the Game?), *Kantipur*, May 28, 2011; Kul Chandra Neupane, *Madhyarat Ma Sitaula Ko Abharodh* (Sitaula's obstacle in the mid-night), *Kantipur*, May 31, 2011; Kiran Bhandari, *Kangress Antim Din Ma Kasari Lachilo Bhayo?* (How Congress was Soften at the End?), *Nagarik*, May 30, 2011.

elites were with the NC and Madhes-based party to push the Maoist to come up with a concrete proposal in implementing peace process-related agreements, it would help ease Nepal's peace process and complete the constitution-writing in the coming days, which, I think, is the primary interest of those Kathmandu elites too. Nepal has missed a chance on May 28, 2011 by bringing India unnecessarily into the debate.

To conclude, people of Nepal still doubt whether the 5-point agreement signed on the mid-night on May 28, 2011 will be implemented before August 28, and a sovereign CA will be able to promulgate the new constitution as a consensus document. If political parties missed the renewed date that is August 28, 2011, it seems very difficult to convince people for another extension of the CA, as they get tired of unhealthy political fighting between the political parties. As a consequence, it is likely that the achievements of the *Janaandolan-II* would be endangered. Also, ethnic violence in the hill and Tarai areas is likely to spread. In fact, it will lead to chaos. That is why, there is no alternative except to make the peace process a success and bring a new democratic constitution through the CA. Such a constitution should be imbibed with internationally established democratic norms and values. For it, the 12-point understanding which was signed by today's major political parties in November 2005, seems to be still valid. If the parties once again read the agreement and duly follow it, the democratic constitution is still possible within the given time. More specifically, if Maoists go through their past agreements and start implementing them, more than 90 per cent of the problems would be resolved. Such a move would also compel other political parties, especially the Nepali Congress and CPN-UML, to engage them in addressing the issues raised by the new aspirant groups. They also need to come up with pro-people policies and programs to retain their position in the following elections.

As far as external power is concerned, it will be helpful for Nepal to overcome today's political stalemate if major external powers relevant in the region could put moral pressure on all Nepali political parties to bring the peace process to an end, and draft a democratic constitution without making Nepal a battleground to demonstrate their sphere of influence. Moreover, the democratic civil society activists globally, and particularly in India, could help the process if they come forward in favour of the struggle for sovereignty and unity of Nepali people for a democratic constitution. We believe that Nepal-India relations are too deep-rooted, pervasive and multi-layered, that cannot be dealt with only by the political establishment; people-to-people solidarity of two countries is extremely essential.

Chapter III

Conflict Transformation: A Nepali Case

Indra Adhikari

The term, 'conflict' is commonly used now a days. It refers to the pursuit of incompatible goals by individuals or groups. Boulding explains it an extreme situation "when a potential position of two beheviour units are mutually incompatible"[1]. It is a situation of competition when individuals or groups identify "a goal they want to secure in order to satisfy material interests, needs or values"[2] and are aware "of the compatibility of the potential future positions in which each party wishes to occupy a position that is compatible with wishes of the others"[3]. When these perceptions lead to actions that contradict the goals of others, then a conflict dynamic occurs. Such dynamics however can be categorized "subjective" and "objective"[4] in nature that covers overall dimensions, nature and source of conflict. It is also observed that the objective aspect of conflicts are based on the resource based interest of parties and are caused by scarcely supplied or lack of their access to the resources. Such resources may not necessarily be material-based like land, food, water and other commodities and services, but be explicitly value-orientated like socio-political position, power and recognition. The subjective aspect of conflicts is on the other hand action

---

1 Kenneth E. Boulding, *Conflict and Defence: A General Theory*, Cited in Pooja kataria, *Conflict Resolutio: Conflict: Forms, Causes and Method of Resolution*, Delhi: Deeps and Deep Publications, 2007, p12.

2 Aurangzeb Haneef, "Theory and Practice of Conflict Resolution", in Moonis Ahmar (ed.), *Different Perceptions on conflict resolution: Need for an Alternative Approach*, Karachi: University of Karachi 2005:47.

3 Boulding, Conflict and Defence, n.23, p12.

4 Aurangzeb Haneef, "Theory and Practice of Conflict Resolution", in Moonis Ahmar (ed.), *Different Perceptions on conflict resolution: Need for an Alternative Approach*, Karachi: University of Karachi 2005, pp47-48.

and reactions of individuals and groups guided by negative psychology and revengeful attitudes. Such attitudes can be emotionally orientated by the shadow sides of "human nature" as Hobbes highlighted: fear, anger, anxiety, jealousy, mistrust, hostility. Clouding perceptions within the conflicting parties, such negativity paves the way for protracted conflict, ignoring the notion of rational communication that helps transform it into peace.

Conflict can be divided broadly into intra and inter state categories. Inter-state conflict occurs directly or indirectly due to incompatible or conflicting national interests between the countries[5]. Several factors such as personal, class, caste, ethnic, communal regional, internal political and psychological factors may be responsible in creating intra-state conflict. The main differentiations between the two types of conflict are the actors that are conflicting for their respective advancement or advantage: these are states, and individuals or groups respectively. Sometimes the intra-state conflict leads the inter-state conflict vis-à-vis, irrespective to the intensity because of the "linkage politics" and nationalities. Issues of people of Nepali origin in Bhutan, the LTTE in Sri Lanka and its impact in Southern India, people of Indian origin in tarai of Nepal are some of the examples of linkage politics and nationalities in South Asia that sometimes create inter-state conflict and controversy. Refugee, migration, linkage between the cross-border terrorists groups, and border issues and its misuse by smugglers and terrorists are the major source of inter-state tension in south Asia.

South Asian experience shows that both the conflicts may adopt the violent and non-violent means to achieve the targeted goal. Such means generally indicate the sensitivity, intensity and seriousness of the conflict. The former by and large occurs for the sake of either separatism or systemic change that indicates an extreme form of decent and frustration of intra-state aggravated parties. And the latter occurs mainly due to the 'sense of relative deprivation'[6] so that it makes the state assure their rights on the basis of equality, address and accommodate the demands of the party amicably by initiating structural reform and adapting the policy of inclusiveness and empowerment. Such initiation helps create an adjustable atmosphere so that the conflicting parties can turn from incompatibility

---

5 Peter wallensteen, *Understanding Conflict Resolution: War, Peace and the Global System*, New Delhi: Sage Publications, 2002

6   Pranab Bardhan, *Scarcity, conflicts, and cooperation: Essays in the Political and Institutional Economics of development*, New Delhi: Oxfort University Press, 2005, pp.169-207.

to compatibility or agree for the process of transformation towards its complete resolution. The process make them change their goals, shift priority, distribute resources, compromise on the issues, share control by externalizing it arbitration and other legal procedures.

Thus, the idea of identification of issues— nature of procedure in which the conflicting parties agree on certain rules and parameters and avoid certain extreme conflict forms— is important to lead it towards transformation. Confidence building methods and measures require to be developed for such transformation by initiating cooperation, changing perception, enhancing communication and developing positive attitudes towards one another. Role of civil society or other groups also is important to transfer such conflict either by intervention or through persuasion, bargaining, coercion, mediation, and empowerment. Baral suggests that "fractioning conflict and cost involved in conflict also are important actions in enhancing the prospect of conflict transformation[7].

To categorize the elements of conflict is a very complex task, though all sorts of conflicts have 'certain basic common elements'[8] that help demarcate the differentiations. In Nepali context, the nature of conflict is typed as value-based, reaction-based, personality-based and ideology-based. All sorts of the roots of conflicts are either individually or commonly interwoven and overlapped, and are playing vital role not only in creating conflict but making it multi-facet and more complicated also. So it is also equally difficult to conceptualize the relationship between and among the divergent roots of conflict as mentioned above.

Additionally, the nature, cause and element of conflict in modern complex society are rapidly changing, and mushrooming respectively day by day. The development of science and technology, means of mass-communication and its contribution to rising sociopolitical awareness increase the expectation of the people. But the traditional structure of the state may not deliver service in the same pace to meet such expectations, hence accelerate conflict[9]. No method is universally applicable for

---

7 Lok Raj Baral, "Some Reflections on Conflict Resolution Research in South Asia", Moonis Ahmar (ed.), *Conflict Resolution Research in South Asia*, Karachi: University of Karachi and Hanns Seidel Foundation, 2010, p.225.

8   Peter Wallensteen, *Understanding Conflict Resolution: War, Peace and the Global System*, New Delhi: Sage Publications, 2002.

9 Adhikari, Indra, "Political Security and Legitimacy", *The Kathmandu Post*, 2 July 2005; Indra Adhikari, Nepal: Contextualization of comprehensive security, The Kathmandu Post, 4 January 2004. Lok Raj Baral (ed.), *Non-Traditional Security: State, Society and Democracy in South Asia*, New Delhi: Adroit Publications, 2006. Dhruba Kumar, *Nepali*

resolving all sorts of conflict of every society. Nether there is an abstract blueprint that suggests about how to transform it into peace. Thus only observation of attitudes, behaviour and contradictions (ABC) are suggested to understanding conflict[10], to identify the "diagnosis-prognosis therapy"[11] in accordance with its nature and roots of conflict, and to deal with for its peaceful resolution. And it may also be applicable to evaluate or measure its level of transformation after initiating the process towards complete resolution and settlement.

That is way, the phrase, 'conflict transformation' indicates the level of change in the conflict resolution process. It helps measure about how the conflicting parties are agreed on the peaceful settlement and whether they are honestly following the terms and condition of such agreement in accordance with its spirit. Conflict can be transformed, if the appropriate mechanism and, method to regulating such mechanism and to understanding issues and problems is devised holistically so that reflects realities, contexts and complications. Thus efficiency of the mechanism, and strong commitment and statesmanship in the political leaders of transforming parties are equally important to timely succeeding the process. Otherwise the people may loose the hope of the transformation and expected change; conflict emerges one and another form on horizontal basis, if the particular conflict transformation process is lingered or failed.

Conflict transformation is a process of concluding a dispute or conflict in which the adversary parties, with or without the assistance of mediators, negotiate or otherwise strive toward a mutually acceptable agreement or understanding, taking into account each other's concerns[12]. Any conflict resolution can be defined as a new formation that is acceptable to all actors and can be made sustainable by them only. The trends of emergence of conflict suggest that mostly the sources of conflict are indigenous in nature and means and methods of resolution of such conflict also should be searched at local level where the formation of conflict is rooted. The logic is that the indigenous method can be only a sustainable solution. If

---

State, Society and Human Security: An Infinite Discourse, Dhaka: Bangladesh Institute of International and Strategic Studies, The University Press Limited, 2008.

10   Johan Galtung, Peace by Peaceful Means: Peace and Conflict, Development and Civilization, New Delhi: Oxfort University Press, 1996, pp.71-72.

11 Aurangzeb Haneef, "Theory and Practice of Conflict Resolution", in Moonis Ahmar (ed.), Different Preceptions on conflict resolution: Need for an Alternative Approach, Karachi: University of Karachi 2005:60.

12 Louis Kriesberg. æConflict: Social" in Adam Kuper and Jessica Kuper (eds.) The Social Science Encyclopedia. London: Rutledge; 1999. p. 413.

some outside parties, as a mediator is called, use the carrot and stick policy to pressure the parties either to accept its measures or to be ready to bear the punishment, then there can be no acceptability or sustainability, unless one assumes that the 'mediator' is a part of the conflict formation[13]. It should be neither the outsider nor certainly above the conflicting parties. Most importantly, the successful transformation of the conflict depends on whether the indigenous resolution method has managed an adequate post-conflict arrangement, and addressed maturely the transition and questions of reconciliation[14] or not. Against this theoretical background, this paper mainly deals with Nepali experience on conflict transformation process and the Maoist conflict and its transformation process particularly.

History of Conflict in Nepal

Talking about the intra-state conflict, what is understood in Nepal is that it includes state and non-state actors or systemic and extra-systemic forces. Generally Nepali state structure itself is conflict-prone as in other states in south Asia. Discriminatory state in nature by tradition, feudal, bureaucratic and hierarchical society, and elite based centralized political system are major characteristics of the Nepali state. The fundamental civic and political rights, identity politics, demand for social justice for ending all forms of discriminations, and claim for separate states are now hot issues in Nepal. Thus it can be said that the contradictory character of Nepali society and state is the major source of conflict. On the one hand, the state has been practicing to be more monopolistic, uni-cultural and centralized, homogenized since its formation and the society is multicultural, heterogeneous since then on the other. Such state never tries to pursue policy of accommodating all groups on its own through the mechanism developed within the constitution and other legal framework. The regime regardless of its character—oligarchic, absolute monarchy/ traditional authoritarian, constitutional monarchy in democracy— failed to adopt the policy of inclusiveness and empowerment. On the contrary, the elites in the government not only under the Rana and Shah but also elected by the people continue the old feudal and semi-feudal cultural practices during the 1950 - 2006 period that always alienate the people.

---

13 Johan Galtung. *Peace by Peaceful Means*. Oslo: PRIO, 1996 p.89 cited in Dev Raj Dahal. "Conflict Resolution: A Note on Some Contending Approach" in Ananda P. Shrestha and Hari Uprety (eds.), *Conflict Resolution & Governance in Nepal*. Kathmandu: NEFAS, 2003 p. 20.

14 Dev Raj Dahal. "Conflict Resolution: A Note on Some Contending Approach" in Ananda P. Shrestha and Hari Uprety (eds.), *Conflict Resolution & Governance in Nepal*. Kathmandu: NEFAS, 2003.

Such practices and orientation of political elites provided an appropriate ground for not only the emergence of oppositions and extremists within and out of the system but also making them thrive in one or another form for a long time

It can be observed that internal insurgencies in different periods are mainly the output of such wrong policy practices of the state. Thus Nepali conflict is the conflict mainly over and against regime. Nepali Congress (NC), the oldest democratic party of the country formed in 1947 waged the violent war against the Rana Oligarchy despite its leadership being influenced by and involved in Gandhian non-violent movement in India. As a result, the tripartite agreement between the King, the NC and the Rana was signed with the mediation of India in Delhi with a strong commitment of establishing multiparty democracy and constitutional monarchy. After 1960 when King Mahendra staged a coup and imposed the party less Panchyat system under the dynamic and active leadership of the King, the violent and non-violent conflict was continued between the regime and the anti-systemic political forces, especially the NC and communists twice. Then the opposition forces lunched peaceful movements demanding the establishment of the civil and political rights compelling the royal regime not only to reform the Panchyat system in 1980 but also open the multiparty system in 1990. The democratic change in the polity of the state in 1990 limited the role of traditional monarch to the "constitutional" one. Unfortunately the parties that fought against the traditional forces for democracy also could not address the issue of people amicably while they led the government. The single facet conflict—party less vs. multi-party— became multi-facet during the democratic era in 1990s. There was an indefinite conflict within the systemic forces (inter and intra party conflict, between the parties and the king, among different factions in the palace) and the state and the Maoists which was out of the system, at a time while the ethnic groups, people from Tarai, the King, the leftists and rightists political parties were dissatisfied with the constitutional provision of 1990. It created an inherent conflict within the so- called systemic forces that led the problem of adoption of change. The conflict within the system was somehow value-based and ideological but remained mainly reaction and personality based. But the conflict between the state and the Maoists was partially value- based and partially strategic. Thus major stakeholders of the change in 1990 could not work in spirit of liberal and inclusive democracy but compromised its values with the traditional forces. As a result, democratic forces became weak, and the reactionaries ware benefited from the system. The conflict within the system and its reflection in governance created strong ground for growing and thriving extremists in the country. The royal action after October 2002 and escalating the Maoist insurgency after 1999 was the output of such conflict within the systemic political forces. The existence of democratic forces was in the crisis after 2002. The multi-polar conflict was thus converted into bio-polar one, while the leaders from civil society, intellectuals and key political leaders cashed on the situation shaking hand with the Maoist to restore democracy. It resulted in 12-point agreement between the seven agitating political parties against the royal action after 2002 and the Maoists.

Formalization of Conflict Transformation

The Comprehensive Peace Accord (CPA) is the first formal agreement signed on January 6, 2007 by the Interim Government formed by the Seven Party Alliance (SPA) and the then CPN (Maoist) which has now been renamed the United Communist Party of Nepal-Maoist (UCPN-Maoist). It not only declared the "End of conflict"[15] for "giving permanency to the ongoing ceasefire between the parties—Government of Nepal and the UCPN-Maoist"[16]— but directed senior leaders of the parties to be sincere in "the main policy for long-term peace"[17]. It is also an output of the several other important efforts made by the SPA and the UCPN-Maoist in different periods of time and contexts. Its preamble also acknowledges many of the previous agreements including the letter sent to the United Nations by both the sides with the similar viewpoints after the successful Mass Movement in 2006[18]. The CPA along with the ongoing peace process of Nepal is a fully indigenous process as there is no formal national/international mediator. It is, as mentioned before, an output of the several confidence building measures that gave the gate pass to the UCPN-Maoist to enter into the mainstream politics. The process of main streaming the UCPN-Maoist was initiated and formalized by allowing its members in the reinstated Parliament in 2006 and Interim Government in 2007. The treatment of the state and society to the UCPN-Maoist as to other parliamentarian political parties helped them assimilate with and

---

15 Article 6 "End of Conflict", Comprehensive Peace Accord held between the Government of Nepal and CPN(Maoists), 22 November 2006 as published in Uddhab P. Pyakurel, *Maoists Movement in Nepal: A Sociological Perspective*, New Delhi: Adroit Publishers 2007, p. 184.

16　Article 6.1, *Ibid.*

17 Article 6.2, *Ibid.*

18　12-Point understanding signed on 22 November 2005; 25-Point Code of Conduct agreed on 25 May 2006; 8-Point agreement signed on 16 June 2006; others formal-informal consensuses reached between the SPA led Interim Government of Nepal and the UCPN-Maoist. See, Preamble of CPA, Ibid, p.175.

adopt the culture of the multiparty democracy. It created a well-matured ground for making the interim constitution as per the spirit the historical *Jana Andolan* 2006.

"Declaring the beginning of the new chapter of peaceful collaboration between the parties", the CPA initiates for "forward-looking political resolution", and commands both the parties to go through the spirit of earlier consensuses by internalizing and respecting the respective issues of either side. The CPA is the key document that initiates radicalizing the mainstream political parties[19], and main streaming the UCPN-Maoist bringing it in the competitive party politics through a peaceful manner.[20]. That is why the spirit of 12-point understanding between the SPA and the Maoist followed by other agreements was for establishing "absolute democracy"[21], as a full-fledged democracy was possible only after "ending autocratic monarchy"[22] and assuring equality and justice to the people. Thus, the concept of the federal structure of the state was assured by amending the Interim Constitution, and the notion of inclusive and participatory democracy was accepted as a major requirement for leading socio-political transformation to a greater extent.

Thus, the peaceful abolition of the 240-year old institution of monarchy and establishment of the Federal Democratic Republic are the biggest achievements of the Jana Andolan-II. It is proved by the representation of marginalized communities such as Dalits (8%), ethnics (38%), Madhesis (33%), women (more than 33%) and other minorities in

---

19 It, on the other hand, obliges the SPA "to ensure the sovereignty of people through election of Constituent Assembly (CA), restructuring of the state and socio-economic and cultural transformations". Premble of CPA as published in Uddhab P. Pyakurel, *Maoists Movement in Nepal: A Sociological Perspective*, New Delhi: Adroit Publishers 2007, p.184; Point 3 of 12 Points Understanding between the SPA and the Maoists, 22 November 2005

20 It orders the UCPN-Maoist to reiterate their commitment "towards democratic value accepting competitive multiparty democratic system of governance, civil liberty, fundamental rights, human rights, full press freedom and concept of rule of law". *Ibid*, and Points 4 of the 12-Point Understanding between the SPA and the Maoists, 22 November 2005.

21 However, the phrase was defined on the basis of their (the SPA and the Maoist) respective understandings and policies. On the one hand, it was defined by SPA as the end of the autocratic nature of monarchy bringing it under the constitution along with the establishment of other universal principles of democracy, and on the other, the Maoist defined it as removal of the institution of monarchy and establishment of republic country, Nepal.

22 Point 1 of 12-Point Understanding between the SPA and the Maoists, 22 November 2005.

the elected CA The process of democratization of Nepal Army bringing it under the civilian control and professionalization of the Maoist combatants are major directives of the CPA. The restructure of the state is another issue that makes the system more inclusive based on caste, ethnicity, gender, region, religion, etc. The focus has been given to transform the UCPN-Maoist from an insurgent group into a 'civilian political party'. Thus, it orders the UCPN-Maoist to follow a couple of measures such as return the property confiscated during the insurgency to the owner; allow other political parties for political campaign in the country in general, and in the UCPN-Maoist controlled villages in particular.

The Agreement on Monitoring of Management of Arms and Armies reached between the Government of Nepal and the UCPN-Maoist on 28 November 2006, is one of the major forward moving steps towards the conflict transformation, since the management of Maoist combatants and their arms are most important and difficult issues. To facilitate the work of the arms and armies management, the United Nations Mission in Nepal (UNMIN) was established on January 23, 2007. It started working in Nepal as per the United Nations Security Council Resolution number 1740[23]. Its responsibility is limited only to "facilitating, monitoring and supervising the peace process"[24] about whether the activities of the respective parties confine within the boundary of the agreements. In fact, the UNMIN has no right to play decisive role for the peace process but to facilitate the respective parties for following and implementing the agreements in letter and spirit. The task of registration of the Maoist combatants, formation of a Joint Monitoring Coordination Committee (JMCC)[25] and their verification had been over by the UNMIN[26] within a year[27].

---

23 For more on the UNMIN, log in www.unmin.org.np

24 Letter to the UN by the Government of Nepal, Agreement of the UN with Government of Nepal and the Maoists.

25 Accordingly, the UNMIN recruited a total of 126 monitors including 15 UN monitors, 111 Gurkha ex-servicemen who had served in the Indian and British Armies for the management and verification of the Maoist cantonments and weapons. The monitors were kept under the Joint Monitoring and Coordinating Committee (JMCC) of the Agreement on Management and the Monitoring of Arms and Armies that was constituted by three members representing UNMIN, ex-PLA and NA.

26 The type of weapons registered so far are 91 mortars (of which 55 were locally made), 61 machine guns, 2,403 rifles, 61 automatic weapons, 9 sub-automatic guns, 114 side arms, 212 shot guns, 253 miscellaneous and 244 home-made weapons.

27 The management process of the combatants of the UCPN-Maoist began on 8 January after a Joint Monitoring Coordination Committee (JMCC) was formed and the UNMIN announced the first result of the verification of Maoist combatants on 27 December 2007

Hurdles for Smooth Transformation of the Conflict

The structure, role and responsibilities of the Army Integration Special Committee, which has been formed "in order to inspect, integrate and rehabilitate the Maoist combatants",[28] are neither effective nor authorized to independently work as required. It was formed for technical purposes and has nothing to do unless there is a political consensus among the major political parties in the CA. The issue of management of Maoist combatants was politicized to the extent that stopped the whole peace and the constitution writing process. The advocacy and counter-advocacy on the issue of the Maoist combatant's management has made the process more complicated. The UCPN-Maoist's demand to make a "national army" by integrating all its combatants in NA, and its opposition view on entry non combatants into the Nepal Army have almost derailed the peace process but also politicize the Nepal Army. It has been reported that both the Nepal army and the Maoist combatants could not resolve their past antagonism after the CPA was singed. But doubt and distrust between the old rebellion groups continued against each other even after the UCPN-Maoist became part of the system and the government. Ram Bahadur Thapa, the then Defence Minister after the CA election mentioned, referring to the Maoist party's intelligence report, that the topmost officers of the NA have been mobilized by foreign power[29]. Prime Minister Pushpa Kamal Dahal took an oath for the post in the security arrangement of the Maoist combatants, as it was not recognized as a state security force. The expression of the Minister of Defence and attitudes of PM on NA proved that the Maoist party and its government could rely on neither the information nor security guards of the NA. The attitude of Maoist leaders in government was confined to promoting their own combatants and party intelligence in guarding and spying that undermined psychologically the institutional role and responsibility of NA. The mistrust and controversy began while 7,000-8,000 original Maoist combatants[30] reached 30,852 during the entry into the cantonments, and the numbers of Maoist combatants and their registered weapons did not match[31]. The JMCC of the UNMIN also

28 Article 4.4, *Comprehensive Peace Accord* held between the Government of Nepal and CPN(Maoists), 22 November 2006.

29 Indra Adhikari, *Chisido Sena-Sarkar Sambandha* (Cooling Civil-Military Relation), *Kantipur*, February 1, 2009.

30 Highly controversial tape record of Prachanda's indoctrination programme in the Shaktikhor Cantonment, Chitwan.

31 30,852 PLA members registered at the seven main cantonment sites and 21 satellite cantonment sites. The number includes "522 weapons for perimeter security and 96 weapons registered outside of cantonments" *The Rising Nepal*, 10 March 2007, as given

declared ineligible some thousands of them as "new recruits" that reduced the strength of the Maoist combatants in cantonments up to 19,603— 15,757 men and 3,846 women. The situation further weakened the peace process while the debate was initiated about how to manage the Maoist combatants, how many are genuine combatants and "eligible for possible integration in the security agencies fulfilling standard norm"[32] and how the rest should be rehabilitated in the society?.

The UCPN-Maoist has not been ready to manage its combatants even after the latter were kept in the cantonments. If one follows Kharipati decision of the UCPN-Maoist which came just after the party led the government, there were mainly two strategies of the UCPN-Maoist regarding the management of its combatants; the first one was to try to integrate all verified combatants into the NA, along with the senior combatants into the higher rank of NA so that the NA as an institution will be either influenced or weakened through infiltration and division. The second was to keep them in the cantonment for long if the UCPN-Maoist could not succeed in integrating all of them into the NA. By prolonging the life of the temporary cantonment with its combatants, the UCPN-Maoist wanted to benefit financially and politically, as it has been receiving a huge amount of money from the cantonments,[33] and it has been used as a camp for training the people and hiding criminals[34]. The Central Committee of the UCPN-Maoist decided on July 2, 2010 that even if total integration into NA is not possible, its combatants would be under an institution or in a group. It seems that the ultimate motto of the UCPN-Maoist is to keep its combatants under its command forever, if not at least till the next election, so that the psychological strength of its leadership and bargaining capacity of the party remained high. They always threat others that they may "capture power", if their agenda are not accepted by other parties. Contrary to it, the non-Maoists parties are guided by the fearful psychology thinking that the Maoist captures the state power. They feel that only the Nepal Army can rescue them and the State in this situation, since they do not have their own party combatants for their security. Such mutual psychology of fear of the Maoist and non-Maoist parties has helped neither facilitate the conflict

---

in *Nepal Update*, January-April, 2007, p. 91. *The Rising Nepal*, 10 March 2007, as given in *Nepal Update*, January-April, 2007, p. 91.

32 Agreement on Management and the Monitoring of Arms and Armies reached between the Government of Nepal and the UCPN (Maoist), 28 November 2006.

33 See Uddhab Pyakurel (2008) "Sociology of the Maoist' Cantonment," *Kantipur*, 23, January 2008.

34 Interview of Subodh Pyakurel on Kantipur TV on June 26, 2010.

transfer process, nor conflicting parties themselves.

Weaknesses of the Process

There are several provisions that prohibit both NA and the ex-combatants[35]. In fact, only five out of the nine restricted activities under the CPA, and only seven out of 19 clauses under the AMMAA[36] were implemented by the Maoists. The UCPN-Maoist started recruiting youths in cantonments just after it signed the CPA with guarantee of handsome salary and job in Nepal Army[37]. Some of the new recruits were school-going children; some were abducted [38]by it for the purpose. All received military training with weapons since the ceasefire was declared in spite of warning of national/international organizations[39]. Even the then government did

---

35 The agreement prohibits mainly: (1) to hold, carry and display arms, use of violence and armies for creating terror and fear; (2) to intimidate and use any type of violence against people—kidnap, murder, and torture to hurt or render mental pressure against any individual; (3) to recruit additional armed personnel or conduct military activities; (4) to collect cash or goods and services or levy against one's wishes and against the existing law; (5) to restrict free movement of people and goods; (6) to spy on military activities of either sides; (7) to publicize for or against any side and support or protest against any side, (8) damaging and seizing public/private/governmental and non-governmental property, etc. As the CPA was a detailed and comprehensive agreement, it was categorical even in each and every small issue such as leave of the Maoist combatants put inside the cantonment. It has a provision that no more than 12 per cent of the total retained force of the Maoist combatants can be on leave under the deferent cause-medical referrals, visiting families—of a given cantonment.

36 Agreement on Monitoring of Management of Arms and Armies reached between the Government and the UCPN-Maoist on 28 November 2006

37 The Maoists openly established "recruiting center"s, with the assurance of a good salary (with a promise of Rs. 7,000 salary per month) and job guarantee in Nepal Army, See, INSEC Online report, "Maoists Running Recruitment Camps," www.inseconline. org browsed on September 3, 2006

38 It has been proved that the seven children of Bhaludhunga Secondary School of Bishnu Paduka School were, in fact, abducted on September 6, 2006 and they were given military training in Motipur VDC of Morang after conscripting them in Ratna Sakunta Brigade Second Battalion. For details, see "Maoists Recruiting Children against Code of Conduct", www.inseconline.org, September 19, 2006. It is reported that some recruitments are voluntary where those who were not physically fit to get jobs in Nepal army and police force, join the PLA with the hope of the merger of the PLA and Nepal Army soon.

39 Even Internationally recognized organizations such as the Office of the High Commissioner for Human Rights (OHCHR) and UNMIN reported it. See, United Mission in Nepal Press Conference on 8 April, 2008, Kathmandu available at http://www.unmin.org.np/?d=media&p=press accessed by the author on July 6, 2010; see also UNMIN Election Report No 3, 6 April 2008 available at http://www.unmin.org.np/downloads/publications/2008-04-06-UNMIN.Election.Report.3.ENG.pdf accessed by the author on July 6, 2010.

not initiate any measure to stop the process. Rather, the UCPN-Maoist supreme leader, Prachanda with pride claimed that his party successfully increased the number of its combatants from 7-8 thousand to 32,250 through new recruitment.[40] Also, the UCPN-Maoist continued its activities of extortion, intimidation, abductions, ill-treatment, violation of rights of internally displaced people[41] and even killings after the CPA too, though the numbers of such activities are considerably low. They continued their so-called parallel governments till the completion of CA election, and tried to stop political activities of other political parties till today.[42]. Though UCPN-Maoist leadership issued a directive to end human rights abuses in September 2, 2006, no evidence has been found which assures the fulfilment of earlier commitment made by the UCPN-Maoist leadership, hence the question of accountability against the UCPN-Maoist leadership.

On the other hand, neither the Truth and Reconciliation Commission[43],

---

40 The video Tape which was his one and a half hour long address to the Maoist combatants at Shaktikhor Cantonment. In the address he urged his caders to remain calm till they capture power and establish "people's Republic" as envisaged by Mao and Lenin. Some excerpts of the video is available at http://www.google.com/search?q=Prachanda+Shakt ikhor+Video&hl=en&client=gmail&sa=X&rls=gm&prmd=v&source=univ&tbs=vid:1 &tbo=u&ei=0f8xTPGrG4SYrAfEvrDHBA&oi=video_result_group&ct=title&resnum =1&ved=0CB0QqwQwAA, accessed by the author on July 5, 2010.

41 Of these, most of the deaths in the Maoists custody were because of "extreme beatings and torture" by them after abduction (See "Maoists abduct, kill teenager", *The Kathmandu Post*, September 16, 2006. The Maoists issued a statement claiming that the boy died after "accidentally falling off a cliff). Cases of abduction, intimidation, beating of people and extortion are rising by the day (Ameet Dhakal, "Life beyond Communism", *The Kathmandu Post*, September 1, 2006). It was reported that many industries were closed due to Maoist intimidation and "the majority of Nepali entrepreneurs were on the verge of being displaced due to the Maoists' extortions" (See "FNCCI warns of protests if Maoist extortion continues," www.ekantipur.com September 17, 2006) during the ceasefire. Hotels in Nepal faced the threat of closure due to extortion drives and "illogical demands" by the Maoists (See "Nepal: Maoist threats forcing closure of hotels," *The Indian Express*, September 5, 2006). Maoists abducted youth as young as 13 years and have not spared even students studying in grade seven (For details, see "Maoists abduct 3 minors in Bardiya"*Kantipur*, July 11, 2006; "Maoists abduct four, thrash one", *Kantipur*, August 5, 2006; "Maoists keep up abductions, extortion" *Kantipur*, August 18, 2006; "Maoists continue abductions, intimidation, extortions", *The Kathmandu post*, August 2, 200). They detained 15-year-old youngman to 60-year-old man in their "labor detention camp" (see http://www.kantipuronline.com/kolnews.php?&nid=83978).

42 According to the OHCHR report, the rebels were responsible for the death of at least 16 civilian, mostly innocent villagers and for abduction of at least 184 individuals since the ceasefire declaration of April 26.

43 Nepali democracy faced ups and downs in the past because the guilty were spared in the name of "reconciliation" after each and every successful movement. The regressive forces had made a comeback and hatched a conspiracy against the democratic system due

nor the Commission for Investigating the Displaced People was formed to manage the peace process and provide justice to the victims during the conflict. So, interest of conflict between the rival forces resumed again while the UCPN-Maoist succeeded in making total combatants up to 32,250 without any disturbance of the then government. Later, Nepal Army also initiated the new recruitment[44] process of soldiers advertising in a government owned national dailies[45].

The narrowly defined terms "integration and rehabilitation" that corporate only to the combatants is not enough to provide justice to the people victimized by the conflict. It has not recognized the necessity of justice to the rest of the conflict victims such as injured, handicapped, displaced, trafficked, disappeared, raped, toured, assaulted and verbally and physically harassed people. The division in Martyrs declaration putting them in the basket of Maoists and non-Maoists shows that there is still conflict between the Maoists and non-Maoists parties.

Similarly, the election of CA for the making of a new constitution was the major task. Because at that particular time, the state moves from the divided past to a shared future required the capability and feasibility not only to create a just order, but to perform its basic state functions also. But after CA election, no further effort has been made so that the peace process reaches to the logical end. Neither the State Restructuring Commission for making federal structure nor the State Reconciliation Commission as dictated by CPA and the Interim Constitution of Nepal

---

to failure of the then government to punish the guilty proved in the Mallik Commission Report in 1990. Again, it got repeated in the country as the recommendation of Raymajhi Commission report 2006 got ignored and was not implemented. That was one of the causes of creating mistrust and dissatisfaction over the new government formed right after the successful Janaandolan II. Unnecessary delay in implementing the declaration of the House of Representatives which made very radical announcements as per the mandate of the movement, was another shortcoming of the government. Any excellent declaration having no implementation has no meaning and does not support in the process strengthening and deepening democracy. The Maoists, who played a major role on their part in derailing the democratization process in Nepal from the very beginning, have continued killings, extortion, abductions and recruitment activities after they declared truce and signed various agreements, including the 25-Point Code of Conduct.

44 According to the provision of CPA, the Maoists combatant would be managed within six months of CA. When it became impossible, the then government was convinced that the professionalism of the NA should not be captive because of the delay of the management of the Maoist combatants. Then, the process of new recruitment on the vacant posts in technical area of the NA was initiated to fulfil the posts. The recruitment was not additional but fulfilment of the vacancy within the existing strength.

45 Gorkhapatra on November 2, 2008.

2007 could be materialized.

Conversion of conflict: Vertical to Horizontal

The process of militarization of political parties, radicalization of the society and ruining of the state authority are the interconnected and newly emerged challenges for peace after the CPA was signed. The non-Maoist political parties themselves started to militarize their parties that not only encourage conflict in different mode but also discouraged the process for transformation of the past conflict. They rationalized such initiatives for the defence of their own cadre of the parties. Guided by the tit-for-tat policy against the Maoist offences, most political parties who have some sort of influence in one and other way in the country have formed the militant or semi-militant organizations as given below.

Table 1

Main militant groups formed by the political parties/groups

S.N.	Youth Organisations	Mother Organisations	Geographical Influence
1	Young Communist League	UCPN (Maoist)	All over the country
2	Youth Force	CPN (UML)	All over the country
3	Madhesi Youth Force	Madhesi Janaadhikar Forum (MJF)	Eastern, Central and Mid Western Terai regions
4	Chure Bhawar Shanti Sena	Chure Bhawar Ekta Samaj Party	Central and Mid Western regions
5	Security Brigade (Rakshya Bahini)	Nepal Sadbhawana Party (Rajendra Mahato)	Central and Mid Western regions
6	Madhesi Commando	Nepal Sadbhawana Party	Central and Mid Western regions
7	Terai Madhes Sewa Surakshya Sangh	Terai Madhes Loktantrik Party	Mid Western and Western regions
8	All Nepal Democratic Youth Organisation	Rastriya Janamorcha Party	Mid Western and Western regions

9	Tharu Sena	Tharuhat Swayatta Parishad	Certain Districts of Mid Western and Western regions (for e.g., Dang, Kapilbastu and Bardiya)
10	OBC Regiment	Pichhada Varga Mahasangh	Central Terai region
11	Limbuwan Volunteers and Limbuwan Liberation Army	Sanghiya Loktantrik Rastriya Manch / Limbuwan Rajya Parishad	Eastern region
12	Kirat Limbuwan Volunteers	Pallo Kirat Limbuwan Rastriya Manch	Eastern region
13	Janasurakshya Bal	CPN-Maoists	Some districts
14	Madhesi Raksha Bahini	Sadbhawana Party	Some of the Terai districts
15	Khas Kshetri Unity Society	Khas-Kshetri Unity Society	Some regions

Source: Collected form different sources

In fact, the restoration of democratic system after the successful Jana Andolan-II provided a background for enhancing their movements. The aim of Nationwide Janajati Movement was to establish a secular state status and ethnicity based autonomous federal structures. Dalit movement was to end caste-based discrimination. Similarly, the Madhes Movement of August 2007 led by the MJF started to declare Nepal as a federal democratic republic and full proportional representation system for the election of CA. Similarly, Chure Bhawar movement (August-October, 2007) known as anti-Madhes agitated opposing the demand of Madhes Movement— 'One Madhes, One Pradesh' and to amend the Election Commission Act in increasing the relaxation for inclusive candidacy (from 20 per cent to 30 per cent). Similarly, the Tharu Movement[46] demanded to

---

46 The Tharu Movement demanded the government to withdrawal its ordinance (which had defined the identity of all communities residing in the flat-land as Madhesi. It had also demanded to replace the terminology "Madhes" by "Tarai-Madhes," and recognize the Tharu as a separate ethnic identity in Madhes and form a federal state for Tharus with

recognize their Tharu identity within the Madhes, to frame a federal state for Tharus and to establish right to the local natural resources-*Jal, Jamin* and Jungle. Federal Limbuwan Movement is also an ethnic movement, especially launched in nine districts of the Eastern hills with the demand of formation of an Autonomous Limbuwan State. These were the major social/political movements witnessed after the CPA was signed and most of these movements have demanded proportional share in each and every government body. The government of Nepal tried to be engaged with these movement groups and signed the following agreements to address the problem of respective groups.

Table II
Agreements with the Movement Groups after CA

S.N	Name of the Group	Date of Agreement with Government
1	Janajatis	August 7, 2007
2	Madhesi Janadhikar Forum	August 30, 2007
3	Chure Bhawar Pradesh Ekta Samaj	September 13, 2007
4	National Badi (a hill Dalits group) Rights Struggle Committee	October 15, 2007
5	United Democratic Madhesi Front	February 28, 2008
6	Federal Republican National Front	March 2, 2008
7	Federal Limbuwan State Council	March 19, 2008

Awareness and expectation were increased by the catchy slogan of the UCPN-Maoist during the insurgency that radicalized the entire society. But these rising expectations remained unfulfilled after the political change. Even if they came in the peace process, participated in the government and parliament, became the single largest party in CA election, and then formed the government under their leadership, the UCPN-Maoist could not make any policy change towards peaceful and democratic ways[47]. In

their prior-rights on the local natural resources: water resource, jungle and land (*Jal, Jangle ra Jamin*) available in their particular territory.

47 Indeed, the SPA and the Maoists reached an agreement several times to "reinstate the displaced civilians in their homes and to return all land, houses and property seized unjustly". But till the date, they have neither returned the property nor allowed people to stay in their homes in the village. The Maoist party has played a dual role while talking

fact, their modus operandi to run the country proved to be more corrupt, irresponsible, unaccountable, incompetent to provide the good governance and less honest to the expressed commitment. As a result, hopelessness and frustration was increasing among the various deprived communities who had no expectation from other parties, and have been helping the UCPN-Maoist with high hope for change.

In addition to the movement of social groups, there are more than hundred other armed and semi-armed groups active in different geographical regions of the country. Among them most are in tarai and the rest in the eastern hill, Chure Pradesh and all over the county except Himalayan Region. The table given shows the trends of armed groups in Nepal after CPA.

Table III
Armed/Semi-Armed Forces Born After Peace Accord
(November 22, 2006 – June 30, 2009)

1	Akhil Tarai Mukti Morcha	39	
2	Bahun Chhetri Newar Saamuha	40	Nepal Mukti Morcha
3	CPN [Maoist (United Bidrohi Morcha)]	41	OBC Regiment
4	Chure Bhawar Shanti Sena	42	Nepal Rakshya Dal
5	Deshbhakta Army Nepal	43	PalloKirat Limbuwan Rastriya Monch
6	Gorkha Mukti Morcha	44	Paribartan Nepal
7	Gorkhaland Mukti Sena (Tista Kangada)	45	Rajan Mukti Samuha
8	Gorkha-Line Mukti Sena Samaj	46	Rajdhani Army
9	Janabadi Ganatantrik Tarai Mukti Morcha	47	Ranabir Sena

to implement agreements—the Maoist leadership welcome "displaced people" in the villages by words and circulates secret order to their local cadres not to implement, whatever the leadership said, in action. Then the Maoists' behavior in the village has not changed at all, except the armed activities (For details see http://www.kantipuronline. com/kolnews.php?&nid=83973).

10	Jana Samrakshan Sena	48	Rastriya Army
11	Janabadi Kirant Workers Party	49	Rastriya Army Nepal
12	Janatantrik Tarai Mukti Morcha (Goit)	50	Rastriya Samanantar Jwala Mukhi
13	Janatantrik Tarai Mukti Morcha (Himmat Singh)	51	Revolutionary Left Wing (National Red Guard)
14	Janatantrik Tarai Mukti Morcha (Jwala Singh)	52	Samyukta Janatantrik Tarai Mukti Morcha
15	Janatantrik Tarai Mukti Morcha (Prithvi Samuha)	53	Samyukta Mukti Morcha (Ulfa)
16	Janatantrik Tarai Mukti Morcha (Visfot Singh)	54	Saghia Limbuwan Rajya Parishad (Lawoti)
17	Karebian Dog	55	Sanghia Limbuwan Rajya Parishad (Palung)
18	Khambuwan Rastriya Morch	56	Sanghia Limbuwan Rajya Parishad (Lingen)
19	Janatantrik Party Nepal	57	Sanghia Lontantric Rastriya Morcha
20	Kirant Janabadi Workers' Party	58	Save the National Army Nepal
21	Liberation Tigers of Tarai Elam	59	Shahi Mukti Morcha
22	Limbuwan Democratic Volunteers Force	60	Shantikalagi Tarai Kranti
23	Limbuwan Mukti Morcha	61	Shiva Sena
24	Madhesi Mukti Force	62	Sudur Parswim Krantikari Party
25	Madhes Raksha Bahin	63	Sup Kranti Dal
26	Madhesi Special Force	64	Tarai Army
27	Madhes Sena	65	Tarai Bagi

28	Madhesi Bises Dasta	66	Tarai Camando Lig
29	Madhesi Commando	67	Tarai Cobra (Naagraja)
30	Madhesi Janaadhikar Forum	68	Jarai Janakrantikari Bal
31	Madhesi Mukti Tigers (Raman Singh)	69	Tarai Ganatantric Mukti Morcha
32	Madhesi Tigers	70	Tarai Parishad
33	Madhesi Virus Cleaners Party	71	Tarai Uthan Sangathan
34	Mangolian Revenge Group	72	Taraibadi Madhesi Mukti Force
35	National Terrorist Encounter	73	Tharuhat Swatta Rajya Parishad
36	Nepal Ajinger X Samuha	74	Trishul Sena Nepal
37	Nepal Gatantric Sena	75	Samyukta Jatiya Morcha
38	Nepal Gorkha Sena		

Source: Bishnu Pathak and Devendra Uprety. Tarai-Madhes: Searching for Identity Based Security. CS Center, Situation Update No. 88, October 14, 2009

Talking about the objectives of different armed and semi-armed groups, some of them are working for the reinstatement of Hindu state; few of them are for the reinstatement of the institution of monarchy. However, most of such groups claim having a political intension based on ethnic identity. Tarai-Madhes and eastern hill areas are the most affected regions today by such groups. It is argued that the conflict escalated after the CPA because of the unfulfilled hope of people[48] in general, and ethnic community on the issue of ethnicity based autonomous state in particular. The Maoist cashed the sentiment of the people by proposing ethnicity based autonomous states[49] during the conflict but turned out of the

---

48 Uddhab Pyakurel, *Sambidhan Sabha Ka Lagi Purba Sarta* (Preconditions for the Constituent Assembly), *Nepal Samacharpatha,* 27 March, 2007.

49 Even if they comprise less than 30 per cent population in the particular regions, they purposed the autonomous state. They proposed for a Limbuwan state for those Limbu (with 1.6 per cent national population) which occupy 27 per cent population in the area. Kochila state was proposed for less than 24 per cent population of such groups. Gurung

agenda after it won the election of CA. A large numbers of UCPN-Maoist cadres and supporters belonging to Madhesis, Tharu, Newar, Limbu and other communities started going away from the Party to start their own movements, since it signed the CPA and agreed to promulgate the Interim Constitution 2007 without conceiving the federal structure. Interestingly, they have become aggressive and skillful in armed activities through the knowledge gained by their involvement with the UCPN-Maoist during the insurgency. The cadres indoctrinated by the armed tactics of the UCPN-Maoist has mostly led the armed groups to attack and weaken the state for building more pressure.

The state power and government policy are the major components whether to intensify more violence or resolve it. Main causes of spreading violence horizontally in the country even after introducing the peace process to resolve a conflict can be thus be mentioned[50]: Low level of socio-political cohesion; High level of political violence occasioned with state repression; Political conflict over organizing ideology of the state; Major recent change in the structure of political system; Existence of proportionally small urban middle class; Rampant corruption and government unaccountability; low absorbing capacity of foreign aid and its utilization; and High level external penetration. The indicators analysed above show how a state can be weak, unstable and conflict prone[51] and how newly emerging problems overlap making the conflict transformation process more complicated. Most problems rise becoming complex mainly due to either "low regulative capacity[52]" or very limited "presence of the state" that not only affected government-run development and other activities[53], but helped encourage the violence activities.

In fact, the SPA government lost its cohesive power before the UCPN-Maoist even if it tried to implement most of the commitment for making a suitable atmosphere for the peace process. It was reported that the government freed all the UCPN-Maoist cadres from prison, withdrew all

---

state was proposed for less than 22 per cent population of Gurungs in the particular region. And Magar state was proposed for 28 per cent Magars in the regions.

50 Dhruba Kumar. "Nepali State and Politics: Inevitable Crisis and Harrowing Transition" a Report submitted to the Center for Nepal and Asian Studies, December 12, 1997. p. 20 cited in Dhruba Kumar. "Proximate Causes of Conflict in Nepal" *Contribution to Nepalese Studies*. Vol. 31 (1). January, 2005 p. 60.

51 *Ibid.*

52 Ram Kumar Dahal. "Nepal's Neighbourhood Ties During the Interim Government" in *POLSAN Annual Journal on Nepalese Foreign Policy*, Vol. 6 & 7, 1998: 99-115.

53 *The Kathmandu* Post, September 16, 2006.

the cases filed in the courts, lifted the terrorist tags on the UCPN-Maoist, etc. for making a suitable environment for strengthening the peace process. The situation adversely encouraged the UCPN-Maoist as if it could get more than their expectation and started bargaining further. The tough time has begun for both the UCPN-Maoist and the whole process with the people starting counter-action[54]against the UCPN-Maoist activities by taking law and order in their hands. When the UCPN-Maoist led the government after the CA election in 2008, the situation worsened[55].

The weak and personalized character made the conflict management process more ineffective. But Nepali transition and peace process could not go smoothly because of lack of effort to institutionalize it. In fact, it was like the personalized issue especially between the two actors—the then PM Koirala and the UCPN-Maoists' Supremo Pushpa Kamal Dahal. Many important decisions taken between them were neither documented nor shared with their colleague in their parties; people could have no basis to interpret/analyze it. As a result, the concerned parties were polarized as per the ideology rather than as per the spirit of several formal agreements, if there was crisis of confidence between two leaders. The motive of both was to secure their importance permanently in the power and polity of the nation, so that they could change and play the rules of the game in accordance with their respective interests. For them, to establish a stable system, which was expected for fulfilment of people's aspirations—civil

---

54 Maoists were beaten and even killed by the villagers when people found the Maoists guilty of killings and beating up innocents. The transport entrepreneurs and hoteliers protested against the Maoists and Federation of Nepalese Chamber of Commerce and Industries (FNCCI), on September 17, 2006, they warned to launch a nationwide protest if the Maoists continued extortion and intimidation. Getting excited by such counter attacks in the village and in city, US Ambassador James A. Moriarty expressed skepticism toward the possibility of holding constituent assembly elections in a free and fair manner. He said, "You can't have peace and violence at the same time contradictorily". He mentioned, "Everybody realizes that the Maoists are engaged in lot of violence right now even here in Kathmandu. There is a lot of extortion, beating, intimidation of people going on, that sort of activities will obviously threaten the peace process (See, *The Kathmandu Post*, 16 September 2006 and also "Sorry if I offended anyone: Moriarty," *The Kathmandu Post*, 16 September 2006). Donors working in the development sector in Nepal have started rolling back their programs from the districts due to strong pressure from the Maoists Department for International Development (DFID) of the United Kingdom working for poverty reduction and development in poor countries, including Nepal (See, *The Kathmandu Post*, September 1, 2006). Concerns shown by United Nations Resident Representative and Humanitarian Coordinator in Nepal, Matthew Kahane acknowledged on September 16, 2006 about the rapidly increasing Maoist influence in the countryside.

55 Indra Adhikari and Uddhab Pyakurel, " Internal Conflict in Nepal after the Comprehensive Peace Agreement (CPA)", paper presented in a seminar organized by Banaras Hindu University, 5-8 March 2010.

liberty, freedom, basic needs and identity— became secondary. That is why, recreating the conflict, resuming the conflict and sustainability of the conflict resolution is dependent on the capacity, responsibility, honesty, accountability and transparency of the respective elites or leadership engaged in the peace process. But misunderstanding and threat to the peace process can be created, while "elite conflict occurs…[and] an elite attempts to undermine another elite's capacity to extract revenue from non-elites"[56].

Similarly, use of many good and catchy, vague, ambiguous and ambivalent terms is the third characteristics in each and every agreement that allows the signatories to define the agreements as per their interest. The government's modus operandi to deal with the movement groups further helped increase the armed and semi-armed groups. It had no culture to recognize the opposition and listen to the voices raised through peaceful means. Thus many peaceful movements were compelled to be converted in violent mode. Such established precedent gave sense that violence means only can get the attention of government to their demand, hence incensement of anti-systemic and extra-constitutional mode of struggle day-by-day. On the other hand, UCPN-Maoist and the government left their prior agendas-peace, progress and democracy by starting playing double roles with multiple tones. It was proved by their ambivalent positions on "ending autocratic monarchy" and "establishing federal structure"[57].

Neither the media nor the civil society groups, which had played a vital role during the Jana Andolan-II, were critical, as if their actual job of civil-society is over. As a result, no critics came for the non-implementation of clauses agreed/signed by the parties, and non-adherence to the code of conduct signed/agreed by the UCPN-Maoist and the interim government. The civil-society was divided as per the party ideologies—Maoists and non-Maoists, and participated in the restored parliament as their respective representatives. It made them watchdog. The issues raised by them were taken subjectively that encouraged violating the code of conduct and

---

56 Richard Lachmann. "Class Formation Without Class Struggle: An Elite Conflict Theory of the Transition to Capitalism" *American Sociological Review*. Vol. 55 (3), June, 1990. p. 403.

57 The Maoist leadership had no problem in accepting the monarchy if the people want, and the SPA leader, then PM Koirala, started talking about baby king. Both rationalize that they want to ending the "autocratic [character of] monarchy" rather the institution of monarchy, if it remains under the constitution. Both the forces were reluctant to frame the provision on federal structure in the Interim Constitution but tried to engage with regressive and traditional forces, they both had changed their position about the federal issues only after they faced a big threat by Madhes assertion.

interpreting it in favour of one's own interest. Ultimately, the situation shifted from politics of consensus to the politics of confrontation.

More importantly, the UCPN-Maoists deliberate attempt to create anarchy and instability became instrumental in increasing the number of armed and semi-armed groups in Nepal. The UCPN Maoists' leadership responded to them provocatively, so that an opportunity could come to vitalize the role of their combatants, kept in cantonment, and to catch the fish in muddy water. They on the one hand said that "Anarchy and instability help the UCPN-Maoist to consolidate power for further revolution for people's republic" and blamed some genuine movement groups as criminal outfits, imperialist's outfit, etc. on the other[58]. It is proved by the proposal and action of the UCPN-Maoist while the Madhesh movement had taken place.

There are some specific causes which helped Madhesh to become the heartland of the armed conflict after the UCPN-Maoist 'renounced' violence. These are:-

- Political/institutional vacuum due to lack of existence of the state and the mainstream political parties.

- Tarai strategic geographical area for criminals.

- Tarai history of high rate of violence and crime, even if law and order was maintained.

- Vulnerability of tarai and its strategic importance for international players.

- Regional interest for madhesi leaders as second priority, division and competition for their petty interest rather than unity for the interest of the region.[59]

Conclusion

It can be said that organizational transformation from armed rebels to peaceful politicians depends on three preconditions—faction, followers and friends. (1)The rebel group's degree of internal cohesion during the

---

58 Dr. Baburam Bhattarai said "The *naike* (derogatory word for leader) of the criminal group [read that as Madhesi People's Rights Forum] must be arrested and the outfit must be outlawed" (Speech of Dr. Bhattarai on March 23, 2007).

59 As per the demand, Madhesi parties were exempted by the provision of inclusive candidacy in the CA. The amendment was not made mandatory for those political parties which fill up less than 30 per cent candidates in the election.

peace process, (2) its level of popular support among the population at large at the time of the transition, and (3) the amount of legitimacy that the international community is willing to grant to the rebels through the transition period helps in examining how the rebellion groups are being transferred.[60] But when the UCPN-Maoist opts for playing with their two-line struggle, it seems that they have lost their internal cohesion over the party cadres. In fact, this weakness of the Maoist party ultimately provides a clue not only for its cadres to continue criminal activities along with extortion, intimidation, killing, abduction, etc., but also for other groups who were waiting for a favourable situation to initiate the armed movements to influence the state. The issue of integration and rehabilitation of the Maoist combatants has alone stopped the whole process. That is why we find some commonality in most of the groups today if we follow their movement and demands seriously. In every negotiation talk between the government and the armed groups, there has been a common demand for eventual integration of their combatants into security forces, mainly the Nepal Army. Militants' integration into security forces has become one of the major hopes of most armed groups. In other words, possible integration in security agencies and rehabilitation in society with handsome amount of money from the national treasury has already becomes a precedence. The violent armed activities become the guiding principle to the unemployed youth. In other words, the agreement between the government and the UCPN-Maoist for the management of the latter's combatants encouraged others to take to arms. These groups are also interested in entering into the security agencies through back-channel negotiations. The trend is likely to be present for years to come due to the high rate of unemployment of the youth. Today, youth of Nepal can easily join any of such armed groups with the motto of just entering into the security forces, which previously used to be very difficult unless one had a political influence. Another cause of possible sustainability of such armed groups in Nepal is social respect if one joins in the security forces, especially in Nepal Army.

---

60 Mimmi S. Kovacs. *From Rebellion to Politics*. Sweden: Uppsala University, 2007. p. 8. as cited in Indra Adhikari and Uddhab Pyakurel, " Internal Conflict in Nepal after the Comprehensive Peace Agreement(CPA), paper presented in a seminar organized by Banaras Hindu University on 4th-5th June 2010, India.

Chapter IV

Democracy and Problems of Democratization in Nepal

Indra Adhikari

Two Greek words, *Demos* (People) and *Kratos* (rule), are combined to form the term 'democracy' which means a people-centric principle and practice of politics. In a broad and inclusive system of government, democracy is both participatory and constitutional[1]. Democracy and social justice are an integral part of each other, as are liberties and democracy. It includes freedom and justice, but freedom alone does not make the process of democratic government. Freedom should relate to power based on popular sovereignty[2]. Fundamental rights of citizens and recognition of opposition or dissent is the measuring yardstick of democratic governance. So democracy is both a process and ideology that demands institutions, procedures and conduct of free and fair elections. Parties are also organic to the democratic process, as no other alternatives to parties have been developed as yet for regulating electoral politics, the legislative and the executive organs of government[3].

Since democratization includes both a process and ideology, it has been more difficult in a semi-traditional country. Hence, the crisis of 'democratizing democracy' continues due to the reasons identified here from our perspective.

---

1 George Sorensen, *Democracy and Democratization: Process and Prospects in a Changing World*, (Bolder: Westview Press, 1998), p.118.

2 David Held, *Models of Democracy*, (Cambridge: Polity Press, 1987), p.271.

3 Adam Prezworski, *Democracy and the Market: Political and Economic Reforms in Eastern Europe and Latin America,* (Cambridge: Cambridge University Press, 1991), p.10.

Positive and Negative Factors for Democratization

The process of democratization in Nepal began in 1951, following the end of the century-old oligarchy of the Ranas. The interim constitution of Nepal (1951) provided fundamental rights to the people. The constitution stated that it would be the duty of the state to promote the welfare of the people through a social order based on freedom and justice.

However, the internal conflict within the interim government, consisting of representatives of the Rana ruling elite and the Nepali Congress (NC), and the later developments that precipitated intra-party conflicts within the NC, allowed the king to be assertive. Such developments diluted the premise for the election of a constituent assembly composed of representatives elected by the people. As a result, the king suspended the entire provisions of the interim constitution relating to the executive power of the council of ministers, and declared through the Special Emergency Power Act, 1954 that " The executive authority was vested in the Monarch which he could exercise either directly or through officers as appointed by him for that purpose". It made the king the real executive head of the state and government, and he ruled continuously by hiring and firing prime ministers and cabinets until the Constitution of the Kingdom of Nepal, 1959 was promulgated. By this time, the king had consolidated power and declared himself as sovereign. The political parties had become weak and had no other option but to accept the Constitution offered by the sovereign king in February 1959.

Under the Constitution, the first general election was held on 18 February 1959 and it gave a mandate to the NC which had two-thirds majority in the Parliament. However, the experiment of the multi-party democracy or parliamentary system was short-lived, lasting only eighteen months. King Mahendra was not satisfied with his limited role under the Constitution, though he retained supreme executive power and extensive discretionary and emergency powers. In December 1960, using the emergency power, he dismissed the first elected government, dissolved the Parliament, detained political leaders, banned political parties and took over the legislative and executive power by announcing a party-less Panchayat system, said to be "rooted in our soil and suited to our conditions". The party-less regime continued until it was overthrown by the people through a mass movement in 1990.

The Constitution of the Kingdom of Nepal, 1990 was a major departure from the previous constitutions because of its introduction of Nepali people as sovereign. However, the exercise since 1991 exposed that the actual sovereignty still vested in the king. Even if convinced that "… the source of sovereign authority is inherent in the people and desirous of conducting the government of the country in consonance with the popular will", the king claimed, on 4 October 2002, that power has been vested with him and that by using that power he dismissed an elected government headed by Sher Bahadur Deuba.

On the other hand, Article 3 of the Constitution lays down that the "sovereignty of Nepal is vested in the Nepali people and shall be exercised in accordance with the provisions of the Constitution". But the Sovereign people have no power to change the four fundamentals of the constitution—multi-party, constitutional monarchy, sovereignty of the people and fundamental human rights. It is, therefore, a rigid Constitution that cannot be amended by the 'sovereign people'. It is more so "in absence of other alternative provisions for reflecting the popular opinion on certain crucial areas that may not necessarily go along with the demand of time and situation or people themselves may want to bring about changes on them"[4].

The Monarchy after 1990

The process of democratization and the role of the monarchy have become contradictory in Nepali politics. The Constitution declares the king as the symbol of Nepalese nationality and the unity of the Nepali people, who compose different multi-ethnic, multi-lingual and multi-religious groups. The king has no executive and other powers except where mentioned at 'his discretion' without 'advice and recommendation' and the consent of the council of ministers and some constitutional bodies[5]. Theoretically, the king has no other role except making palace rules for the royal family members and palace bureaucracy. In practice, however, the king was not satisfied with his limited role and was, therefore, looking for an opportunity to be an active king after 1990.

It is said that immediately after the promulgation of the Constitution,

---

4 Lok Raj Baral, *Participatory Democracy: Concept and Context*, unpublished paper.

5 Article 35(1) of the 1959 Constitution states that "The executive power of the Kingdom of Nepal shall, pursuant to this Constitution and others laws, be vested in His Majesty and the Council of Ministers". Article 35(2) clearly states, "Except as otherwise expressly provided as to be exercised exclusively by His Majesty or at His discretion or on the recommendation of any institution or official, the powers of His Majesty under this Constitution shall be exercised upon the recommendation and advice, and with the consent of the Council of Ministers. Such recommendation, advice and consent shall be submitted through the Prime Minister".

King Birendra expressed his grievance by pointing out that his role was more limited than the President of India. The several roles shouldered by him also comprised of nomination of upper house members, appointment of ambassadors to other countries, mobilization of Royal Nepal Army (RNA) etc. He had, however, rejected the advice of the prime minister on the question of deployment of the army against the Maoists and defied the citizenship bill passed by both Houses of Parliament, though the king has no authority to exercise veto against bills introduced in the lower house, such as finance bill, etc. Later, King Gyanendra dismissed the elected government headed by Sher Bahadur Deuba on 4 October 2002 accusing him of being 'incompetent' to hold the election within the given deadline, and took over the executive power. The king re-emerged as the real executive head of the state by misusing and misinterpreting Article 127 of the Constitution[6]. Since then, he has been firing the prime ministers asserting that he would not like to be an inactive king. The history of post-1950 politics is thus being repeated, though the actors and the context are different.

Parties, Government and Democratization

The election Commission had registered twenty parties in 1991, twenty-four in 1994 and thirty-nine in 1999 elections. Among them, five parties — NC, Communist Party of Nepal-Unified Marxist-Leninist (CPN-UML), Marxist-Leninist (ML), Rastriya Prajatantra Party (RPP), and Nepal Sadbhawana Party (NSP) — had established themselves as national parties in the last general election (1999) that "secured a minimum of three percent of the total votes cast in the election to the House of Representatives"[7]. In spite of the existence of the number of parties, the party system is not effective in the country due to ideological aberrations and lack of confidence vis-à-vis the monarchy. Moreover, the process of democratization has been weak due to the fragmentation of political parties due to intra- and inter-party conflicts. For example, five parties [NC, CPN-UML, United People's Front, NSP-Anandi Devi group, Nepal Workers' and Peasants' Party (NWPP)] were agitating on the streets against the king's 4 October 2002 dismissal of the Deuba government. CPN-UML, however, left the movement on the pretext of other coalition partners not accepting the candidacy of its general secretary Madhav Kumar Nepal for

---

6 Article 127 of the Constitution of Kingdom of Nepal, 1990 - power to remove Difficulties: "If any difficulty arises in connection with the implementation of this Constitution, His Majesty may issue necessary Orders to remove such difficulty and such Orders shall be laid before Parliament".

7 Article 113 (2), D, of the *Constitution of the Kingdom of Nepal-1990*.

the post of prime minister. Later, it joined the Deuba government, which was reappointed by the king.

The elected government has been changed at least once a year - twelve elected governments have ruled Nepal between 1991 and 2002. These governments have been changed due to three reasons. First, the culture of intra-party conflict or non-cooperation with the government by a faction of an other party other than the party of the prime minister, and non-cooperation of the opposition or inter-party conflict[8]. Second, the king's intervention to be an 'assertive monarch' and non-cooperation of RNA to the government became significant under the so-called constitutional monarchy. Finally, the challenge posed by the 'ultra-left' Maoists' armed rebellion derailed the established system. Prime Minister G.P. Koirala was compelled to resign from the post after non-cooperation of RNA on the issue of curbing Maoists at Dunai and Holari in the western hills. The king dismissed the government headed by Sher Bahadur Deuba accusing him of being an 'incompetent' prime minister but surprisingly reinstated him two years later, and the reasons for such a dramatic turn was not known.

Election

One of the indicators of democratization is periodic elections. Three general and two local elections have been held after the restoration of democracy in 1990. All general elections held in Nepal after 1990 were mid-term elections except the first one in 1991. The beleaguered prime ministers invariably use elections as an 'exit strategy', i.e., they avoid the internal party conflicts using the weapons of election. Elections in Nepal are also not free from muscle, money and mafia power as the incumbent government tries to take advantage using all such means[9]. Moreover, parties are indifferent to improving the election system because of their short-sighted calculation of winning the election. As a result, no substantive change could be seen in the pattern of three national elections held in the country. Thus, the democratization process seemed to stress on 'electocracy' that has hardly promoted the spirit of inclusive democracy. The process was further halted due to Maoists violence, and no one knows when competitive electoral politics would return in the country.

---

8 Opposition party, CPN-UML had boycotted the Parliament for fifty-six days demanding the resignation of G.P. Koirala from the post of prime minister, in 2001.

9 Bishnu Pratap Shah, "Study and Training/Workshop on Electoral System and Research Methodology Inaugural Address" *Nepal Journal of Contemporary Studies*, Vol.1, No.1, March 2001, pp.1-8.

Militarization vs. Democratization

Militarization has increased on the pretext of the Maoists. In Nepal, as in other South Asian countries, the unchanging mind set of the ruler and security personnel, find security in the military approach to resolution or containing of conflict[10], which makes the process of democratization more complex. The state of emergency imposed for nine months between 26 November 2001 and 25 August 2002 saw the curbing of fundamental rights of the people. People suffered both the security forces and the Maoists who threatened, arrested, tortured, killed, abducted and were responsible for the disappearance of innocent people.

In democracy, military must be under the control of the civil government, but the RNA regularly held press conferences bypassing the civil administration. The government increased the budgetary allocation for the security forces and transfer of funds from the development to the security sector rose in accordance with RNA's demand. Between 2001-02 and 2002-03, an estimated cost of security expenditure[11] amounted to Nepali Rs. 39,634 million, which is equivalent to 10 percent of Nepal's 2000-01 GDP at factor cost[12]. In the following year between 2003-04 and 2004-05, the total budgetary expenses for combined security forces amounted to Rs. 29 billion, exclusive of the supplementary spending and foreign military assistance[13]. RNA pursued the role that led to an increased recruitment of armed personnel and weaponization with sophisticated gadgets. In 2001, the recruitment spree went up to 78,000 with the addition of 30,589 personnel over the 47,411 put at the 20th session of the then House of Representatives. According to its newly adopted ten-year defence plan, the RNA added two divisions and five Brigades to the existing three divisions. In the fiscal year 2003-04, the RNA recruited 6,440 personnel[14]. It is also planning to recruit 8,500 personnel in the current fiscal year making the total 100,000. On the other hand, Nepal's

---

10 Lok Raj Baral, "Security in Democracy and Pluralism: The Case of Nepal", paper presented at the Regional Seminar on Non-traditional Security in South Asia, organized by Nepal Center for Contemporary Studies (NCCS), on 16-17 November 2004, Kathmandu, Nepal.

11 Budgetary allocation, supplementary expenses and foreign military aid combined.

12 Dhruba Kumar, "Consequences of the Militarized Conflict and the Cost of Violence in Nepal", *Contributions to Nepalese Studies*, July 2003.

13 Ministry of Finance, *Public Statement on Income and Expenditure of the Fiscal Year 2004-2005*, Kathmandu: Ministry of Finance, 2004.

14 Bijay Ghimire, "Sena Dwara Thap Eghara Arab Maag" (the army demanded an additional eleven billion rupees), *Kantipur Daily*, 31 August 2004.

civil police have around 48,500 personnel and the Armed Forces number 18,000 making a combined strength of 1,44,500 men in uniform[15].

The Terrorist and Disruptive Activities (Control and Punishment) Act (TADA) has several clauses or sections that directly affect the constitutional order[16]. Its amendment through an ordinance in 2004 facilitated the security forces' unquestionable authority to arrest, search, detain, and use necessary force to accomplish their objectives. Under this Act, people can be arrested and held in preventive detention for up to 365 days. Similarly, there are several cases where the security forces have defied the judiciary's order in the case of constitutional 'right against preventive detention', which is no less a cause for concern for democratization.

Judiciary

The rule of law is one of the backbones of democracy. A powerful judiciary is the main defender of human rights. According to the present Constitution[17], extraordinary power rests with the Supreme Court to declare the law as void, if such laws are inconsistent with the Constitution. For the settlement of any constitutional or legal question involved in any disputes of public interest or concern, the judiciary has the extraordinary power to issue necessary and appropriate orders to enforce such rights or settle the dispute. The roles and the decisions of the judiciary are, however, not clear. The judiciary has given contradictory verdicts in case of dissolution and restoration of the House of Representatives and its credibility was under question when the Supreme Court upheld the dissolution after the king asked for its opinion on the same. What was more surprising was that the Court even went to the extent of endorsing the elections during the emergency imposed by the Deuba government to combat Maoist insurgency.

Civil Society and Human Rights

Civil Society in Nepal is increasingly becoming strong and mature after the restoration of democracy in 1990. Human rights groups and other associations have been raising their voice against RNA's atrocious activities such as illegal detention, disappearance, kidnapping, harassment, torture

---

15 Dhruba Kumar, "Emergency, Militarization and the Question of Democratic Recovery", paper presented at the National Seminar organized by Nepal Centre for Contemporary Studies (NCCS) on 2-3 January 2004, Kathmandu.

16 "Terrorist and Disruptive Activities (Control and Punishment) Ordinance 2001, *Informal*, 2001.

17 Article 84 of the *Constitution of the Kingdom of Nepal, 1990.*

and killing of innocent people as well as the extortion and abduction activities of the Maoists. They also played an important role of opposing the king and his government, both neither responsible to the people nor to the Parliament (upper house). The civil society has been opposing the promulgation of the TADA ordinance that legalizes unlawful detentions and creates human rights crises in the country.

In 2004, according to the Informal Sectors Service Centre, the recorded deaths by the state were 1,324 in comparison to the 819 deaths by the Maoists. Similarly, the number of security forces and the Maoists who have disappeared are 1,234 and 331, respectively, from May 2001 till very recently. According to Amnesty International, the number of recorded appeals from Nepal in a year, in comparison to those registered from different countries of the world, is the highest. Civil society groups have also shown concern over the present political vacuum and recommend the Constituent Assembly for progressive and participatory democracy as solutions. Besides, the Nepal Human Rights Commission has cautioned the security force to respect human rights. The spokesperson for RNA accuses human rights organizations as one-sided and claims that the RNA was 'fighting the Maoists for democracy'[18]. The security forces have arrested and detained some lawyers for their alleged involvement in the Maoist activities. The Human Rights and the Bar have opposed such actions. According to the Nepal Bar Association, among the ten arrested lawyers, two were released, and the whereabouts of the other eight lawyers are yet unknown[19]. Human rights activists and the civil society also raise their voice against forced recruitment, especially child recruitment, in the Maoist militia.

Media

Both electronic and print media have been playing an important role in the democratization process. Following the 4 October Royal takeover, when there was neither an elected government nor a Parliament, the media played the important role of the opposition. The daily papers and FM radios that have been providing factual information to the people are more or less independent. Media became important in the absence of the Parliament. Among the media, private media is urban centred, while the government media such as Radio Nepal and Nepal TV, as well as *Gorkhapatra,* have biased views against the Maoists and other agitating political parties, and therefore, censor the news or programme under government pressure.

---

18 *The Himalayan Times*, 10 December 2004.

19 *Rajdhani,* 28 February 2004.

Non-government sector media or press has also played an oppositional role. Nepal is in the 106th position in the list of freedom of press[20].

Unfortunately, media personnel suffered because of government and the Maoists. Journalists were killed by both the government and Maoists and harassed by security forces. The number of journalists reportedly murdered in custody is few. The most prominent till date are the journalists who have disappeared after being abducted by the Maoists. Besides this, three more journalists were killed by the security forces after 27 August 2003, and the whereabouts of ten journalists are still unknown[21]. Both the security forces and the Maoists tortured many others.

King Gynendra, who appointed and dismissed three governments consecutively since the dissolution of the Parliament in May 2002, took over the executive power of the state by imposing a state of emergency in the country on 1 February 2005. The king tried to rationalize his actions against the elected government on the claim that Prime Minister Deuba was 'incompetent'. He promised to hold general elections within a certain timeframe, after negotiating with the Maoists to protect people's sovereignty, democracy, life and property[22].

Except for imposing a ban on political parties, the king tried to restrict political activities and put political leaders under house arrest. Activities of civil society, including media and the NGOs, were controlled. Stern action was taken against the private FM stations and newspapers. The protest movements launched by the parties, students union, human rights activists, civil society and other professional organizations demanding full democracy were also ruthlessly suppressed using army and police forces[23].

Similarly, the royal actions compelled parliamentary political parties to join hands and protest against the king's move. In May 2005, a Seven Party Alliance (SPA) was formed with the Nepali Congress (NC), Nepali Congress Democratic (NC-D), Nepal Workers and Peasants' Party (NWPP), People's Front of Nepal (PFN), Nepal Sadhbhavana Party (Anandi Devi) and United Left Front with the primary objective of 'ending the despotic monarchy'. Though the NC-D and CPN-UML were dismissed in the Royal government by the king on 1 February 2005, they

---

20 *Reporters without Borders Report*, 2004.

21 *The Himalayan Times*, 19 April 2004.

22 See full text of the King's proclamation at http://nepalnews.com/archive/2006/feb01/news09.php

23 "Excessive use of force: OHCHR", *The Kathmandu Post*, 20 April 2006.

too joined the alliance in order to augment the tempo of the movement. Prior to this, a four-party alliance[24] had continually protested against the king's 4 October 2002 move.

In June 2005, election to the Constituent Assembly (CA) was agreed upon by the SPA, citing it as a vital means to resolve the problems faced by the Nepali people ruled by a handful of "high caste Hindu males" from the hills, who continued to be in power within the feudal structure of the Nepali state established by the Shah ruler in the eighteenth century. The agreement to move ahead for a Constituent Assembly paved the way for making the SPA-Maoists alliance a peaceful movement against the autocratic regime of the king. Several rounds of separate talks were held between the SPA and the Maoists in the country and in India, before finally reaching a twelve-point agreement on 18 November 2005 to fight for 'full-fledged democracy'. The international community, including the UN Secretary General Kofi Annan, welcomed the agreement[25]. The main issues of the twelve-point agreement were:

- Ending autocratic monarchy through nationwide democratic protests, establishing complete democracy through the restoration of Parliament, forming an all–party government with complete authority, holding elections to a Constituent Assembly through dialogue and understanding with the Maoists;

- Keeping the Maoists' armed force and the Royal Nepalese Army (RNA) under the supervision of the United Nations during the election of CA, conducting elections in a free and fair manner and accepting the results of the election;

- Expressing commitment for free political party activities, absolute democracy, competitive multi-party system, civil liberties, human rights, the concept of rule of law, and observance of fundamental rights by the Maoists;

- Expressing commitment for letting leaders, activists and the people displaced during the armed conflict to be resettled in their homes, for returning the land, houses and properties seized unjustly, and for creating an environment to allow free political activities by the Maoists;

---

24 In the four-party alliance, there were NC, NWPP, PFN, and Nepal Sadbhavana Party (Anandi).

25 *The Kathmandu Post*, 25 and 28 November 2005.

- Undertaking self-criticism and self-evaluation of past mistakes, making a commitment not to repeat such mistakes in future by both sides and settling any problem emerging between the parties through peaceful dialogue at the concerned level or at the leadership level[26];

- Boycotting the municipal polls terming it as a trick to legitimize the illegitimate and autocratic rule of the king;

- Maintaining friendly relations with all countries of the world and good-neighbourly relationship with India and China.

The royal government ultimately held the municipal election on 8 February 2006. According to the Election Commission, all candidates in the twenty-two municipalities were elected unopposed, though nominations were only filed for about half of the total of seats 4,146 in forty-eight municipalities. Apparently, 2,251 posts remained vacant as no candidates registered their names and those who filed papers were declared winners (unopposed) for the 1,277 posts[27]. However, the intention of the government to go to the election turned out to be a farce when the United States reacted that "Nepal's municipal election called by the King represented a hollow attempt to legitimize his power"[28]. The US criticism followed the sharp reactions of India, UK, EU and Japan. These governments came out openly against the government headed by the King stating that the municipal election without the participation of the SPA, which had secured more than 90 per cent of the seats in the dissolved House of Representatives, was meaningless and the poll was "a step backward from democracy". The pro-democratic political parties and the Maoists played an important role to foil the election using every means. Even the SPA leaders had urged the Maoists to foil the election by using force. The Royal government reacted to the external opinion as "an intervention" in its internal affairs and a "part of a ploy to destabilize Nepal". In an interview, Tulsi Giri, one of the Vice-Chairmen of the Royal government said that parliamentary election would also be held in the same manner as the municipal polls by the next year (2007).

Subsequently, on 19 March 2006, the SPA and the Maoists conducted

---

26 For full text of 12-points agreements, see http://www.nepalitimes.seacem.com/ issue/274/FromtheNepaliPress/9190

27 For municipal election details, see http://www.nepalnews.com/archive/Municipal_ polls_2062.php

28 www.nepalnews.com, 10 February 2006.

a long dialogue in India and formally agreed to strengthen their coalition with an announcement of a second Memorandum of Understanding (MoU). In the meantime, the Maoists declared a 20-day economic and transport blockade in all district headquarters, including Kathmandu from 14 March 2006. Disclosing their intention to intensify the protest against the monarchy, the SPA and the Maoists discussed how to make the protest more effective against the royal regime but convenient for the people. The Maoists also agreed to lift the blockade programme on 20 March as it affected the life of the people badly. The SPA agreed to reciprocate the lift of the blockade by announcing a four-day general strike from 6 April 2006. The proposed general strike, which shifted into *Janaandolan-II*, continued for nineteen days and compelled the king to give in. It was indeed an unprecedented movement that achieved everything short of gaining a republican order. All other major demands were promised by the king, as dictated by the SPA.

The election of the CA was endorsed by the very first session of the reinstated House of Representatives (HoR) on 30 April 2006. The HoR passed a resolution tabled by Prime Minister Girija Prasad Koirala on 17 May 2006, depriving the king of most privileges enjoyed by him, and declaring the reinstated House as 'sovereign'. The 'historic declaration' also called 'House Proclamation' 2063 (B.S), decided to collect tax from the king, declared Nepal as a secular state, changed the name of Royal Nepal Army into Nepal Army, and put the military under the Parliament. In addition, the HoR proclamation provided the authority to the house to decide on royal succession and prepare another national anthem suitable for the spirit of the movement. By a single stroke of parliamentary decision, the Raj Parishad (counseling body to the King) was abolished and the palace bureaucracy known as Raj Parishad Seva was annulled.

On 25 May 2006, a Ceasefire Code of Conduct was signed between the Government of Nepal and CPN (Maoist). Two rounds of talks were held for holding the summit meeting between Prime Minister Koirala and Chairman Prachanda of the Maoist party. Such a 'summit meeting' was held between the top leaders of SPA and Maoist at the Prime Minister's residence on 16 June 2006, where it was concluded to effectively and honestly implement an eight-point agreement, mainly a combination of the SPA-Maoist twelve-point understanding signed in the previous year and the 25-point ceasefire Code of Conduct signed on 25 May 2006. Further, they expressed commitment to a multi-party system, human rights, press freedom, civic liberties and the rule of law. It was also decided to request the UN, to help in the management and monitoring of arms and armies of both sides, during the election. They agreed to draft an interim constitution and form an interim government, which included the Maoists, before the election, and to dissolve the reinstated HoR after making alternative arrangements and dissolving the 'people's governments' of the Maoists across the country[29]. The meeting paved the way for the formation of an interim constitution drafting committee that has already publicized its draft, though there is no consensus among the political forces on some issues of the drafted constitution.

Problems and Prospects

Politics in Nepal is once again becoming problematic because of the ambivalent attitude of the SPA government. The Maoists are increasingly becoming suspicious of the actions of the government. Prime Minister Koirala came under criticism for trying to compromise on basic issues such as monarchy, army and Parliament. Parliament is being prolonged, undermining the demands of the Maoists and other civil society members. The parties have yet to start any discussion on holding the Constituent Assembly election and on forming an interim government with the Maoists. The other agenda, which is state restricting and making of Nepal into a republic, have also been sidetracked, vaguely stating that the issue of monarchy would be settled only by the people during the Constituent Assembly election. The peace process has also not accelerated as was expected, due to lack of trust between SPA and the Maoists. The Maoists want a political settlement first and the disarming of the PLA, while the other parties and some foreign countries want the demobilization of the PLA first. Nevertheless, the SPA government too does not want to prioritize the interim arrangement without settling the issue of the Maoist's arms. They argue that it is not possible for the unarmed SPA and the armed Maoists to remain together in the interim government. The Home Minister, the chief of the negotiating team of the government, said "the constituent Assembly election can't be expected to be impartial, until and unless the fear in those who faced the barrel of guns is allayed first". Thus, the issue of Maoist weapons has come as a great stumbling block between the SPA and the Maoists.

Another obstacle is the Nepal Army issue. The Maoists claim equal treatment between Nepal Army and PLA, and have asked for it to be put in temporary barracks until the Constituent Assembly election. The government, however, is not ready to accept this demand. For SPA, the

---

29 The full text of the eight-point SPA-Maoist agreement is available at http://ekantipur. com.16 June 2006.

Nepal Army would remain within the barracks, but under the control of the government. The National Army would not be disarmed, but its activities would be supervised by the UN. People have raised questions on the restriction of the Nepal Army, which never favoured the Nepali people and was always mobilized and used to suppress people's movement by the Shah rulers since 1950. Thus, if Nepal Army is not democratized, the system will not work properly because ambitious leaders can always misuse the army for their personal gains as has happened in the past. The present 'democratic' government too, has neither initiated the process of democratization of the army nor punished the commander-in-chief of the Army under whose command other security sectors such as Armed Police Force, Civil Police and National Investigation Department had worked for suppressing the people's movement. While the government removed chiefs of the other three security sectors from their posts, it did not touch the army generals, including its chief. Instead, interestingly, the government has appointed Rukmangad Katuwal as commander-in-Chief. Katuwal had allegedly played a vital role in suppressing *Janaandolan-II*. Now an Army related bill is tabled by the SPA government in the Parliament aiming at accelerating the democratization of the army.

The international community, including the US, India and the other key players influencing Nepali politics, do not want to include the Maoists in the government. The US envoy has expressed his government's position on the Maoists comparing the latter with the Hezbollah and Hamas terrorist groups. The interest of the international and regional players has not only created mistrust between the key players and the Maoist, but also between the Maoists and the SPA government. If such a situation continues, the SPA would not be able to continue the peace process. Both SPA and the Maoists have repeatedly committed to the settlement of all problems faced by Nepal. However, the peace process lingers on because of the increasing mistrust between the two and lack of consensus within the SPA on key issues. On their part, the Maoists have neither given up killing nor stopped the kidnapping, extortion and terrorizing of the people or recruitment into the PLA[30].

In spite of lack of agreement on these issues, both the Maoist leadership and the government have been frequently expressing their

---

30 According to Human Rights NGO, INSEC, since the April Revolution, the Maoists have killed thirteen people, mostly innocent villagers. Of these, three were shot dead and three others beaten to death. Similarly, they have abducted 371 people in the intervening months. Intimidations and extortion are rising by the day; see Ameet Dhakal, "Life Beyond Communism", The Kathmandu Post, 1 September 2006 and INSEC online report, "Maoists Running recruitment camps", 3 September 2006.

commitment to abide by the agreements. Rights groups, civil society, intellectuals and people from different walks of life have warned the two not to take any steps against their understanding and jeopardize the peace process. Although the situation is not so pessimistic, the government's failure to work to the expectation of *Janaandolan-II* is a cause of concern to the Nepalese army. It can, however, be hoped that both the SPA leaders and the Maoists are under pressure from the people and are not expected to foil the spirit of the movement.

Chapter V

Genesis and Growth of the Maoist Movement in Nepal[*]

Uddhab Pd. Pyakurel

Background

This chapter examines the origin and development of Maoist movement in Nepal. The hypothesis of the research is that the Maoist movement has capitalized on the agenda of socially, culturally and economically marginalized people of Nepal, especially women, the dalits and ethnic groups. To substantiate the hypothesis, this chapter looks into the history of the formation of the Communist Party, with radical agenda, its shift to the 'revisionist' position, and eventually marginalization of some of the sections of Nepali masses because of its own inner party conflicts. There are about a dozen communist parties in Nepal. Each of them accuse the other of being a 'revisionist', 'liquidationist', etc. The essay examines the chain of circumstances faced by the Maoist following the armed revolt in 1996. Besides, the chapter also details the Maoist movement in Nepal with reference to four basic criteria of a Social movement. These are ideology, environment, organization, and strategy. Before going to discuss those criteria, we shall discuss history of the Communist Parties in Nepal.

History of Communist Parties in Nepal

Unlike the history of other parties, the history of the communist parties in Nepal is quite of recent origin. Nepal was isolated from the rest of the

---

* This is the revised version of one of the chapters of a book by Pyakurel, Uddhab Pd. *Maoist Movement in Nepal: A Sociological Perspectives* (New Delhi: Adroit Publishes, 2007)

world during the 104-year-old Rana oligarchy. The Nepalis people came to know about the rest of the world only after the Nepalis military joined the First World War. However, some Nepalis were becoming aware of politics even before that and had also participated in the Indian independence movement. The Nepalis who started political movement in Nepal were in India either for their education or in exile in the 1940s. Although a nascent communist movement had emerged in 1947 during the Biratnagar Jute Mill strike, the Communist Party of Nepal (CPN) as a force of the democratic struggle in Nepal, came into existence only in 1949. In 1950, the communist party, which denounced the Delhi compromise between the Nepali Congress (NC), King Tribhuvan and the Ranas, was having just a fledgling entity. Earlier, the party was not very clear about its role during the democratic movement in 1951, which is termed as a 'revolution' in Nepalis history. NC was the leading party, which used weapons to overthrow the Rana regime in the movement. The movement ended when the King and the Ranas signed an agreement before the then Indian Prime Minister Jawaharlal Nehru. The accord, also called 'Delhi Compromise,' paved the way not only to end the Rana oligarchy, but also paved the way to form the interim government in Nepal. The agreement was termed as 'betrayal' by the CPN.

The CPN, which was infuriated with the NC after the latter joined the interim government, started tying up with other small anti-NC parties and made United Front in July 1951. Apart from that, the party tried to prove its credentials by adopting an anti-Indian stance by declaring the NC as 'Nehru government's toy.' Later, CPN was banned till April 1956 after it claimed responsibility for the January 1952 revolt.

The first convention of the CPN was held secretly in January 1954. It elected Manmohan Adhikari as the General Secretary. Adhikari was already holding the post after replacing Puspa Lal in 1951. Although the first Congress had been advocating republican state replacing the monarchy, the party shifted its stand and accepted the king as the country's head in 1955. Since there had been never-ending leadership struggle within the party, Keshar Jung Raimajhi replaced Manmohan Adhikari during Adhikari's visit to China. In the 1959 General Elections, the party took part in the elections and won four seats out of the 109 seats in the lower house.

The leadership clash in the CPN had turned into ideological conflict and led to the division of the party into two factions in 1960. These were the pro-Peking and the pro-Moscow factions. Such a division became visible when Keshar Jung Raimajhi, the then General Secretary of CPN, welcomed the dissolution of parliament by King Mahendra calling it a progressive step. However, the king's action was termed by other politburo members including Puspa Lal Shrestha and Manmohan Adhikari as 'military terror.' Three distinct views —Raimajhi wanted to work with the king, Puspa Lal wanted to work with NC to restore the parliamentary democracy, and Mohan Bikram Singh wanted to hold an election to the Constituent Assembly—were seen in the party in the Durbhanga Plenum in 1961. Among them, the first one was adopted as its party line by the CPN. In April 1962, Raimajhi was expelled from the party on the charge of supporting the autocratic king. He was replaced by Tulsi Lal Amatya at the party's Third Convention in Benares. Another party was formed under the leadership of Puspa Lal in May 1968 at the Gorakhhpur meeting. In September 1974, Mohan Bikram and Nirmal Lama took the lead to organize the Fourth Conference at Benares, which paved the way to constitute another communist party named CPN Fourth Convention. The Fourth Convention, led by Mohan Bikram Singh as General Secretary, was very clear on the question of armed revolution. It proposed to follow the path of armed struggle in 1979. However, the party gave up the idea after the announcement of the national referendum in the same year. It is said that the proposal adopted by the CPN Fourth Convention in 1979 is the very course that the Maoist took from 1996.

The CPN organized Nationwide District Secretary's Conference in 1979, which forced Nirmal Lama to leave the post of General Secretary. The Conference charged Lama as supporter of the referendum declared by the king. This conflict among the leaders ultimately led to another split in 1983 in the leadership of Nirmal Lama and Mohan Bikram Singh. The former led the same CPN Fourth Conference, and the latter founded CPN (Masal). CPN (Masal) had been seen as one of the founder members of the Revolutionary Internationalist Movement (RIM) in March 1984 in London. The aim of the RIM was to engage in a worldwide grouping of the revolutionary parties committed to the scientific principles of Marxism-Leninism-Mao Tse-tung thought.

It was during the period when Lama and Singh were busy fighting for the post and blamed each other as ideology shifter or revisionist that another faction of the youth communist leaders started armed revolt in Jhapa district in Nepal in 1971. Jhapa lies across the border of Mechi River. The revolt was the first uprising in Nepal with the ideological and physical support of the Communist Party of India (Marxist and Leninist)'s youth of Naxalbari area, which is the dividing line between India and

Nepal. (Hachhethu 2002:70). By this revolt, some eight 'class enemies' were wiped out in the name of the campaign to eliminate class enemies. There is a claim that the Jhapa uprising was the gateway for the process of forming CPN (UML), which became the largest communist party of Nepal after 1990.

On the other hand, the party-breaking trend had been seen as a continuous process. In the Fifth Congress in 1985, Masal once more broke up into CPN (Masal) and CPN (Mashal). The latter was formed under the leadership of Mohan Baidhya. Mashal became the crucial organization for launching the 'people's war' when Puspa Kamal Dahal alias Prachanda took over the post of general secretary from Baidhya. To summarize, the CPN (Fourth Congress) was divided into three factions—the Fourth Congress, Masal and Mashal during its 11-year journey since 1974. Among these three, the first one joined the United Left Front (ULF, an alliance of seven left factions' under the co-ordination of Sahana Pradhan) on the eve of the 1990s mass movement. The front launched the 1990s movement after joining hands with the NC. However, the other two formed the Samyukta Rastriya Janaandolan (United National People's Movement, UNPM) under the leadership of Baburam Bhattarai. The UNPM was not satisfied with the achievement gained by the 1990s movement and asked people to continue the movement after the NC and the ULF called it off. The main demand of UNPM was the people's sovereignty and to hold the election of the Constituent Assembly to write the constitution.

In March 1991, Masal again splited into two factions on the issue of whether the party would take part in the 1991 elections or not. The factions, subsequent to the split, were 'Masal' led by Baburam Bhattarai, and 'Mashal' led by Mohan Bikram Singh. The first faction decided to participate in the 1991 elections in order to use the opportunity to 'expose the monarchy and the parliamentary system' (Pristhabhumi, 21 March 1991 cited in Thapa (ed.) 2003:21), and the second faction decided to stay underground. For contesting the first general election under the 1990s constitution, five radical forces—Fourth Conference, Mashal led by Prachanda, a small faction of Masal led by Baburam, Sarbahara Sramik Sangathan and NCP (Janamukhi)—came together, formed a new underground party by the name CPN (Unity Centre) and decided to contest the elections. They took part in the election by floating another party named United People's Front, Nepal (UPFN). The declared objectives of UPFN were to 'expose the inadequacy of the parliamentary system'. It got nine seats out of 205 in the House of Representatives in the 1991 election and became the third largest party in the Parliament. After submitting a

14-point demand to Prime Minister Koirala in 1992, the Unity Centre joined hands with the Masal and two other smaller parties to launch a series of protests against the first elected Koirala government. Among the protests, the protests of April 6, 1992 turned violent in which more than a dozen people were killed in the police firing.

Analyzing Prachanda's political line with a Marxist-Leninist-Maoist ideology, the CPN (Unity Centre) at its Unity Congress in December 1991 passed 'a resolution to initiate a 'people's war' to bring about a new democratic revolution' in Nepal (Thapa 2003:43). The decision became the cause of another split of the party into Prachanda faction and Nirmal Lama faction. It was divided in May 1994 where Lama left the party CPN (Unity Centre), and formed another party by the same name. Others stated that the action taken by Lama was only because of his distrust in armed uprising. After the split, the Prachanda-led Unity Centre went underground to prepare for its next phase of struggle. At the same time, the division in the mother party into a two tier, the Unity Centre, organization and UPFN, which was formed to contest the election; UPFN also cracked into the Baburam Bhattarai group and Niranjan Govinda Baidhya group. Both the groups went to the Election Commission for recognition. However, only the latter got formal recognition from the commission. This decision of the commission became a pretext for the first group to boycott the mid-term election in 1994. Ultimately, the group gave up the parliamentary electoral politics and started preparation for the armed revolt.

Having gone through ups and downs in its organization through splits and unities, CPN (Unity Centre) organized its Third Plenum in March 1995. At the plenum, the party was renamed CPN (Maoist). It also came up with a major decision for raising arms against the state. The decision taken was, "for the true liberation of the people all efforts must be concentrated for the development of a people's war that would usher in the new people's democratic form of government" (Thapa and Sijipati 2003:45). The party also gave up its policy of taking part in parliamentary elections. In September of the same year (1995), the party adopted the "Plan for the Historic Initiation of the 'People's War" and passed 'seven theoretical premises' (Thapa and Sijipati 2003:45 - 47). Following this, the party started a series of public meetings or campaigns including the famous *Sija* campaign[1], which the party termed as 'final politico-ideological

---

1 Sija is the shortcut term of Sisne and Jaljale. These are two different villages of the eastern part of Rolpa District, where the party organized the political campaign and carried out some social work to mobilize party members to propagate the ideology of Marxism-Leninism-Maoism. Rolpa belongs to mid-western part of Nepal.

preparation.' In October 1995, a clash between the *Sija* campaigners (the Maoist) and the cadres of mainstream political parties, specially the NC and RPP activists, was reported. It was a campaign in which the local people also participated. In November 1995, the clash led to the police suppression of the participants of the campaign. The security force launched 'Operation Romeo.' Random arrest, torture, rape and extra-judicial killings became the normal practice. This 'brutal' suppression was the turning point of the Maoist to establish speedy rapport with the people by expressing sympathy or concern for them. 'Operation Romeo' became the vehicle to unite the villagers and the Maoist for a common agenda 'to escape and protect the life from the state repression'.

In January 1996, the underground party fixed the 13th February 1996 as the date for starting the 'People's War'. On February 3, 1996, the open political wing of the party led by Baburam Bhattarai had presented its 40-point memorandum to the government. It warned the government that the UPFN would begin an armed struggle against the state unless appropriate measures towards fulfilling the demands were initiated by February 17. Citing the government's indifference to UPFN demands, the party cadres including Baburam Bhattarai went underground and launched an attack on February 13, 1996 in four different places in four districts in the name of 'People's War'. The first four targets of the Maoist were Agricultural Development Bank in Gorkha District, and three different police posts in Rolpa, Rukum and Sindhuli District.

Various scholars have considered the demands presented to the government, as well as the issue of the denial of the recognition of the party by the Election Commission, as critical causes for the eruption of 'People's War'. (Karki and Seddon 2003:17). In fact, having a look at the strategic preparation of People's War, one can say that those causes are only a farce. It is because the leaders strategically made two parties—one underground, and the other open—to prepare for the armed conflict. Both the parties aimed to expose the inadequacy of achievements of the 1990s movement. The party, led by Baburam Bhattarai, entered into electoral politics with the explicit objectives 'to expose the inadequacy of the parliamentary system'. Another justifiable evidence for such a position was that the UPFN started attack on the government institutions even before the 17 February deadline. It seems that the attack was guided by the underground party's decision of January 1996 rather than the UPFN's given deadline. Another aspect is that the UPFN had presented a similar 38-points demands to the UML government in December 1994. The government claims that the Maoist had begun their attacks before the government could formulate its response on their demands.

However, people had a doubt that if the election commission had favoured the Bhattarai group by recognizing his faction as a party, the UPFN faction would not join the war. Even Prachanda expressed doubt about Baburam's 'jump' from pure intellectual ideology into the underground and *rebellion* war (*Janadesh* 2006:19). Prachanda's 'benefit of doubt' over the communist leaders is valid in Nepalese politics because rarely the communist leaders came back and continued with their ideological stand if they once entered into the election politics. Most of the Communist leaders left their ideology and shifted to the right once they went to take part in the election in Nepal. Keshar Jung Raimajhi, Radha Krishna Mainali and Gore Bahadur Khapangee are those, who from radical left, changed to conservative royalists after engagement within the electoral politics. Another example is of CPN (UML). Most of the leaders of the party were from 'Jhapa uprising' background (a replication of the Naxalite movement of India), but after having adopted the path of socialism through competitive parliamentary democracy, they have forgotten their ideology as well as ultimate goal, viz., socialism and classless society. Now they seem to be more liberal than other liberal democrats like the NC.

Some Elements of The Maoist Movement

For Ghanashyam Shah (1990), as mentioned earlier, revolts, rebellions, reforms, and revolutions are various forms of movements. The Maoist Movement, following Shah, can be conceptualized as a revolution, which means it is 'a form of politics characterized by the extensive use of violent or other illegal means in competition for control of government power and authority' (Wolfenstien cited in Singh 2005:9). Referring to environment, ideology, organization, and strategy as four dimensions, Mohanty tries to provide a framework for study of the revolutionary movement (Mohanty 1977:10). Most studies on social movements speak out at least four components—ideology, strategy, organization, and objectives—as essential components of a movement (Louis 2002:31). Attempt has been made here to discuss these aspects in the context of the Maoist movement in Nepal.

Ideology: The general meaning of the term 'ideology' is that it is a system of ideas concerning a phenomenon, especially the social life. Ideology not only provides the motivating force but also defines the aims and objectives of the movement. The Maoist claim that they are guided by Marxist and Leninist theories and that they apply whatever Mao had applied in China. Accusing all other communists as revisionists and liquidationists, they claim that they are the only real followers of Marxism-Leninism-Maoism. The Maoist of Nepal quote Mao: 'Mao enriched qualitatively the theoretical treasure of Marxism-Leninism by successfully fulfilling the necessity of class struggle in the imperialist era.' For Prachanda, contribution of Mao in relation to People's War should be understood in the context of the necessity of developing class struggle in the history (Prachanda 1993:182).

The Maoist take the position of Marx and Angels that the violent revolution has a universal character in the class society. They believe in Lenin's clarity on systematically developed theoretical concepts regarding necessity of armed struggle in the course of implementing it in the Russian revolution. Based on the theoretical assertions of Marxism-Leninism on violent revolution and the experience acquired from their practical applications, Mao developed the comprehensive theory of 'People's War' in the course of accomplishing new democratic revolution in China. They claim that the theory of 'people's war' developed by Mao represents the apex of Marxist-Leninist military science and will be applied universally in all kinds of countries according to the situation. (Prachanda 1999:146).

Ideologically, they believe that revolt is the only path for changing the society. They advocate that the 'People's War' will end all kinds of other war' (Prachanda 1999:185). Therefore, they tried revolting against the Panchayat regime in 1990 when strong alliance of NC and ULF were trying to defeat the Panchayat through peaceful movement. Those who believed in peaceful means to change the society are, according to the Maoist leaders, foolish and irrationals. Responding to Sayami's argument about the achievement of 2006 people's movement in Nepal, Baburam Bhattarai, one of the topmost leaders of the Maoist, tried to give credit of the achievement to the armed revolt launched by the Maoist. Sayami had stated that the 19-day-long peaceful movement achieved much more than the 10-year-long war in which some 15,000 lives were lost (*Kantipur*, May 3, 2006). Likewise, Bernstain's contention that 'capitalism transforms peacefully into socialism was termed as a 'counter revolution tradition' by Prachanda. Bernstain had said, "through the methods of voting, demonstration and pressure we can bring about reforms for which a violent revolution was necessary hundred years ago". (cited in Prachanda 2004:121). The goal of political struggle, according to Kautsky, is "to win the state power by changing parliament to the master of government through a majority in it" (*ibid.*). For Prachanda, parliament and parliamentarian democracy means nothing. He said, "in relation to the parliamentary system and parliamentarism, there have been life and death struggles in the International Communist Movement since the birth of Marxism" (*ibid*: 120).

The Maoist of Nepal claim that the party has been ideologically following the tenets of Marxism-Leninism-Maoism, and its ultimate aim is to apply Mao's thought in Nepal. First, it tried to mobilize the masses to follow Mao, according to whom the masses are the "creators of history". It took to arms following its belief in the Maoist thought. To Mao, 'people with no army have nothing of their own.' Prachanda says, "in whatever way they are equipped with weapons, trained and powerful in the beginning, their fall is inevitable when they stand against the interest of the masses. Final victory is theirs that fight for defending the interest of broad masses however weak they seem militarily in the beginning" (Prachanda 1993:183).

Apart from such belief in people's army and war, Mao had also shown his belief in people's power rather than the weapons. He used to say, "weapons are an important factor in war, but not a decisive factor; it is people, not things, that are decisive" (Prachanda 1993:183-184). It seems that the Maoist in Nepal followed the double standards of Mao on people and army, and tried to attract the general public by raising 'situational local issue related slogans'. Although the Communist ideology was against the 'identity issues', they tried to bring these issues to the forefront. These issues not only touched the native and suppressed people, but also the migrants, labourers, peasants, women, Dalits etc. They even tried to win support by creating hostility among the different groups in the society; the cadres of the Maoist used to say that after their rule prevails in the society, the migrant landlords will have to give up the lands they occupied. The Maoist sells such agenda to the native people, most of whom belong to the ethnic communities.

However, the Maoist has had no constant policy; after they gained high support of native and ethnic communities, it is now trying to get support from the high caste and elite community advocating the necessity of social harmony in the society. According to its leaders, harmony is needed for achieving its ultimate goal of 'Communism through Socialism.'

Environment: Environment is another important component of the movement. Every incident will be guided and influenced by the environment. I examine the given socio-political and cultural situation, which has given space to the Maoist movement in Nepal.

As mentioned earlier, Nepal is a highly diversified society. Pluralism is its integral feature. Nepal is spread over an area of 147,181 sq. km. It has a population of about 23.5 million. The country is divided into three topographic zones as under:

- One is the mountainous region which is inhabited by the people of Tibetan origin, i.e., Bhote, Sherpa, Thakali etc. The region covers 15 per cent of Nepal's land and 0.7 percent of the total population. It comprises 15 districts.

- The second is the hilly region which covers 36 districts with approximately 68 per cent land of Nepal. Caste-and ethnic-settlements overlap in this region. Out of total 36.4 per cent ethnic population of Nepal 25.8 per cent reside mainly in this region. Likewise, 40.3 percent, out of total 57.5 per cent caste population of Nepal is found in this region.

- The third is the Tarai region, which is considered a traditional homeland of tribal people, i.e., Tharu, Rajbansi, Dhimal, etc. Apart from that, the people of Indian origin have also settled in Tarai. The region covers 17 per cent of the area of Nepal, and has 24 districts. As per the 2001 census, Nepal has as many as 100 caste-and ethnic-groups, and 90 languages and dialects. Based on caste, ethnic, regional, cultural and linguistic considerations, the Nepalis population is broadly classified into three major categories: *Parbatiya* (hill people) and *Medhesia* (plain people); jati (caste groups) and janjati (ethnic/tribal groups); and high-caste and low-caste Hindus. Nepal therefore, has long been considered as a pluralistic state although every regime has mostly favoured the dominating language, religion and culture.

Of the total of 100 caste/ethnic groups, the number of people comprising each of these groupings ranges from 3.6 million to a little less than 1,000. The largest group is the Kshatriya with 15.8 per cent of the total population, and the smallest Kusunda numbering only 164. The social composition of Nepalese population is made up of 57.5 per cent caste group, the constitue 36.4 per cent ethnic groups and 6.2 percent others 6.2 per cent (Pfaff-Czarnecka 1997; Gurung 2003:5). There is, of course, a debate over the status of the Newars. The issue is whether they are to be treated as a marginalized group or not has been contentious because the socio-politic-economic status of Newars as a group is much higher than the other groups of the society. The caste groups are characterized by a four-layer hierarchy consisting of Brahmans, Kshatriyas, Baisyas and Shudras. The people of Terai, except those who migrated from the hills, are called Madhesis and distributed in over consist of both caste and ethnic groups. In fact, the term Madhesi has been identified an ethno-regional identity of the Indian Origin Terai people. They constitute over 31 per-cent of the total population of Nepal. The Madhesi caste-groups alone constitute about 19.5 per cent of the total population. This, of course, includes the Dalits of Terai. There are 59 officially defined ethnic groups in Nepal. They are the *Adibasi/Janjati* people who are considered as the indigenous people of Nepal. Among the 59 groups, 18 are settled in the mountains, 24 in the hills, six in inner Terai, and 11 in Terai proper. Among 36.4 per cent of the total population of *Adibasi/Janjati in* Nepal, Magar with 7.14 per cent population is the largest group in the hilly region, and Tharu in terai with 6.75 per cent population in Tarai.

Out of 90 languages recorded in the 2001 census, 12 have 1 per cent speakers each. Nepali, which is recognized as the 'language of the nation' as well as the official language, is the language of a little less than half (48.61 per cent) of the population; it is the of *lingua* franca of Nepal. Although Nepal was constitutionally declared a 'Hindu Kingdom', its people belonged to various religions. As per the 2001 census, 80.6per cent of the Nepali people practise Hinduism, 10.7 per cent Buddhism, 4.2 per cent Islam, 3.6 per cent Kirat. People of other religious such as Christian, Sikh, Jain, etc., constitute less than 1 per cent (Gurung 2003).

In the prevailing situation, the hierarchies of relationships have been discriminated against and deprived on the basis of gender, caste/ethnicity, and region. The lower strata, particularly women, Dalit, Janajatis and Madhesi people, were deprived from equal and equitable treatment and sharing of resources. Because of the policy of 'Nepalization' accelerated by the Nepali state for 238 years, the hill high caste Brahman-Kshatriyas and the ethnic group Newars have long been in a privileged position. The following table shows the socio-politicol-economic position of the above-mentioned groups.

Table 1: Human Development by Caste and Ethnicity, 1996

		Dominant Groups			Marginal Groups			
		Brahman	Kshatri-ya	Newar	Madhesi	Janajati	Dalit	Nepal
1	Life Expectancy	60.8	56.03	62.2	58.4	53.0	50.3	55.0
2	Adult Literacy Rate %	58.00	42.00	54.80	27.50	35.20	23.80	36.27
3	Means Years of Schooling	4.4647	2.786	4.370	1.700	2.021	1.228	2.254
4	Per Capita Income (Nos.)	9921	7744	11953	6911	6607	4940	7673
5	Life Expectancy Index	0.957	0.522	0.620	0.557	0.467	0.422	0.500
6	Educational Attainment Index	0.490	0.342	0.462	0.221	0.280	0.186	0.295
7	Income Index	0.237	0.181	0.289	0.160	0.152	0.110	0.179
8	Human Development Index (RDI)	0.441	0.348	0.457	0.313	0.299	0.239	0.325
9	Ratio to HDI Nepal = 100	135.87	107.31	140.73	96.28	92.21	73.62	100.00

Source: NESAC. 1998. *Nepal: Human Development Report 1998*. Kathmandu: Nepal South Asia Centre

The above-mentioned table indicates the socio-economic position of Nepal's various social groups. The Newars, who are also in the list of the ethnic population in Nepal, have the highest Human Development Index (HDI). The Brahmans are ahead of Newars only in life expectancy and education related index. Kshatriyas are behind the Newars and Brahmans in all aspects of HDI. Although the Janajatis are ahead of Madhesis in life expectancy and education related index, Madhesi's position is ahead of the Janajatis in HDI. Dalits score the lowest in every aspect of HDI.

Table 2: Integrated National Index of Governance (INDG), 1999

S. N.		Dominant Groups		Marginalized Groups				
		Bahun/ Chhetri	Newar	Madhesi	Janajati	Dalit	Other	Total
1	Court	77.0	13.6	7.6	1.7	0	0	235
2	Constitutional Bodies	56.0	24.0	12.0	2.8	0	0	25
3	Cabinet	62.5	9.4	15.6	12.5	0	0	32
4	Parliament	60.0	7.6	17.4	13.6	1.5	0	265
5	Public Administration	77.6	17.6	3.7	1.2	0	0	245
6	Party Leadership	58.8	10.9	15.8	15.2	0	0	165
7	Leadership: Local Elected Bodies	55.5	15.7	16.2	12.0	0	0	191
8	Leadership: Commerce and Industry	16.7	47.6	35.7	0	0	0	42
9	Leadership: Educational Arena	77.3	11.3	7.2	2.1	1	1	97
10	Leadership: Cultural Arena	69.1	17.9	0	4.9	0	0	123
11	Science/ Technology	58.1	29.0	9.7	3.2	0	0	62

12	Civil Society Leadership	75.9	14.8	7.4	1.9	0	0	54
	Total	66.5	15.2	11.2	7.1	0.3	1	
	Population %	31.6	5.6	30.9	22.2	8.7	1	
	Difference In Population %	+ 34. 9	+9.6	- 19.7	- 15.1	- 8.4	-1	

Source: Neupane, Govinda. 2000, Nepalko Jatiya Prasana (Question of Caste/ Ethnicity in Nepal). Kathmandu: Centre for Development Studies

If one analyzes the table, one gets to know that all social groups in Nepal, excepting the Brahmans/Kshatriyas and Newars, have under-representation in key institutions and positions. The proportion of Brahmans and Kshatriyas are exceedingly high, excepting in the fields of commerce and industry. In commerce and industry, Newars and the Madhesis share dominant positions. The Brahmans/Kshatriyas occupy the third position. The position of ethnic groups and Dalits remains the same as in Table No 2.

Table 3: Share of Caste/Ethnic Groups in Prestigious Occupations

CasteEethnicity	Legislative, Senior Officials, Managers and Professionals	Technical and Assistant Professionals	Clerks or Office Assistants
Brahmans of Hill Area	9.09	4.83	4.13
Dalits of Hill Area	0.45	0.31	0.55
Dalits of Tarai Area	0.30	0.26	1.06

Ethnic People of Mountain and Hill Area	2.72	1.51	1.94
Ethnic People (Thakali) Mountain and Hill Area	8.24	3.21	1.88
Ethnic People (Newars)	6.29	3.70	3.80
Ethnic People belonging to Tarai Region	1.30	0.78	1.84

Source: *Nepal Human Development Report 2004,* Kathmandu: UNDP

The position of the Brahmans remains high in all prestigious occupations. Interestingly, an ethnic group known as Thakali, occupies the position next to the Brahmans. Among the ethnic groups, the hill ethnic groups are ahead of the Terai ethnic groups. The Dalits position is the same in respect of HDI and Integrated National Index of Governance (INID). However, the Terai Dalits are ahead of the other Dalits in respect of the white-collar colour jobs of the lower level, such as clerks, office assistants, etc.

Table 4: Caste/Ethnic Composition of HOR and Party Central Committees

	House of Representatives*			Parties' Central Committee (** & ***)					
Caste/ Ethnicity Total Number	1991	1994	1999	NC **	UML **	RPP **	JM ***	NSP ***	NWPP ***
	205	205	205	29	46	41	38	29	9
Bahun	37.6	42.0	37.6	62.1	65.2	19.5	44.7	-	22.2
Chhetri	19.1	19.5	20.5	10.3	10.9	31.7	7.8	-	11.1
Newar	6.8	6.3	6.8	3.4	13.0	4.9	10.5	-	66.6
Hill Ethnic Groups	15.2	12.2	14.7	13.8	6.5	26.8	21.0	-	-

Tarai Communities	21.0	20.0	19.5	10.3	4.3	17.1	5.2	100	-
Others	2.9	2.0	2.5	-	-	-	10.5	-	-
Total	102.6	102	101.6	99.9	99.9	100	99.92	100	100

Sources: * IIDS, 2000. *The Fourth Parliamentary Election.* Kathmandu: Institute for Integrated Development Studies. ** *Nepal Human Development Report 2004,* Kathmandu: UNDP p:190. *** Lok Raj Baral, Krishna P. Khanal and Krishna Hachhethu. 2002. 'Responsiveness of Nepali Political System'. (Unpublished Report)

Table 4 gives two kinds of information. The first part examines the representation of different communities in the House of Representatives (HoR). The data shows absence of increase in the composition of representation from ethnic and other communities during the three elections. However, the representation of Kshatriyas has increased; Brahmans have maintained constant hegemony. In fact, the Brhamans had three times more representation than the size of its population. Interestingly, though the state and the political parties raised voices favouring the representation of the 'marginalized' groups, the presence of these groups (hill ethnic groups, Terai communities and others) in the three recent parliaments, have substantially decreased.

To show the representation of the different groups in the parties at the central level, it is interesting to note that all major parties somehow show the same kind of representation coming from higher caste groups (Brahmans and Chhetris). The UML, which has been trying to show its status as a party of the proletariat and the 'marginalized,' has the highest representation from Brahmans. In fact, the ethnic and Terai representation is higher in the NC than in the UML. In Rastriya Prajatantra Party (RPP), the representation of the marginalized groups seems better. However, the members made by the RPP in the name of the representation from different communities, are rather more from the elite class than the Brahmans, Kshatriyas and Newars. Most of the elites from different groups, who were allies of the king, joined the RPP when Nepal turned into a democracy in 1990. It is said that the RPP elites are neither progressive, nor do they represent the 'marginalized' groups.

Another remembrable feature of Table 4 is that the representation of two parties—the point worh nothing in the case of NSP and the NWPP— seem more homogeneous than the other four parties. Both the parties, according to their documents, have been formed to raise the voice of the 'marginalized' groups. The question is that if the party itself has not addressed the diversity by accommodating all the groups in the party on the basis of their proportion of population, how can a leader of the same outfit raise such a question at different forums? On the issue of inclusion and representation, the position of Jana Morcha (JM) seems a bit progressive although the representation from the Terai group is poor in the party.

Table 5: Land Holding Position of Caste/Ethnic and Religious Groups

S. N.	Caste/Ethnicity	Landless	Semi-landless (below 0.2 Hectare)	Farmers with the land In-between 0.21 to 1 Hectare	Small Farmers (1.01-2.00 Hectares)	Lower Middle Farmers (2.01-4.44 Hectares)	Middle Farmers (4.01-10 Hectares)	Big Farmers (over 10 Hectares)	Total Family
1	Nepal	24.44	6.98	27.59	20.15	13.42	6.25	1.17	4174374
2	Ethnic Community								
	Santhal, Jhangad, Kisan, Munda, etc.	58.46	4.91	10.44	7.07	9.5	8.76	0.87	16910
	Gurung	26.85	6.36	30.53	21.5	11.1	3.25	0.41	110574
	Tharu	22.83	6.36	17.93	15.65	19.25	15.18	2.79	235500
	Rai	20.04	4.89	24.97	24.24	17.69	7.4	0.76	125297
	Tamang	16.69	6.93	31.29	26.73	14.18	3.85	0.32	239755
	Limbu	15.83	4.57	27.06	25.0	18.67	7.95	0.91	67916
	Magar	14.41	5.88	33.33	26.53	14.71	4.51	0.63	296313
3	Caste group								
	Tarai Dalits	43.98	9.89	26.19	11.3	6.01	2.29	0.34	231880
	Hill Dalits	15.32	15.24	44.55	17.25	6.14	1.27	0.24	308796
4	Religious groups								
	Muslims, Churautes	40.37	6.29	19.54	13.18	11.19	7.4	1.94	148036

Source: Central Bureau of Statistics 2002 Ka cited in *Nepal Human Development Report 2004,* Kathmandu: UNDP p: 194

For a country, where the economy is primarily based on agriculture, land is the main form of the property of the people. Property determines the economic status of the people. It can be clearly seen from Table 5 that the Dalits in Terai and the Muslims overall suffer from lack of access to land. The economic position of the major ethnic groups like Magars, Tamangs, Tharus, Gurungs, Rais, Limbus, etc., is somewhat better. Exceptions are the Santhals, Jhangads, Kisans, and Mundas. Six out of ten people from Santhal, Jhangad, Kisan and Munda groups are landless. The position of Dalits in the hills is again somewhat better than the Dalits from the Tarai. Tharus, who belong mostly to the Tarai region, are better placed in terms of land holding.

Table 6: Educational Status of the Caste/Ethnic and Regional Groups

Caste/ Ethnicity	Literate %	SLC and Equivalent %	Intermediate or Equivalent %	Graduate or Above %
Nepal	53.74	100	100	100
Hill people				
Thakali	72.42	0.13	0.12	0.10
Newar	72.18	11.87	13.27	13.51
Limbu	59.64	1.40	1.01	0.68
Rai	58.77	2.30	1.72	1.25
Magar	57.70	4.58	3.08	2.16
Tamang	42.00	2.07	1.13	0.75
Tarai				
Upper caste	73.92	4.11	5.63	6.95
Tharu	46.54	3.52	2.75	1.69
Dalit	21.06	0.63	0.46	0.31
Hill				
Brahmans	75.64	29.91	34.85	41.48

Kshatriya, Thakuri, Sanyasi	60.90	21.99	20.17	18.25
Dalits	41.93	1.32	0.86	0.51

Source: Central Bureau of Statistics 2002 Ka cited in Nepal Human Development Report 2004, Kathmandu: UNDP p: 193

Table 6 shows the educational status of the different groups in Nepal. The data indicates that the educational status of the hill groups is better than that of the Terai. There is a notable margin between hill and the Terai upper caste people. About difference of 2 percent is seen between two upper caste communities in the literacy rate, but in the higher education, the difference is seven times greater. In respect of the Dalit groups, the literacy rate of the Terai Dalits is only half the literacy rate of the hill Dalits. The educational status of Thakalis and Newars (both are considered as ethnic communites) is higher than the Kshatriyas and Thakuris. Among the hill people, the position of the Tamang group, one of the major ethnic groups in Nepal, is the poorest.

Table 7: Gender Participation in Economic and Political Activities

Sector	Details	Male %	Female %
Economic level (job sector)	Agriculture and forest	52	48
	Fuel and water supply	78	22
	Public adm.	88	12
	Education	74	26
	Health	71	29
	Other community, social and private work	85	15
Political level	National level (MP)	94.2	5.8
	District level	93.3	6.7
	Village level	92.3	7.7
	Ward level	80	20

Source: Central Bureau of Statistics 2002 Ka cited in *Nepal Human Development Report 2004,* Kathmandu: UNDP pp: 192-193

Women are the other marginalized group in Nepal. As participation is considered as a major indicator of the empowerment, Table 7 shows the low participation of women in every sphere of economic and political reality in comparison to men. Women out number men by 0.26 percent in Nepal. However, they are on the margin (nowhere) in the economic and political level. They are significantly visible only in the agricultural and forest sector. In other spheres, men have 4 to 16 times more participation than women. It is interesting to note that the participation of women is the poorest at national level politics, where all policies are being finalized.

The next section of this chapter analyzes the constitution and election manifestos of major political parties. This has been done to see how the constitution and the major political parties have addressed the socio-cultural and regional diversity in Nepal. Apart from that, the study also examines the Maoist's policies and programs, as it has been instrumental in attracting the marginalized groups.

The 1990 Constitution: The constitution is a supreme legal framework, which provides the main guidelines for the government. The constitution is not an abstract/shapeless document. It represents a document, which reflects the interest of the major political actors in the country.

After being disenchanted by the policies and programmes of the autocratic Panchayat regime, people from all walks of life took part in the mass movement of the 1990s with the hope of emancipation, good governance and development. There was wide-ranging participation in the movement. Dalits, ethnic groups, women, religious groups, regional communities, linguistic groups, and civil societies, all joined in the movement in a big way. With the success of the movement, the participants tried to get their share from the democratic government. They expected their agenda to be incorporated in the 1990 constitution. The question is, whether the constitution provided for space raised by the stakeholders of the 1990s movement. Table 8 shows the responses of the state towards the varied groups through the constitution of the Kingdom of Nepal 1990.

Table 8: Constitutional Provision for the Different Communities in 1990 Constitution

S. N	Issue	Constitutional Provision
1.	Nation/state	1 Nation constitutes of people irrespective of religion, race, caste or tribe 2. Strengthens national unity and harmony amongst various religions, castes, tribes, languages, race and communities 3. Multi-ethnic, multi-lingual, democratic, independent, indivisible, sovereign Hindu and Constitutional Monarchical Kingdom
2.	All marginalized groups (ethnic/ gender/caste/ class)	1. All citizens are equal before the law 2. No discrimination on grounds of religion, race, sex, caste, tribe or ideological conviction. 3. Eliminate all types of economic and social inequalities 4. Maintain cultural diversity preserving and promoting language, script and culture of the different communities 5. Pursue a policy, which will help promote the interests of the economically and socially backward groups and communities by making special provisions with regard to their education, health and employment.
3.	Religion	1. Officially Hindu kingdom 2. Freedom to profess and practice own religion as handed down to him from ancient times, having due regard to traditional practices 3. Prohibition to convert persons from one religion to another 4. Right to maintain independent existence of every religious group, and for this purpose right to manage and protect its religious places and trusts.
4.	Language	1. Nepali in the Devnagari script is the national as well as the official language of Nepal 2. All the other languages spoken as the mother tongue in various parts of Nepal are the national languages of Nepal 3. Right to operate schools in its own mother tongue upto the primary level.
5.	Civil Society	1. Freedom to form unions and associations 2. Freedom to assemble peacefully and without arms 3. Freedom of opinion and expression 4. Freedom to move throughout the kingdom and reside in any part thereof 5. Freedom to practice any profession or to carry on any occupation, industry or trade

Source: The Constitution of the Kingdom of Nepal (1990), Kathmandu: His Majesty's Government, Ministry of Law, Justice and Parliamentary Affairs, Law Books Management Board, computed by the author.

As already discussed, although the 1990 constitution aimed to be democratic in nature by making provision for freedom and equality, the caste/ethnic, religious, regional (Terai and remote areas) and linguistic groups were not happy with the 1990 constitution. It was because the constitution declared only Nepali language as the official language and the state a unitary structure. Apart from that, on the issue of religion, the constitution remained the same as the previous constitution of 1962. That notwithstanding, all groups tried to join the democratic process by memberships of different political parties and institutions. New forums like parties, identity related organizations and NGOs were formed not only to ensure democratic rights, but also to contribute to the country over all development. After the installation of democracy, about six dozen new political parties emerged. Following this phenomenon, many frontier organizations of the parties came into existence. Within a year of the democratic system, some 15,000 NGOs were registered. Most of these were either Dalit or ethnicity oriented, or gender or language or religion-based. All the NGOs started selling their agenda to the people.

On the other hand, media came to enjoy freedom and autonomy soon after the installation of democracy. The electronic media, especially Radio Nepal, started broadcasting the available news freely. The print media was also democratized during the period. Many FM radios, private television channels, and print media got permission from the government. Such increased media activities led to people's awareness. The agenda, raised at different forums, eventually reaches the people if there is strong and unfettered media. That was the case with Nepal, too, after 1990; everyone got to know of the exploitative policies of the state with regard to say, a particular community, and the hidden interest underlying every policy or programme of the state. In summary, the 1990s constitution directly infuriated the people, but because of the democratic provisions in the constitution, people from all walks of life benefited indirectly.

The Election Manifestoes of Parties: Political parties are inevitable aspects of the democratic system. There is a strong tie between the people and the people. The parties represent the people by getting their votes, and run the country. Governments are formed by political parties; gaining majority support is the main democratic regiment of a norm to govern the state. Having realized this fact, those who had taken part in the democratic movement to bring about emancipatory democracy, tried to compel the main political parties to address their agenda at the policy - as well as the implementation-level. Their demand was to implement the agenda provided in the constitution and to accommodate it by bringing a new policy if that was not covered by the constitution.

In democracy, each and every political party reaches out to the people with its policies and programs and after being elected, it is under obligation to go through the 'blue print' called election manifesto. This section explores the election manifestos of the parties with regard to two aspects. The first is to examine how the parties addressed the issues of the people that arose in the 1990s mass movement. The second is to analyze or not whether the parties confined themselves to the policies and programs they declared earlier. Table 9 examines the election manifestoes of six major political parties in the last three general elections of Nepal. The analysis has primarily been done keeping in view the aspect of caste/ ethnicity, region, and language.

Table 9: Election Manifestos of the Parties in the Elections of 1991, 1994 and 1999 (on Caste/Ethnicity and Regional Groups)

Party	Issues	Provisions
NC	Ethnicity/ language	**In 1991** Preservation and promotion of different languages, cultures and traditions existing in the country; elimination of regional and community disparity in development **Added in 1994** Use of mother tongues in education and communication; establishment of institute relating to culture of different communities **Added in 1999** Set up culture centers to promote songs, dances and cultures of different communities; set up an independent council of janajati; protect and promote knowledge, skill, art and culture of indigenous groups; empowerment of indigenous groups in education and health programs
	Region	**In 1991** Equal opportunity for jobs in police, army and civil service without discrimination; distribution of citizenship certificates
	Caste/Dalit	**Added in 1994** Special provisions in education and law to marginalized groups; scholarship for *Dalit* students; **Added in 1999** Representation of Dalits and backward communities in all parties, parliament etc.,; set up an independent council for Dalits; utilization of Dalit's skill and knowledge

UML	Ethnicity/ language	**In 1991** Secular state; abolish constitutional/legal provisions of discrimination on caste/ethnicity, language, religion, and culture; make constitutional provision for the representation of backward janajati to National Assembly; autonomy to local elected body for the promotion of caste/ethnic, language, religion and culture; primary education in the mother tongue **Added in 1999:** Set up academy for ethnic, language, religion and cultural development
	Region	**In 1991** End region-based discrimination in recruitment in army
	Caste/dalit	**Added in 1994** Abolition of untouchability; reservation for backward communities and areas in education, health and civil service
NSP	Ethnicity/ language	**In 1991** Freedom of religion; primary education in the mother tongue **Added in 1994** Reservation of 30 percent seats to hill ethnic people in government and semi-government jobs
	Region	**In 1991** Reservation of 50 percent seats to Tarai people in government and semi-government jobs; set up a separate battalion of army for Tarai people; making voter list of 1980 referendum as cut off year for distribution of citizenship; recognize Hindi as the second national language; federal government
	Caste/Dalit	**In 1991** Free education and scholarships to Dalits

RPP	Ethnicity/ language	**In 1991** Protection and promotion of language, culture, tradition and religion of Janajati; promote interest of janajatis in social, economic and political spheres; representation of janajatis in governance **Added in 1994** Introduce a language course in different mother tongues upto secondary school; special provision to include in education and job; representation in leadership at social, economic and political spheres; restructure National Assembly as a representative body of janajatis, Dalits and Madhesis **Added in 1999** Follow UN provisions related to indigenous concerned; include in National Planning Commission; equal respect to languages of all nationalities like that of national language; respect to right of education in mother tongue; public holiday on festivals of all communities
	Region	**In 1991** Respect for causes/demands of Tarai people; equal opportunity to Tarai people in military, police and civil services; end of citizenship problem **Added in 1999** Representation in Public Service Commission; respect Madheshi sentiment in local leadership in both parties and in elected bodies
	Caste/Dalit	**In 1991** Priority to overall development of Dalits and backward communities **Added in 1999** Strict implementation of Muliki Ain; protection and promotion of traditional skills and professions of Dalits; representation in party

UPF	Ethnicity/ language	**In 1991** Secular state; equal status to all languages; right to use mother tongue in education, court and legislature; reservation for Dalits and ethnic groups in National Assembly; **Added in 1994** Ethnic autonomy **Added in 1999** End of domination on caste, linguistic, religious groups; make National Assembly as Ethnic House
	Caste/Dalit	**In 1991** End of untouchability; reservation for Dalits and backward communities in education, health and employment
NWPP	Ethnicity/ language	**In 1991** Freedom of religion and protection of tradition of religious tolerance **Added in 1999** Protection and promotion of language, literature and culture of different communities
	Region	**In 1991** Resolve citizenship problem

Source: Hachhethu 2003; Election Manifestos (1991, 1994, 1999) of NC, UML, RPP, UPF, NWPP and NSP.

Table 9 shows that issues which have been incorporated in the election manifestoes of the different political parties have many overlappings. The freedom that reinstated along with the multi-party parliamentary democracy in 1990 led to the conducive environment not only for the formation of various forums of interest groups and organizations, but also for holding of peaceful protests in order to make their voices and demands heard. Using such freedom, Dalits, women, and the ethnic communities expressed their grievances by forming different forums. Slowly, the elected governments started to address their agenda, such as including the broadcast of news in regional languages over the national radio the establishment of the National Committee for Development of Nationalities

(NCDN), the setting up of a women commission, and the National Dalit Commission, etc. Inability to declare Nepal as a secular state and lack of support to the affirmative programs by the government for empowering the marginalized community were the main causes which led to the frustration of the ethnic/caste and religious communities. The Maoist 'capitalized' on this and got positive responses from the suppressed and marginalized classes of Nepal.

The Policies and Programmes of the Maoist Party: The Maoist party (the then CPN Unity Centre) began mobilizing the oppressed ethnic communities in its struggle since 1991 when it adopted the twin agenda of secular state and linguistic and ethnic equality. Ever since, it has taken various initiatives for settlement of their issues. The significant ones were the formation of All Nepal Nationalities Association (1994), adoption of Ethnic Policy (1995), Ethnic Right to Self-determination (1997), establishment of Ethnic Department at the central level and formation of 11 ethnic/regional fronts (1998), Ethnic and Regional Coordinating Committee (May 2001) and United Revolutionary People's Council (September 2001). In the meantime, the Maoist party not only tried to cash in on the sentiments of the suppressed groups by raising radical slogans, but also began implementing policies and programmes by declaring autonomous zones, frontier organizations, etc. It launched the insurgency in February 1996 with a Charter of 40-point demands. Of these demands, seven were related to nationalism, 13 to political, 13 to economic, and 7 to socio-cultural issues. Among seven socio-cultural issues, five (ethnic autonomy, devolution, secular state, ending ethnic oppression, and equality of languages) were in consonance with the ethnic agenda.

The Maoist, for the first time, declared the first district Janasarkar (people's government) in Rukum district and appointed Purna Bahadur Gharti, a member of 'marginalized' caste group, as convenor of the Janasarkar on December 20, 2000. By June 2001, the Maoist had declared district Janasarkars in three districts—Salyan, Jagarkot and Rukum. It adjusted the political boundary of 24 hill districts into 21 districts, as it has not been properly done on the basis of the official political map of Nepal. The Moist party tried to merge two or more districts in to this Janasarkar District (Sharma 2002:12, Seddon 2002:16). It declared 21 district-level Janasarkars in November 2001. These were: Rukum, Rolpa, Salyan, Jajarkot, Dailekh, Achham, Bajura, Jumla, Kalikot, Dolakha, Dhading, Gorkha, Tanahun, Parbat, Palpa, Lamjung, Sankhuwasabha, Remechap, Sindhuli, Sindhupalchowk, Gulmi, Nuwakot, Rasuwa, and Terathum.The caste/ethnic compositions of those areas are given in Table 10.

Table 10: Caste/Ethnic Composition in the 24 Districts with Maoist Influence

District	Ethnic	Dalit	Newar	Total
1. Nepal	34.6	8.7	5.6	48.9
2. Rolpa	43.78	16.77	0	60.55
3. Rukkum	23.15	6.16	0	29.31
4. Salyan	4.89	2.83	0.69	8.41
5. Jajarkot	8.69	24.9	0	33.59
6. Kalikot	0	2.35	0	2.35
7. Dolakha	28.73	7.22	7.75	43.7
8. Ramechhap	37.69	11.72	14.09	63.5
9. Sindhuli	41.37	20.55	6.49	68.41
10. Sindhupalchok	43.93	6.08	11.09	61.1
11. Gorkha	36.83	10.48	8.11	55.42
12. Achham	0	29.36	0	29.36
13. Dhading	40	9.28	9.58	58.86
14. Tanahu	39.25	12.68	7.98	59.91
15. Dailekh	9.87	22.5	0.5	32.87
16. Parbat	15.81	20.57	2.49	38.87
17. Palpa	53.56	10.35	3.61	67.52
18. Lamjung	38.04	14.7	3.8	56.54
19. Sankhuwasabha	58	4.4	5.6	68
20. Terhathum	39.5	4.19	2.76	46.45
21. Gulmi	22.4	18.4	1.84	42.64
22. Jumla	0	13	0	13
23. Bajura	0	19.9	0	19.9
24. Rasuwa	72.73	2.02	2.8	77.55
25. Nuwakot	46.5	2.78	7.6	56.88

Source: ISRSC, 2004, computed by the author.

Table 10 shows the composition of population of the caste/ethnic and Dalit group where the Maoist has already declared 'People's Government.' The population composition in these 24 hilly districts show that in each of the 12 districts more than half of its population is from ethnic/caste communities. In six districts, their population form 33 to 50 per cent, and in the remaining six districts their share is less than 33 per cent. The Maoist declared two types of autonomous areas based on caste/ethnicity and region. Out of 24 districts, where the Maoist government has been formed, 18 districts have 33 to 68 per cent ethnic/Dalit population. Having a look at such a scenario, one can conclude that the Maoist have gained appreciative support from the ethnic/Dalit population.

Between 1998 and 2000, the Maoist formed about a dozen ethnic/ regional front organizations. These fronts were formed on the basis of nationalities and religions. Among 11 front organizations, only two (Madhesh and Karnali) are based on region. The rest are formed on the basis of the different nationalities. The Maoist nominated all the heads of the fronts from the same identity. It is said that the Maoist has applied the policy to lure the 'marginalized' groups. The names of the front organizations with their heads, are in Table 11.

Table 11: Caste/Ethnic and Region Based Frontier Organizations of the Maoist and its Leadership

No	Name of Organization	President
1.	Magarat National Liberation Front	Suresh Aale Magar
2.	Tamang National Liberation Front	Ganga Bahadur Tamang
3.	Tamuwan National Liberation Front	Mohan Tamu
4.	Limbuwan National Liberation Front	Bhakta Raj Kandangwa
5.	Nepal Dalit Liberation Front	Thaman Pariyar
6.	Tharuwan National Liberation Front	Ram Charan Choudhary
7.	Madheshi National Liberation Front	Jaya Krishna Goit
8.	Karnali Regional Liberation Front	Khadak Bahadur Bishowkarma
9.	Thami Liberation Front	Chun Bahadur Thami
10.	Majhi National Liberation Front	Tul Bahadur Majhi
11.	Newa Khala	Dilip Maharjan

Source: Sharma, 2001; 2002 and *Janadesh*, Year 15, Vol. (13) 2006

Apart from the 11 fronts, the Maoist declared nine regional autonomous governments and their leaders were deployed as head of the government in January and February 2004. The strategy to win the sentiment of the 'marginalized' group has again been repeated here. Of the nine regions, six are named and formed on the basis of ethnicity, and three are on the basis of region. The details of the Maoist declared regional autonomous governments are given shown in Table 12.

Table 12: The CPN (Maoist) Regional Autonomous Government

S No	Name of Autonomous Regions	Areas	Head
1.	Kirat Autonomous Region	Hill area of Mechi, Koshi and Sagarmatha zones	Gopal Khambu
2.	Tambsaling Autonomous Region	Hill areas of Bagmati Narayani and Janakpur zones except Kathmandu valley	Hit Bahadur Tamang
3.	Newar Autonomous Region	Kathmandu valley	Yet to be announced
4.	Tamuwan Autonomous Region	Hill areas between Kali Gandaki to Budhi Gandaki	Dev Gurung
5.	Magarat Autonomous Region	Hill areas from west of Kali Gandaki to Dhulagiri, Rapti and Lumbini zones	Santosh Buddha Magar
6.	Tharuwan Autonomous Region	Western Tarai areas from Rapti to Mahakali zones	Ram Charan Choudhary
7.	Madheshi Autonomous Region	Tarai of Awadhi, Bhojpuri and Maithali speaking areas	Matrika Yadav
8.	Bheri-Karnali Autonomous Region	Hill areas of Bheri and Karnali zones	Khadga Bahadur Bishwokarma
9.	Seti-Mahakali Autonomous Region	Hill areas of Seti and Mahakali zones	Lekh Raj Bhatta

Source: Computed by Sharma, 2002; 2003 and *Janadesh* special issue 2006

In short, the Maoist tried to capitalize on the sentiments of the 'marginalized' community by making provisions and forming frontiers of nationalities. They tried to provide space for a higher proportion of Janajati representation. For example, of the then 55- members Central Committee in 2002, 21 are from Janajati (Sharma 2002:26); of the 37 members of the United Revolutionary People's Council, 17 are from Janajati and 2 from Dalit. Again, of the 23 district 'People's Government' chairpersons, 15 are from Janajati, 7 from high caste, and 1 from Dalit (Gurung 2005). The Maoist party still has the problem of representation at the top level; all the three-fold Maoist organizations (the party, the UPF and the PLA) are headed by hill Brahmans. Out of 7 members of the party standing committee of the Maoist, only 2 were from the ethnic community.

Organization: Nepal's Maoist have attempted to emulate the classic Chinese communist structure of 'three magic weapons': party, army, and united front. It has followed the Chinese three-fold system, within which it has generally emphasized the development of the party over the army and both of these over the united front. For Mao Tse-tung the party, peoples' army and united front are the three weapons for a people's revolution. This has been 'embraced' by the Nepalese Maoist. The objectives and principles of these three weapons are also different. The party has to involve its members in spreading the party's ideology as well as formulating policies related to the 'People's War'; the army has to engage for attacking 'enemies' and defending the areas under its control, and the united front has a responsibility to consolidate friendly forces with the view to creating the prerequisites for the proposed 'People's Government' (Sharma 2003:362).

The party, whose overall control remains firmly with the 'Party Headquarters', which in practice means Prachanda, has complete responsibility for all activities related to the 'people's war' and for the formulation of policies. The Standing Committee, politburo, the Central Committee, divisional commands, regional bureaus, sub-regional bureaus, district, area, and cell committees, are the hierarchical layers of the party. Seven to ten members must be in the standing committee of the Maoist. At least 27 members, including some alternative members, must be in the politburo. In the Central Committee, the number of members is flexible. In 1996, there were nearly 100 members in the central committee. At the 2nd National Conference in February 2001, the number was only 55. Neither the standing committee nor the politburo exists in the Maoist's organization today. These, according to the Maoist, will be formed in the forthcoming general convention of the party. There are various central wings under the party headquarters, and also a Central Advisory Body. The advisory body consists of 9 to 11 members, who are elected/nominated from the heads of their frontier organizations. It has five regional bureaus under the Central Committee, including various sub-regional bureaus, and in some places, even special sub-regional bureaus immediate under the regional bureaus.

The People's Liberation Army (PLA), which is under the full control of the 'Party Headquarters,' is responsible for both offensive operations against the 'enemy side' and defensive arrangements. It is said that the Maoist developed and organized the 'People's Army' only after the Kilo Sierra 2 operation also known as Shoot 2 Kill operation of the government in May 1998-April 1999 (*Nepal Samachar Patra*, December 17, 2000). In August 1998, the Maoist Fourth Expanded Central Committee meeting (plenum) adopted the slogan of building 'base areas' and building up military strength in order to challenge government repression. Prachanda retains the top position of the PLA as the supreme commander; total authority regarding the mobilization of the 'People's Army is vested' in the Commander. There are regional, sub-regional and district level military wings under the Central Military Commission. The organizational structure of the PLA is built up with division, brigade, battalion, company, platoon, squad and the militias. There are even poorly armed fighters who have not received full guerrilla training. It is reported that there are certain areas, such as Kathmandu, where 'special taskforces' (special battalion) have been established. Each and every army unit is under the dual control of the military commander and the political commander.

Analysts suggest that the Maoist has only a few thousand hardcore fighters. According to Gen. Ashok K. Mehta (Mehta, 2005:94) of India and Sadip Bahadur Shah, a military expert and retired RNA Lieutenant-General, the Maoist has 4,000 armed Guerrillas, 5,000 militia who have received guerrilla training and 20,000 armed militia (*Samay*, 30 December 2004). Militia members (poorly armed and do not wear uniforms) are not generally expected to carry out the guerrilla duties as mainstream fighters. However, they can be called upon as reinforcements. According to the International Crisis Group (ICG) report of October 27, 2005, the Maoist claim to have more than 10,000 armed guerrillas in their nine brigades. In fact, at the RNA press conference, Colonel Victory S.J. B. Rana had made a somewhat similar estimate - some 9,500 guerrillas and 25,000 militia (*The Kathmandu Post*, 21 May 2005). The number is either under-estimated or exaggerated. For the Maoist, the number is their strength; hence they tend to exaggerate their strength. The ICG report of October 2005, termed the number claim by both the RNA and the Maoist as 'higher estimates'. It states:

Of course, the Maoist and the RNA both have reasons to give higher estimates. The Maoist obviously want to create the impression that they have a mass support base and a considerable fighting force. The RNA is faced with the problem that earlier state estimates of a small Maoist guerrilla cadre simply do not tally with their depiction of the current situation (*ICG report*, 27 October 2005:9).

The concept of the 'united front' was central to Mao's thinking in China. Its principal objective is to "unite with all forces that it can be united with in order to fight a common struggle against the enemy, and the unity is to win revolution, and to the construction" (Kwok-Sing Li (tr. Mary Lok) 1995: 451). The quotation seems a simple idea, but in effect it is too difficult. From the time of the anti-Japanese struggle, Mao formulated and continually emphasized the 'unity-struggle-autonomy' policy: 'develop the progressive force, win over the in-between force, and combat the obstinate force' (ibid: 452). From the beginning of the 1990s, the Nepali Maoist planned to create a particular type of united front, which would not only be a broad coalition of organizations assisting in the revolutionary struggle, but also help in bridging with mainstream parties. Later, the United Front comes on the scene to predominate the Nepali Maoist discourse.

Before 2000, there was a 16-member 'United People's Front.' This was dissolved in February 2000 when the party concluded that it could not play the role of the grand united front that had been envisaged for it. Alternatively, it formed a similar type of organization in the form of 'United People's Committee'. The Committee exists in parallel with the central and local government bodies. The central body of the 'united front,' which is called the United Revolutionary People's Council (Nepal), was made public in September 2001 during the first ceasefire. There were 37 members in the United Revolutionary People's Council (URPC). Its role was to mobilize 'various left, progressive, patriotic and democratic forces'. The front partially reflects the 'people's democratic front' of the early People's Republic of China. The front was headed by Baburam Bhattarai; Krishna Bahadur Mahara worked as assistant convenor and Dev Gurung as secretary (*URPC Press Statement* November 26, 2001). Now, there are 'regional', 'district', and 'village' level people's governments under the URPC. Between 1998 and 2000, there were about a dozen ethnic and regional fronts formed by the Maoist with the aim of creating a grand united front. On the other hand, there were at least 22 front organizations working under the Maoist party (Mehta 2005:96-97). Before the declaration of a state of emergency in November 2001, the front organizations of the Maoist had carried out open or semi-underground activities. However, after the state of emergency in Nepal, all of them went underground. The most influential among these has been the All-Nepal National Free Students Union (Revolutionary) led by Lekhnath Neupane. Other active organizations include:

(i)   The Nepal Trade Union Federation (Revolutionary) led by Salikram Jamarkattel, the All-Nepal Women's Association (Revolutionary) led by Jayapuri Gharti,

(ii) The All-Nepal Janajati Federation led by Suresh Ale Magar, the All-Nepal Teachers' Organisation (Revolutionary) led by Gunaraj Lohani,

(iii) The Nepal National Intellectuals Organisation and the All-Nepal People's Cultural Union led by Mani Thapa, and

(iv) The All Nepal Peasants Association led by Shivaraj Gautam. The leadership of the Nepal National Intellectuals Organization has not been published yet.

With the main tasks of advancing Maoist aims through industrial action and to mobilize a support-base by organizing labourers in various sectors of the formal economy, Nepal Trade Union Federation (Revolutionary) brought together many small unions. These have been the All-Nepal Carpet Workers Union

- All-Nepal Transport Workers Union,

- All-Nepal Hotel and Restaurant Workers Union,

- All-Nepal Construction Workers Union,

- All Nepal Meter Tempo Workers Union,

- All Nepal Press Workers Union,

- All Nepal Thangka Art Workers Union,

- All Nepal Painters Union,

- Nepal Shop Workers Union, Nepal Progressive Newspaper Vendors Union and Himalayan Trekking Workers Union.

To assess the real popular support of a party is a difficult task. Hisila Yami (Parvati), a woman leader of the Maoist, claimed woumen membership in women mass organizations of the Maoist around 600,000 (Parvati 2003: 271). Likewise, Shiva Raj Gautam, chairperson of All

Nepal Peasants Union (Revolutionary), has claimed some 1,950,000 members in its organization (*Kisan Sandesh* 2005:48). It has already been mentioned that there are at least 22 front organizations and they all claim their membership in several thousands.

If the party were to take part in the election, it may have been possible to address the question. Again, if an organization were to work in a transparent manner, the membership of the organization might have been taken as a reliable source to indicate its base among the people. However, both do not seem to be applicable in the context of the Maoist. On the one hand, they have not participated in the election after declaration of the 'people's war,' on the other, the party has equipped itself with arms and weapons, and has worked in an underground manner. In the given situation, it is difficult to analyze whether people took the membership of the Maoist party and front organizations by their own individual will or the Maoist rebels forced them to take membership.

The membership of NC and CPN(UML), the major parties in Nepal, were 250,000 and 450, 000 respectively, in late 1995. However, in the recent three general elections of 1991, 1994 and 1999, the NC got only 2,752,445 (37.75 per cent), 2,545,287 (33.38 per cent), and 3,214,746 (36.15 per cent) votes; respectively the UML got 2,040,102 (27.98 per cent), 2,352,601(30.85 per cent) and 2,734,586 (30.74 per cent) votes (Hachhethu 2002:75). It is to be noted that the Maoist had participated in the 1991 election in which they had won only 9 out of 205 seats in the parliament. They had polled only 351,904 votes (4.83 per cent votes) and became the third largest party in the Parliament. In 1994, a faction of the UPFN led by Baburam Bhattarai boycotted the general election. It joined the 'people's war' in 1996. Another faction led by Niranjan Govinda Baidhya took part in the 1994 and 1999 elections in which it polled only 100,285 (1.32 per cent) and 74,669 (0.83 per cent) votes respectively.

To examine the grassroot hold of the Maoist, we have to await the election results of the 'constituent assembly election' which is in the process. According to the RNA estimate, 'beyond their armed cadres and 14,000 political workers, the Maoist may have some 100,000 supporters' (*The Kathmandu Post*, 21 May 2005). Examining the approximate strength of the Maoist in December 2004, Gen. Ashok K. Mehta categorically mentioned that there were 267,000 people who supported the Maoist. Among them, 4,000 are armed guerillas, 5,000 militias trained as guerillas, 20,000 are unarmed militias, 14,000 are political activists, 24,000 are supporters and 200,000 sympathizers (Mehta 2005:94). The assessment is similar to the prediction made by Retired RNA Lieutenant-General Sadip Bahadur Shah (*Samay*, December 30, 2004).

After analyzing the situation of the three-fold system the organizational structure of the Maoist party can be drawn as follows:

Source: Sharma 2003 in Thapa 2003:379, and Crisis Group Asia Report, 27 October 2005:40.

Strategy: As mentioned earlier, for the Maoist party, 'peoples' army,' and united front are the three weapons for a people's revolution. Its 'single' objective is to capture power through 'people's war'. To attain this objective, the party tried to influence the people to join the war. In the process, it laid to rest the myth that Nepal is a peaceful country whose citizens are naturally averse to violence. The Maoist has consistently maintained that violence has been at the heart of the state power throughout Nepal's history. Prachanda is against the popular notion that Nepalese are peace-loving and non-violent people. But an idea dawning upon him is clearly against the historical fact. To Prachanda, such 'historical fact' is a conspiracy to mentally disarm the people, and to protect their rule from reactionary violence (Prachanda 1996:202). To him, Nepalese society has reached its present style through the course of increasing struggle of the Nepalese people and against deception, conspiracy and repression of the reactionaries. The struggles are local and nationwide, including rural class conflict for nationalism, democracy, and livelihood. According to the Maoist, historical materialism has shown that the process of violent conflict among men is inseparably linked with the situation of division of labour, emergence of private property and development of social class division. Prachanda further says, "we communists are clear on the scientific fact that it is necessary to raise the flag of just war in order to oppose the unjust war being conducted by the exploiting class and to end war forever amongst the human beings". (Prachanda 1997a:205). The policy on armed struggle adopted by the CPN(M) in its third plenum in March 1995 made it even more explicit;

> The reactionary propaganda that the Nepalese people are peace-loving and that they don't like violence is absolutely false. It is an incontrovertible fact that the Nepalese people have been waging violent struggle for their rights since historical times. Till today whatever general reforms have been achieved by the Nepalese people, behind them there was the force of violent and illegal struggle of the people (CPN(M), March 1995).

This point was reinforced by Prachanda in a separate essay. He wrote, "people have not obtained even the least of gains without waging violent struggles. Today, the Nepalese society has arrived at such a point of crisis under the existing political system that there is no alternative on the part of the people other than to squash it" (Prachanda 1996:202). According to Prachanada, to become a genuine Marxist-Leninist revolutionary, one has to support the theory of 'people's war'. Elaborating the three stages of the strategy, he says, "for the success of a revolution in the country like ours that lies in the semi-feudal and semi-colonial condition, it is essential to pass through the three stages of the strategic defence, equilibrium and strategic offence with the strategy of seizing towns from the rural areas" (Prachanda 1999:146, 206). Initially, they adopted guerilla war because it played a key role in the first stage. The Maoist itself compared the guerilla war to the Shah dynasty's state expansion campaign. It was comparable to the world history and said, "the guerilla warfare has been effective when pro-people forces carry on war against anti-people army with relatively more equipped with training and arms". (Prachanda 1997a: 207). Prachanda has mentioned five key conditions for the success in guerilla war in Nepal. These are:

- A correct ideological and political line (Marxism-Leninism-Maoism) of the leadership.

- To be conducted for the masses and by the masses.

- Need for a continuous process of awakening and organizing more and more people through faster and better methods.

- Basic tactics must be followed. Under the tactic of 'hit and run,' Prachanda referred to some sub-tactics. These are: when enemy advances, we retreat, centralizing our forces to fight the enemy, decentralizing it to arouse the masses, finding out the weakest points of the enemy with adequate preparation and to attack by ensuring victory, carrying out dependable geographical and other surveys, always taking the enemy by surprise, maintaining regular alertness, mobility, secrecy, etc.

- Building base area for mobilizing and regularizing the war. (ibid::208-9)

In another essay, Prachanda mentioned six strategies and tactics of war. They are (1) tactics of surprise attacks, (2) to attack the weak enemy first and the stronger one later, (3) to take advantage of contradictions among the enemies, (4) to adopt a policy of intrigue, conspiracy and deception, (5) to apply the method of embargo against the enemy, and (6) to adopt the technique of protracted war. According to the Maoist, these are developed from the experiences of the past wars like Gorkhalese war (Prachanda 1996:197-198) for 'unification'. Mao argues, "Correctness and incorrectness of ideological and political line decides everything. If the line is correct, everything will come in its way; if it is wrong, everything will be lost which one had before". Ananta ally Barsaman Pun, a division commander of Maoist army, says that the concept of 'correctness of the political line decides everything'. Through that, one is able "to educate, organize, and make millions of masses agitate," on the basis of which the ideology of the party is "advancing ahead in the direction of acquiring universal character" (Ananta 2003:214-220). The following are ten tactical principles expressed in the Prachanda Path:

1. Give priority to the work in villages, but do not leave the work in cities, too.

2. Give priority to the illegal struggle, but do not leave the legal struggle, too

3. Give priority to certain strategic areas, but do not leave other areas too.

4. Give priority to the work of war, but do not leave work of the mass movement, too.

5. Give priority to clandestine work, but do not leave open work, too.

6. Give priority to the rural class struggle, but do not leave countrywide struggle, too.

7. Give priority to the guerilla actions, but do not leave political exposition and   propaganda work, too.

8. Give priority to the work inside the country, but do not leave worldwide propaganda work, too.

9. Give priority to the work of military organization, but do not leave work of building front organizations, too.

10. Give priority to depending upon own organization and strength, but don't leave tactical unity and the question of taking help and support from international opinion, too (Prachanda 2004: 20).

Another important strategy of the Maoist is to capitalize the sentiment of the suppressed groups of people like Dalits, women, ethnic/native groups, regionally backward groups like Terai people and Karnali area people, etc., which has been playing a vital role to strengthen the movement. The Maoist advocates the united front at the level of all oppressed nationalities and regions under the policy of 'unite and struggle' in the place of their enemy's policy of 'divide and rule'. Realizing the importance to address the sentiment of the entire suppressed group, the Maoist began to think of the need of a concrete and practical programme to fight against national and regional oppression. They made special efforts to do 'serious studies on the nature of national and regional oppression of the people of different areas, their economic, political cultural and geographic background and to prepare a concrete plan for national autonomy and to build the united front accordingly' (Prachanda 1997b:277-278). After the politburo meeting of January 1997, the Maoist agreed to integrate the demands of all the suppressed groups/minorities as an integral part of their campaign and agreed to give the right of self-determination to the ethnic and regional groups. To 'lure' the ethnic community, the Maoist established an ethnic department at the central level in 2000, which was headed by Dev Gurung.

Origin, Growth and Spread of The Maoist Movement In Nepal

Origin: The Maoist first started its 'people's war' from Gorkha, Sindhuli, Rolpa and Rukum districts. The first two districts are situated in the central-western and central-eastern hill area, respectively, and the last two are located in mid-western Nepal. On February 13, 1996, some hundred Maoist captured the office of the Small Farmers Development Programme (SFDP) of Chyangli Village Development Committee (VDC) of Gorkha. The SFDP programme, launched under the government-owned Agricultural Development Bank, is assisted by the Asian Development Bank since 1974. The Maoist seized the Agricultural Development Bank's cash, loan papers and land registration certificates deposited by peasants. A short speech exposing the mechanism of exploitation of poor peasants and the need of capturing the government institution was made in the presence of the local people. After that, they dispersed.

In Sindhuli, it was the Sindhuligadhi police post, which was captured by the Maoist. This was followed by a long discourse on 'new democratic revolution' to the captured police and their families. They tied down the captured policemen, covered them with quilts and disappeared with large quantities of high explosives and other utilities.

Another attack by the Maoist was on the Athbiskot-Rani police outpost in Rukum. There too they followed the *modus operandi* as was done in Sindhuli. These three attacks were quite smooth. The Maoist did not face any counter-attacks by the state security. However, in Holeri police outpost of Rolpa there was firing from both sides, which went on almost for two hours. Ultimately, the Maoist ransacked the post, seized the store, and took hold of the useful warfare material. They made a short speech before leaving the post explaining the objectives to policemen, their family members, and the curious villagers gathered at the site.

Apart from their actions, as per the Maoist report, a multinational company (Pepsi) situated in Kathmandu valley was attacked and a portion of the building was torched. A distillery 'owned by a comprador bourgeois' was blasted in Gorkha, and the house of a 'notorious feudal-usurer' in Kavre in central-eastern Nepal was also raided on the same day. Along with that, they distributed thousands of leaflets and posters; organized the 'March on' programme, where the slogan raised by the party was 'the path of people's war to smash the reactionary state and establish a democratic state.' The 'March on' program was launched in the major cities and headquarters of more than 60 districts in Nepal (*The Worker*, 1996).

There are lots of statements and presumptions about the principal causes behind the Maoists' attacks at different places. The Maoist in Nepal have been trying to show the causes as those based on 'class discrimination; However, the 'class' is a traditional and a readymade showcard to all who believe in communism. According to the Maoist, they got support from the poor people and assaulted the 'semi-feudal and semi-colonial' Nepali state. They used to say, we communists are clear on the scientific facts that it is necessary to raise the flag of just war in order to oppose the unjust war being conducted by the exploiting class and to end war forever amongst the human beings. In the class society, it is impossible to make a forward leap without a revolutionary war" (Prachanda 1997a:205). However, in reality there are many causes, which led people to join the Maoist.

There are various factors to examine as to why the Rapti zone became the initiating area of the Maoist movement. Of these factors, I have focussed mainly on three: (1) the role of Mohan Bikram Singh, who spread the communist ideology in this area after going underground since 1957, (2) the brutal state repression on the Magar community while they were engaged in the struggle, and (3) the presence of the forest, which offers natural surroundings for guerrilla operations.

No doubt, there is poverty in Rapti zone as well. However, poverty alone has not only been responsible for the hopeless people of Rapti to join the Maoist movement. Tharus, one of the major ethnic groups in Terai, and other Terai communities are very poor in comparison to Magars in Rapti. Again, the situation of Tharus and other Terai communities seem far worse than the Magars on the issue of the exploitation by large landlords. Baburam Bhattarai, the then convenor of the UPFN, accepted this fact and said that the Tharus have to work in a kind of feudal relationship. He wrote, "the feudal relation in Terai is very much strong". To him, "majority of the people are poor peasants and substantial production system is there in the hilly region" (Bhattarai, 2005:3-7). Hence, why is the Terai not influenced by the Maoists' activities? If the movement is class-based, one wonders as to why the movement is these in the hills, where, according to the Maoist, the feudal relation is nominal?

Some districts of the mid-western region like Rolpa, Rukum and Pyathan had been exposed to the communist influence since 1957. Mohan Bikram Singh, one of the senior and very influential communist leaders, started his communist career in this region. Singh sensitized people on the issue of their rights and freedom. Because of their political consciousness and value for democracy and freedom, the people of the region contributed a lot to the democratic struggle of Nepal. Thawang, a VDC of Rolpa district, cast only four votes in the 1980s referendum in support of the Panchayat system. The VDC boycotted the election and returned the empty ballot box in the first Rastriya Panchayat election in 1981. Barman Buda, one of the followers of Singh, started leading the Magar people of the region. He was later imprisoned for five years on the charge of having burnt the picture of the king and queen in the 1980s. He was freed after the mass movement of 1990, and became a member of the parliament from UPFN party. In this election, UPFN won both the seats in Rolpa, and the party was right behind the NC in Rukum district.

The antagonism between the UPFN cadre and ruling NC cadres in Rukum and Rolpa after the first local election of 1992 played a vital role in increasing the Maoist influence in Rolpa and Rukum. In the 1991 election, the UPFN came close to the NC. After the election, the NC started ruling the country with absolute majority in the parliament and the UPFN was busy in the village with the people's awareness campaign. Along with the campaign, the UPFN began 'taking action against those they considered exploiters, usurers and cheats' in the villages. Those affected by the UPFN action were mostly from the NC cadres. The local influential NC leaders were from the background of the previous ruling Panchayat system. It seemed that the initial struggle was the two-party struggle. Later, the nature of the struggle spread into the state versus community.

Being the cadres of the ruling party, many of the local leaders of NC used the state machinery against their opponents. Three special police operations—Operation Romeo, Kilo Sierra-2 and Operation Search and Kill—had been launched in the region. In November 1995, the government deployed a squadron of 165 policemen with 50 special military trained policemen and launched Operation Romeo. The impact of the operation was later described in INSEC Human Rights Year Book 1995 reports, as follows:

> The government initiated ...suppressive operations to a degree of state terror. Especially the workers of the UPFN were brutally suppressed. Under the direct leadership of the ruling party workers of the locality, police searched, tortured and arrested, without arrest warrants, in 11 villages of the district. Nearly 6,000 locals had left the villages due to the police operation. One hundred and thirty two people were arrested without serving any warrants. The arrested included elderly people of 75 years of age. All the detained were subjected to torture (INSEC 1995)[2].

Police, in collusion with the local NC leaders started to file 'false accusations' against its opponents. The District Administration Office (DAO) treated these accusations as 'matter of public order'. The accused were asked to furnish a sum of Rs. 28,000 as deposit for the bail. The sum was far from affordable to the villagers. There was also doubt among the accused about free and fair hearing of the case. In this situation, "the majority of the accused found that the only solution was to run away into the forest or to the city, or the plains, or even to India, in the hope of passing time until their relatives managed to sort out the dispute" (Sales 2003:81). The Maoist, which was to win people's sentiment, started capitalizing on this problem. It sent its 'hooded guerillas' to kill the informers or 'class enemies'. For the Maoist, the class enemies were those who made a 'false accusation' on the people. Those who left the village were compelled to face accusation of supporting the Maoist and taking part in the attack on villages. Baburam Bhattarai, in an interview said that more than 10,000 rural youth, out of a population of 200,000 for the whole district of Rolpa, have been forced to flee from their homes and take shelter in remote jungles. The deplorably cruel situation was created by the government, which sent around 1,550-strong especially trained commando force from Kathmandu (*Himal* 14/5 May 2001:10).

Such operation of the government helped to increase the cadres of the Maoist and eroded the credibility of the government in rural area. The following passage describes the scenario of the village after that operation;

> The organization of the daily life in the village is paralyzed: peasants who leave the village risk being arrested by the police who suspect them of helping the guerillas. Thus tilling animals to pasture, departing for summer residences, going to the forest to collect berries and

---

2 INSEC Human Rights Year Book 1995

mushrooms, which form a not insubstantial part of the village diet, have become either impossible or extremely problematic. Schools are closed. Young men, those who have not joined the guerrillas in the forest, have left to hide in the big cities or in India. It is said that the women plough and the old people keep silent (Sales 2003:81).

The villagers were harassed by the Maoist at night (those who had to be fed) and during the day by policemen (looking for suspects, which Sales (2003) terms 'an impossible living situation'). However, villagers, irrespective of their political inclinations, preferred the Maoist rather than the police. It is so because of the behavior of police who treated the villagers not only as an 'evil' but also as a 'milk giving cow.' In contrast, the Maoist, whose atrocious behavior was similar to the security force in the village, has changed its old *modus operandi*, and started social work, raised socio-cultural agenda and respected the village elders as their parents. Even while Maoist cadres asked the villagers for food, they used to ask for cheap, simple, and easily available things like maize and salt, whereas the demand of the police was for expensive things like chicken and alcohol. Another cause of the villagers' hostility towards security personnel was that they were often beaten without any prior investigation if the police suspected them. An opinion poll conducted by the then *Himal Khabarpatrika* of March 2001 proved that the brutality of security force had been seen as one of the main causes of support for the Maoist. According to the poll, 30 percent of the respondents attributed the rise of the Maoist to high handedness of the security force.

The third factor for the emergence of the Rapti zone as the Maoist initiating area has been the zone's geographical location. More than half of the districts of Rukum and Rolpa are forested, which give 'natural surroundings to the guerillas to hide from state security forces and to launch the training and other sorts of campaigns in the jungle. The dense forest and remoteness made it easier for to the Maoist to hide their cadres from the state security. It became fruitful for their movement, and for supplying their weapons from one part to another. In the case of Terai, where there is 'more influential feudal culture than in the hills,' the Maoist realized that "the geography is negative there to start the insurgency (Bhattarai 2005,3-7)". Such a natural opportunity has been used not only by Nepalis Maoist but also by Naxalites of India (Benerjee 1980:33-34).

Apart from those three causes, the hung parliament and its adverse impact on the stability of the government played a vital role in making the Maoist movement influential. Power game among the parliamentary parties gave a chance to the Maoist to put forward their agenda against the parliamentary democracy. In the mid-term election of 1994, no party got majority in the parliament and people faced five prime ministers within four years. Deuba headed a coalition government from September 11, 1995 to March 6, 1997; Chanda headed the government from March 12, 1997 to October 4, 1997. The people had very negative perceptions towards these two governments. Both the governments were busy in horse-trading in parliament. The MPs used the parliament as a platform to make money and got their bills reimbursed by submitting all sorts of irrelevant dues; Male MPs submitted pregnancy related bills and got reimbursement for their expenditure from the state. The state fund was very much misused during that time. The government decided to give 'Pajero and pension' facilities to the MPs, which was severly criticized by the people. Those agenda were picked up by the Maoist and raised before the general public.

Having a look at Nepal's performance of parliamentary democracy after 1995, one can argue that the movement has its backing from the 'frustrated' masses of the society. In the communist history of Nepal, preparation of such an armed struggle was made in the 1980s and 1990s. In the 1982-83 Ayodhya plenums, Mohan Bikram Singh presented a report on the basics of the preparation of armed struggle, keeping in mind *Baghe Odhar* experience. Prachanda said that he had started to think about the theoretical and practical parts of the armed conflict when he had started to lead the youth league in 1983. Some radical communists of Nepal, under the leadership of contemporary Masal group, rigorously tried to prepare and launch an armed revolt against the Panchayat regime on the eve of the 'mass movement of 1990'. In the preparation phase, Maoist Chairperson Pushpa Kamal Dahal himself was involved in imparting the armed skills training to the cadres by collecting arms. According to him, he with two other prominent leaders Ram Bahadur Thapa "Badal" and Dev Gurung were involved in active collection of weapons. The three were able to buy two guns from Ganesh Bahadur Gurung of Manang district in 1989; another gun was gifted by Lekhnath Bhatta to the party. It is said that Dahal and Thapa "Badal" had a very narrow escape from the police search while they were on the way to Gorkha from Tanahun district with a gun and some explosives provided by Bhatta. With those three guns, the party started a skill training program in Tiranchowk of Gorkha district against the state in Sirubari. Some 16 people participated as trainees (*Nepal*: 2006). After the training, they attempted a revolt in support of the movement, which according to Prachanda, could not be a success because of lack of proper preparation on ideological, political, and organizational level' (*Janadesh* 2006:19).

Realizing the above-mentioned weaknesses to launch armed revolt, they started to gather the scattered 'revolutionaries' and ultimately got success by organizing the CPN (Unity Centre). The 'unity general convention' of the CPN in 1991 has given the mandate to the 'Peoples' War.' After the convention, four types of preparations—ideological-political, organizational, technical and revolt— carried forward by the party for waging the 'people's war.' It tried to use both the underground and open methods 'to strengthen rural class struggle' through an underground party led by Prachanda. They tried to train people by continuing people's movements, mass meetings, and 'Nepal *bandh*' on issues such as nationality, people's democracy, and people's livelihood.' These were done through Baburam Bhattarai-led UPFN which was involved in open politics.

In its review on the great success of the struggles, the leaders of CPN Maoist intentionally and repeatedly put the term 'class' in the forefront. However, Prachanda once accepted the socio-cultural agenda they raised as influential cause. He said that they got people's support because of the "right decision to address the problems based on caste/ethnicity, region, and gender" (*Janadesh* 2006:18). Even today, the Maoist has been strategically bringing the concept of the 'Joint front' to address the socio-cultural issues. However, they termed the concept as "the experience of specific nature" (*Janadesh* 2006:19).

Growth and Expansion: The Maoist started the 'People's War' with only 200 cadres in 1996 (Philipson: 2002:19). Until September 1999, the Maoist was busy in 'struggle, propaganda and mobility.' Within that strategy, the Maoist launched some token/small attacks in its area with a view to draw national and international attention. It ambushed two policemen in Tak VDC of Rukum on May 6, 1996. This is considered as its first attack. On January 4, 1997, the Bethan police post of Ramechap was captured by the Maoist rebels. Three Maoist guerrillas lost their lives in this encounter. These guerrilla attacks were waged for propaganda. Till May/June 1997, it was assumed that the Maoist preserved and showed its effective influence only in 83 Village Development Committees (VDCs) of four neighboring districts of Rolpa, Rukum, Salyan and Jajarkot. The assumption was based on the Maoist's agenda of boycotting the 1997 local election. The boycott was successful only in those 83 VDCs.

The Maoist declared the 'people's army' or 'Central Military Commission' under the leadership of Prachanda only on February 13, 1998. On the eve of the second year anniversary of the Bethan attack on 3

January 1999, the Maoist attacked the Bhattedanda police post of Lalitpur district and seized all the weapons. Lalitpur is in Kathmandu valley and the attacked post was considered as 'the nose of the Kathmandu valley'. In between the 'successful' attack of Bethan and Bhattedanda, a number of small and symbolic attacks like the attacks on police patrols in Kalikatar of Tanahu district, Khahare in Dhading district, *Korbachong Nimri* of Rolpa district, Sourpani of Gorkha district, Jhimpe tower of Salyan district, Phalate of Kavre district, Nirmal Basti of Parsa District, and Laliya of Dhanusha district, were carried out. In all, the Maoist killed five policemen and got some weapons and money from those attacks. Apart from that, they captured the local office of Nepal Bank and looted Rs. 20 lakh from Khahare. The diversified and simultaneous attack, which covered at least four zones out of a total of 14 zones of Nepal, worked as propaganda. These attacks led to a scare among the people as well as awareness about the Maoist anti- social activities.

After the Maoist disturbed 83 VDCs' local elections in Rapti zone in 1997, the government contemplated the programme to 'sweep out' the Maoist from the villages. From May 1998 to May 1999, the government launched the Kilo Sieoro II Operation in 18 Maoist-affected districts. This led to the killing of at least 500 people within a year (Sharma 2003:372). The Maoist attacked Mahatgaun police-base in Rukum on September 22, 1999, killed seven policemen and abducted Thule Rai, the District Superintendent of Police (DSP). It is said that it was the Mahatgaun attack in which the Maoist shifted from an offensive war to a defensive one. On the same night, the Maoist demonstrated its presence and strength in 25 different districts by carrying out simultaneous attacks. When the Ghartigaun police-base camp was captured in February, the government started centralizing the police force by removing the police posts in villages. In April, other two police camps were captured: one was the Tak *Ilaka* (area) police office in Rukum, and the Harmi police post in Gorkha. In-between July and August 2000, three police posts—Panchkatia *Ilaka* police office in Jajarkot, Dhawadi *Ilaka* in Nawalparashi and Mahawari *Ilaka* office in Jhapa—were captured. Till May 2001, the Maoist-related deaths took place in 52 districts, out of a total of 75, in Nepal (*Himal*, May 2001:5).

In September 2000, the Maoist for the first time attacked the district headquarters - Dunai of Dolpa district; and not only captured all the police posts but also looted the money from Dunai Bank. After two days of the Dunai attack, Bhorletar Ilaka police office in Lamjung district was captured. In November 2000, the Maoist captured the Doramba police post in Ramechap. In December of the same year, the Maoist declared its first 'District people's government' in Rukuim district. By its second national conference in February 2001, the party passed 'Prachanda Path' as a party's guiding principle. The principle assumed "a kind of revolution that would be a fusion of the Chinese model of protracted People's War (to expand from villages to towns) and the Russian model of general armed insurrection" (Sharma 2003:375). The conference carried out a slogan 'let us consolidate and expand our base areas and move forward towards a people's government in the centre'.

In April 2001, the Maoist attacked three security bases (Rukumkot of Rukum, Naumule of Dailekh and Mainapokhari of Dolakha) and destroyed them. Again, in May, the Maoist repeated the same incident in Okhaldhunga where Khanibhanjyang Ilaka police office was captured and destroyed. On June 1, 2001, there was the Royal Massacre in Narayanhiti Royal palace, of which the Maoist declared 'the official end of the traditional monarchy from Nepal.'

When the royal massacre took place in Nepal, both the 'people's war' and the intra and inter party antagonism in the parliament were going on side by side. The first struggle was confined to the villages and the last one was in the Capital for acquiring post and power. Apart from that, the struggle between the two factions of NC had increased. The opposition parties disrupted the parliament for more than eight weeks. Taking note of the weaknesses of the state and parliamentarian parties, the Maoist accelerated their activities in the countryside. They increased the attacks after May 2001. The Maoist abducted some six policemen after their attack on Holeri police post in July. The government led by G.P. Koirala tried to deploy the army to free the abducted 69 policemen from the Maoist but failed in the attempt owing to the king's 'non-co-operation'.

The 'non-co-operation' increased the antagonism between the king and the then government on the issue of deployment of the army. Koirala resigned from the post of Prime Minister on July 19, 2001. The situation became very tense. The struggle shifted from bi-polar to tri-polar after the king showed 'non-co-operation' to the democratically elected government. The parties of the triangular struggle were the Maoist, the parliamentary parties, and the king with the army.

After the resignation of G.P. Koirala, Deuba was elected as the new leader of NC Parliamentary Party, and became the prime minister on July 23, 2001. By the time of Deuba's appointment, truce was announced by the government. The Maoist, too, reciprocated the truce. It was enforced till

November 21, 2001. In between, there were two rounds of talks between the government and the Maoist. One was on August 30 in Kathmandu, and the other on 14 September in Bardiya. However, after the Maoist attacked two district headquarters - Dand and Syangja — on November 23, 2001, the truce was suspended and the country again witnessed violent activities. It is said that the truce was used by the Maoist to raise funds as well as people's support by asking for donations, addressing mass meetings, and extending the memberships. On the day before calling off the truce, the Maoist announced the formation of the 41 member United People's Revolutionary Council Nepal under the leadership of Baburam Bhattarai (*Janadesh* 2006:6).

After calling off the truce, the Maoist repeatedly attacked three district headquarters. These were the district headquarters of Dang, Syangja and Solukhumbu. By November 26, the government declared a state of emergency in the country. Within nine months of emergency, there were formidable encounters between the Maoist and security forces. Three district headquarters—Achham, Arghakhanchi, Jumla, along with Saphebagar airport of Achham, Gam base camp of Rolpa, and Bhiman *Ilaka* police office of Sindhuli, were attacked and destroyed by the Maoist during the period. Thousands of people were displaced from their houses, villages, and districts. Table 13 depicts the killing scenario between February 13, 1996 to December 27, 2005.

Table 13: Killing by the State and the Maoist

Period	Killing			Per day killing ratio
	By the security forces	By the Maoist	Total	
Killing up to 27 November 2005	8,283	4,582	12,865	3.65
Killing before emergency (13/2/1996 – 25/11/2001)	992	811	1,803	-
Killing during the emergency (26/11/2001 - 31/8/2002)	3,849	1,952	5,801	2.43
Killing before king's takeover (13/2/1996 - 3/10/2002)	3,849	1,952	5,801	2.43

Killing after king's takeover (4/10/2002 — 27/11/2005)	4,438	2,630	7,068	6.28

Source: INSEC report 2005

The above table shows that between the suspension of the ceasefire and declaration of the state of emergency in November 2001, the brutal killings became rampant from both the sides. The killing during emergency period (26/11/2011- 21/8/2002) had almost doubled in comparison of the numbers to the total killing during five years of the Maoist movement. The number of killing reached 3,538 during the emergency, whereas there were only 1,803 killings till November 25.

Torture, extortion, violation of human rights and destructive activities were on the increase. According to government figures, 1,321 VDC buildings were completely destroyed in the first year of the state of emergency (November 2001-November 2002). The region-wise breakdown of the damage of the VDC buildings were; 316 (82.5 per cent) out of 383 in the Far Western region; 165 (28.7 per cent) out of 575 in the Mid-Western region; 221 (25.5 per cent) out of 865 in the Western region; 334 (27.8%) out of 1,199 in the Central region and 285 (31.9 per cent) of 893 in the Eastern region. Until early 2003, some 440 post offices were destroyed. Another effect of the Maoist movement is the displacement of the people from the conflict area. As per Human Rights Yearbook 2005 published by INSEC, as many as 38,191 people were displaced by the conflict upto the end of 2004. The report further stated that more than 22,000 people had been displaced from their homes only from the Mid-Western region by the end of 2003, whereas the IDP project of the Norwegian Refugee Council estimates the number to exceed, 200,000 as displaced people (INSEC 2005:ix).

On the other hand, the conspiracy against democracy had started in the parliament process itself. On May 22, 2002, the king, "on the recommendation of prime minister", dissolved the parliament. The parliament was dissolved because of the debate in NC over the issue of the extension of the State of Emergency. Deuba proposed the extension of the emergency in the parliament on which his party (the NC) was of the view not to continue it. By the time of the dissolution of the parliament, the government declared the new poll date and reinforced the state of emergency in the country. The next step against the democratization process was the postponement of the elections of local bodies, which had to be held by July 2002. However, by that time the elected representatives were replaced by bureaucrats in the local body. Later, King Gyanendra interrupted the democratic process by dismissing the then Deuba government on October 4, 2002. The King charged Deuba of incompetence by not holding elections. This incident accelerated a three-party struggle between the Maoist, the monarchy backed by the security forces, and the political parties. The daily killings went up from 2.43 (before the king's takeover) to 6.26. Dissolving parliament and doing away with local representatives resulted in a political vacuum at all levels. The situation became convenient to the Maoist to expand their bases at local level. Arbitrary arrests, increasing number of disappearances, violent activities, and random searches, all had a negative impact on the local communities. They were constrained to stay under the Maoists' rule.

After dismissing the elected Prime Minister Deuba and taking over the power, the king appointed two successive governments, the first under Prime Minster Lokendra Bahadur Chand (October 2002) and the second under Surya Bahadur Thapa (June 2003). However, both the governments were sacked by the king on May 30, 2003 and May 7, 2004, respectively. The king charged the governments of incompetence to get the support from major political parties. The first government announced a truce on January 29, 2003. The Maoist reciprocated with ceasefire. It was the second ceasefire declared by the Maoist and the government. They held three rounds of formal talks—the first was on April 24 (in Kathmandu), the second on 9 May (in Kathmandu), and the third on August 11 (in Hapure, Dang). The last dialogue was held while Surya Bahadur Thapa was the prime minister. The second truce came to an end after the Maoist unilaterally called it off on August 26, 2003. On the eve of January 26, 2003, the Maoist killed the Inspector General of Armed Police Force (IGP of APF), Krishna Mohan Shrestha and his wife, while the couple was having a morning walk in Kathmandu.

As already mentioned, spate of the killing increased after the declaration of the state of emergency on November 26, 2001. The figure of deaths noticeably increased after the takeover of power by the king on October 4, 2002. The increase in the number of deaths continued even after the break -up of the second truce. The figure is as follows:

Table 14: **Killing by the State and the Maoist (after Assumption of Power by the King)**

Period	Killings			Per day killing ratio
	By the state	By the Maoist	Total	
Total Killings until 27/11/2005	8,283	4,582	12,865	-
Killing after king's takeover (4/10/2002—27/11/2005)	4,438	2,630	7,068	6.24
Killing after the take over and before the second truce (04/10/2004 – 29/01/2003)	688	337	1,025	8.91
Killing after the break up of second truce (28/08/2003 - 27/11/2005)	3,626	2,211	5,837	7.22

Source: INSEC report 2005

At the end of the second ceasefire in August 2003, the violent conflict further worsened and human rights abuse increased. The per-day killing touched the ratio of 8.91. Prior to the second truce, the ratio was 7.22 and it was 2.43 before the king's takeover. On March 2004, Bhojpur and Beni, the headquarters of Bhojpur and Myagdi districts were attacked along with other small attacks by the Maoist.

The security forces were accused of torture, rape, murder, and arbitrary arrests—but were under impunity. Political opponents were the Maoists' main targets who abducted teachers and students and brought them to indoctrination camps. The state was not able to ensure the safety and security of its citizens. By the beginning of 2004, members of the political parties, civil societies and student organizations joined and assembled on the streets to protest against the 'autocratic' King and demanded for the restoration of democracy. These demonstrations led King Gyanendra to reappoint of Sher Bahadur Deuba as Prime Minister in June 2004.

Deuba tried to make an 'all party' government, but was able to get the support of only UML from Five-Party Alliances which was protesting against the king. UML left the street and the alliance, and joined the Deuba government. Other major political parties, including the mainstream Nepali Congress Party, refused to join the government citing the government as another conspiracy and the continuity of the king's regressive action. Their argument was that the government was formed to continue and strengthen his autocratic regime. Deuba formed a 'multi-party' government with the help of his own party Nepali Congress (D), the UML, and some small parties in the parliament. However, those parties which were on the streets, formed the Four-Party Alliance (FPA), and continued their protest for restoration of democracy.

Deuba government was given the task of negotiation with the parties and the Maoist to settle the existing conflict. Deuba set mid-January 2005 as the deadline for the Maoist for the truce and negotiation. However, the Maoist declined Deuba's offer raising a question on the status of the government.

On February 1, 2005, King Gyanendra finally dismissed the Deuba government by a proclamation. It was the king's second dismissal of Deuba from the post of prime minister. In the proclamation, the king declared that he would assume power for three years. He installed a Council of Ministers under his chair. All the ministers appointed by the king were the supporters of the previous Panchayat system. He suspended all democratic rights and 'installed military rule' in the country. Immediately after this announcement, the army occupied the streets of Kathmandu; political leaders were put under house arrest or detention; telephone and Internet communications were disconnected for several days and the international airport was shut down. Fundamental rights, such as freedom of speech and assembly, were abrogated under the proclaimed state of emergency. However, the king justified his actions by saying that he was forced to take this step to defend multi-party democracy.

The king's move on February 1, 2005, led to a new battle with the parliamentary parties and civil societies in cities while there had already been another battle in the villages with the rebels. Within 11 months of the king's direct rule (from February 1, 2005 to November 27, 2005), about 6,112 political activists and human rights defenders were arrested. At least 1,000 journalists and media personnel became jobless because of the restriction on broadcasting news from all of the 47 FM radio stations. Thousands of political activists and human rights defenders were re-arrested by security forces and a total of 40 persons were restricted from leaving Kathmandu valley (INSEC 2005).

On the other hand, the king's February coup affected the Maoist movements also. The RNA, which had been loyal to the king, was deployed not only to suppress the political party's activities in the cities but also to control the Maoist activities in the countryside. This was the first time that the RNA was properly mobilized against the Maoist movement. Therefore, both the RNA and the Maoist had fought against each other, which led to more than 1,370 killings during the period. During the year 2005, there were several Maoist' attacks. These attacks took place in Bandipur of Sirah district, Mirchaiya of Sarlahi district, Narke of Kavre district, Pandhare of Bhojpur district, Khanda of Argakhanchi district, and Pili of Kalikot district. There was a four-month unilateral ceasefire declared by the Maoist, but the king's government did not reciprocate. The people faced two long general strikes — the first being three days long in February, and the second 11 days long in April. Both the strikes were called by the Maoist.

Interestingly, Nepal found certain positive outcomes by the king's coup to restore peace and democracy in the country. The important outcomes are: -

1. The regime's repressive actions against all political forces helped the parliamentary parties to realize the fact that it is important to be united to fight for democracy and for their existence as well. . This reduced the antagonism within the parties and a Seven-Party Alliance (SPA) was formed in May 8, 2005. Prior to that, the main parliamentary parties were divided; four parties were on the streets to protest against the king's October 4, 2002 move, and two others were in the royal government. However, following the February 1st movement, Deuba and UML realized the king's intention, i.e., the divide and rule policy. The coup not only made the political parties to unite against the autocracy, but they also agreed on a pro-democracy agenda based on common understandings.

2. The Maoist had reached the commitment of peaceful democratic means during the king's active rule. The Maoist, by its party plenum in August 2005 in Rolpa, decided to opt for 'competitive democracy' by giving up the 'people's war'. The Maoist, which was having a tacit understanding with the king to defame democratic forces, left the alliance with the king and decided the momentous decision to join multi-party competition after getting

to know about the king's intention. It was the landmark decision by the Maoist which helped the SPA to rethink over the intention of the Nepali Maoist. The SPA, after several meetings in June 2005, reciprocated the Maoist's acceptance of the election of the CA as the only way to bring the Maoist into the mainstream. The SPA reciprocated the Maoist commitment by accepting the election of the CA, which was one of the three main demands of the Maoist. The two events became the main elements to get the SPA and the Maoist closer, which later on had contributed to the agreement regarding the twelve-point understanding to fight for establishing 'full-fledged democracy' in the country.

3. It directly and indirectly helped people to be aware about democracy and the democratic system. People came to know about the importance of freedom and democracy when the king seized all the means of communication like telephone, news and the movement of the people. Prior to the king's direct rule, many people, mainly the elites, had shown their reluctance over political parties and their *modus operandi*.

4. The king's strategic weapons like the charge of corruption became a setback to the king himself. Some groups of people were unhappy with the democratic parties and their leaderships and charged them of corruption, nepotism, etc. When they found notorious, corrupt and culprit persons in the king's cabinet and advisory boards, the people changed their mindset on political parties and its leaders and started supporting the parties and democratic movement as well. In April, the earlier mentioned Four-Party Alliance (FPA) became the Seven-Party Alliance (SPA) when the Deuba-headed Nepali Congress (Democratic), the UML and the United Left Front joined the FPA. With this began the nationwide protest against 'the king's autocratic regime'.

On November 23, 2005, the SPA signed a twelve-point agreement with the Maoist. The main point of the agreement was to put forth a common front with a view to end the king's autocracy. The SPA declared a four-day general strike from April 6, 2006 to April 9, 2006 against the regime. However, the general strike culminated into the 19-day indefinite. Mass Movement-II. The movement, in which 21 protesters lost their lives, hundreds became disabled, and thousands were injured, compelled the king to address the SPA's agenda for the restoration of the parliament.

There were two main objectives of the Mass Movement II. The first was the wide-spread discontent caused by the repeated failure of the king's direct rule. The second was the hope that the twelve-point agreement between the mainstream parties and the Maoist would bring peace and democracy in the country. An ICG report of 10 May 2006 describes the then developments in Nepal as follows:

> 'King Gyanendra's capitulation on 24 April 2006 in the face of a mass movement marked a victory for democracy in Nepal and, with a ceasefire between the new government and the Maoist now in place, the start of a serious peace process. Forced to acknowledge the 'spirit of the people's movement,' Gyanendra accepted popular sovereignty, reinstated parliament and invited the mainstream seven-party alliance to implement its roadmap—including election of a constituent assembly to rewrite the constitution in line with the parties' five-month-old agreement with the Maoist.' (ICG report, 10 May 2006)

Talking of the growth of the Maoist movement, the causes seem more or less similar to the causes of the origin of the Maoist Movement in Nepal as mentioned earlier: Brutal action of the security forces towards the villagers, geographically favourable hilly area for the guerilla warfare, and poor performance of the government has been the important causes for the rampant growth of the Maoist Movement. Apart from that, the 'capitalization' of ethnic/Dalit sentiment by the Maoist party by deciding the ethnic/regional governments seems another important cause. To instal the marginalized population in the position of power, the Maoist declared autonomous regions and made provision for the representation of ethnic, Dalit and minorities in proportion to their size of population in the autonomous body.

The split of CPN-UML into CPN-UML and CPN-ML in 1995, the sweep out of ML from the 1999 general elections, and the palace massacre of 2001 are other major factors, which helped in escalating the Maoist Movement. The Mahakali treaty between the Government of India and the Government of Nepal led to the split of the UML. According to the then ML faction, the treaty was discriminatory. With the division of the party, radical elements within UML joined the ML. However, after the ML was swept out in the 1999 elections, the cadres with radical orientation started shifting to the Maoist party. When the UML and ML finally merged, most of the ML cadres refused to go back to the UML and joined the Maoist party.

In the midst, the Royal Massacre, which took place in July 2001, became another opportunity for the Maoist to capitalize on people's anti-monarchy feeling. The Maoist was the first political force to declare the end of traditional monarchy by the massacre, and appealed to the people to move forward for the republican state. Prior to that, the Maoist leaders spoke out that they were having a 'tacit understanding' with the king (Kantipur, June 6, 2001; *Nepal Samachar Patra*, June 15, 2001; Singh 2003). The decision and appeal of the Maoist to move forward the republican state became a landmark decision to draw attention of those youth and others who were having reservations over the report related to the massacre issued by the investigation committee. By then it had realized that the people lost their faith in the new king, Gyanendra, and the Maoist started raising the republican issue as a 'cardinal demand' leaving its 'tacit understanding' with the monarchy.

Another cause of its rapid growth was that they not only raised people-oriented slogans but also started implementing those slogans into practice. They deployed their leaders to the Janasarkar and started giving justice through the 'people's court.' It established schools and co-operatives. They offered loans to the poor and needy charging lower interest than the government banks. This was welcomed by the general public and women in particular. It banned gambling and alcohol drinking. It tried to control child marriage and polygamy as it considered these as 'social evils.'

The political situation of Nepal has changed recently by the April 2006 uprising. Prior to the movement, there were triangular clashes between the king's autocratic regime, the parliamentary parties and the Maoist. The SPA and the Maoist came ideologically closer by the 12-point understanding, and made the municipal election, which was declared by the king's regime in February 2006 as a failure. Again, the SPA and the Maoist conducted a long dialogue in India and formally agreed to strengthen their coalition and announced a second memorandum of understanding on March 19, 2006. The second memorandum, according to parties, was essential to give another strong message to those who took the 12-point understanding lightly. They came to a consensus to launch separate and common protest to defeat the king's regime and to establish a democratic system. The Maoist withdrew a 20-day economic and transport blockade after the request of SPA and the civil society which was declared in all district headquarters, including Kathmandu, from March 14, 2006. It was because the blockade affected the life of the people in general. The SPA reciprocated the withdrawal of the 20-day blockade announcing a four-day nationalwide general strike from April 6, 2006. The proposed four-day general strike was diverted into the April Uprising and continued for 19 days until the king declared that he would give up his power and reinstate the dissolved House of the Representatives on April 24, 2006. Millions of people from all walks of life defined the 'shoot-at-sight' order of the king during the 18-hour curfew enforced by the security forces, and risked their lives by coming onto the streets.

During the 19-day general strike, three proclamations were made by the king. Among them were, traditional address on the occasion of Nepali New Year on 14, April 2006, and other two issues, were made with consequent to pressure of the people. The king, in his New Year address, called upon all political parties to join in a dialogue in order to assume responsibility and contribute towards activating the multi-party democracy. He tried to teach political parties about democracy and said, "we believe that there is no alternative to multi-party democracy in the 21st century and the verdict of the ballot alone is legitimate". His intention of the proclamation was to lure political parties in the name of reactivating all representative bodies through so-called elections and to end the ongoing general strike. The political parties ignored the proclamation, and continued protesting because every party knew that the king was not eager to strengthen the democracy, but to continue his own autocratic regime.

After seven days of his April 14 speech, the king issued another proclamation. The speech came out on the 16th day of the general strike announced by the SPA on April 21, 2006. The declared intention of the speech was to hand over the sovereignty to the people by proclamation. The announcement stated, "we, through this proclamation, affirm that the executive power of the Kingdom of Nepal, which was in our safekeeping, shall, from this day, be returned to the people". However, the SPA immediately rejected the announcement terming the proclamation "a betrayal" to diffuse the momentum of the mass movement, and intensified the peaceful protest. The rejection of the king's offer was because the king called upon the SPA to join the government for implementing his agenda. Another fact of the denial of the call by the SPA was that the king expressed high regard for the duty consciousness, valour and discipline of the security forces which suppressed the peace protest and no reference was made to the importance of people's uprising.

When the SPA accelerated the massive protest denying the king's second offer, the king was compelled to accept all the SPA demands, including to reinstate of the House of Representatives which was dissolved on May 22, 2002, and to let the SPA run the country according to their roadmap. The SPA accepted the third offer by the king when he recognized the people's movement and extended his heartfelt condolences to all those who had lost their lives in the people's movement and wished the injured speedy recovery. Earlier, he had been refusing to endorse the people's contribution to the Mass Movement-II.

The first meeting of the reinstated house was held at 1 p.m. on Friday, April 28, 2006 which endorsed a commitment resolution for the assembly. The House declared the House as 'supreme', decided to put the king under normal laws placing him at par with normal citizens provisioning to collect tax, declared Nepal as a secular state and changed the name of Royal Nepal Army to Nepal Army. The Council of Ministers was empowered to appoint the Chief of the Army Staff. It announced to bring the army under the parliament. Apart from that, the House of Representatives' proclamation provided the authority to the House to decide on royal succession.

On May 25, 2006, the Government of Nepal and CPN (M) signed a Ceasefire Code of Conduct respecting the popular mandate expressed through the historic people's movement for total democracy, progress and peace. Both the parties agreed to sign this code of conduct to transform the ceasefire into permanent peace and resolve the problems through negotiations. They both showed their commitment once again towards democratic values including the concept of competitive multi-party democracy, civic liberties, fundamental rights, human rights, press freedom and rule of law through the signature.

The SPA and Maoist held three 'summit meetings' along with a number of informal talks at the Prime Minister's residence. It was at the first summit meeting on June 16, 2006 that an eight-point agreement was signed with the objective of implementing their earlier commitments effectively and honestly. They agreed to draft an interim constitution and to form an interim government along with the Maoist and hold the Constituent Assembly elections. Other points agreed upon were to dissolve the reinstated House of Representatives after making alternative arrangements and dissolving the 'People's Governments' of the Maoist across the country. Further, they both expressed commitment to multi-party system, human rights, press freedom, civic liberties, and rule of law; and decided to request the UN to help in the management and monitoring of arms and armies of both sides during the CA elections through the eight-point agreement.

The third round summit meeting between the SPA government and the Maoist finally produced a historic deal paving the way for formal entry of the Maoist into the political mainstream on November 8, 2006. Following the deal, the government and the Maoist signed a Comprehensive Peace Agreement (CPA) on November 22, 2006 declaring 'an end to the armed conflict ongoing in the country since 1995 by giving permanency to the ongoing cease-fire between the Government and the Maoist'. Another output after the deal was the signing of a tripartite agreement of arms and army management between the government, the Maoist and the UN on November 28, 2006. This agreement includes commitment on all issues such as fate of the monarchy, arms management, interim constitution, interim legislature, interim government and electoral system for CA. They decided to determine the fate of monarchy by the first meeting of the CA, to put the properties of late King Birendra under a trust and to nationalize the ancestral property of King Gyanendra. The king became powerless till the first meeting of the CA determined the fate of monarchy.

Following these agreements, the Maoist combatants were sent to cantonments as seven big cantonments and 21 smaller camps were set up. According to the deal, the arms of the 'people's army' would be surrendered and put under a single lock system; its key to be given to the Maoist and the cantonments would be monitored by the United Nations through Closed Circuit Television (CCTVs) and siren alarm system, which would be set off if there is any unauthorized tampering of the lock. The UN started verifying the arms and monitoring it soon after it arrived in Nepal along with the tripartite agreement of the SPA, the Maoist and the UNMIN. The Government also reciprocated by putting a similar quantity of arms of Nepali Army (NA) under the single lock system.

The reinstated House of Representatives had promulgated the Interim Constitution and formed Interim Legislature. The Interim Legislature had 330 members with 75 seats for Nepali Congress, 73 seats for CPN-UML, 73 seats for the Maoist and remaining 48 seats for civil society, professional organizations and various small party organizations. Of the mixed electoral system for 601 members of the CA–240 are elected directly on the basis of existing electoral constituencies, 335 members are nominated by various parties on the basis of their proportional strength of direct elections and balance 26 members are nominated by the Prime Minister.

Today, everyone is optimistic about the resolution of the decade-long armed conflict in Nepal. Hope was kindled in Nepal when Prachanda, through an extensive interview, disclosed a momentous decision which was taken by his party plenum in August 2005 in Rolpa (*The Hindu*, February 8, 9 and 10, 2006). The optimism is obvious because the SPA and the Maoist have reached several agreements to resolve the conflict.

Another interesting and optimistic point is that every discussion between the government and the rebels has been held at the official residence of the prime minister without any national or international mediators, which is unique in the world. Prachanda, an underground supremo of the Maoist rebels, for the first time appeared in public in Kathmandu at the residence of the prime minister, and has been seen there without feeling insecure for his life after several years of underground activities. This is another achievement of the Nepali peace process. However, the process is not free from conspiracy, power game and vested interest of SPA, the Maoist and other national or international power centres. Therefore, the process has been moving slowly and the time frame decided in several agreements could not be followed. All the same, people are hopeful of the success of the peace process because they have no other option, except to wait and watch how the situation progresses.

Chapter VI

Changing Patterns of Nepali Ethnic Movement and Consequences

Uddhab Pd. Pyakurel

Janajatis in Nepal: an Overview

Though considered as a small country in South Asia, Nepal is a homeland of 100 ethnic/caste groups. The term "tribe" or "ethnic community" often used by western scholars and popular in the writings of Indian anthropology and administration, these groups are popularly known as Adibasi/Janajati (indigenous/nationalities) in Nepal (Dahal 1979; also see Dahal forthcoming). The ethnic groups, who have been popularly known as 'Janajati' in Nepal, alone comprise 59 groups in total. As per the official definition, "Janajati" or "indigenous nationalities" means "a tribe or community as mentioned in the schedule having its own mother language and traditional rites and customs, distinct cultural identity, distinct social structure and written or unwritten history" (NFDIN 2003:32). It is said that the categorization was based on the recommendation of a task force formed by the government of Nepal in 1996 for the identification and uplift of these social categories. However, the National Foundation for Development of Indigenous Nationalities (NFDIN) Act 2002 was brought into existence only after revision on the recommendation of the task force[1]. There is also a provision that the Nepal Government, on the recommendation of the Governing Council of the National Foundation for Development of Indigenous Nationalities (NFDIN), can make change in the schedule of Janajatis by publishing a notice in the Nepal Gazette

---

1 So far the major revisions are concerned, the part of the definition proposed by the task force which stated that Janajatis were not part of the four-tier Hindu varna system has been omitted in the Act. Also the schedule published as part of the Act only lists 59 groups as indigenous nationalities even though the task force proposed 61 groups in the schedule (for details, see Onta 2006: 308-313).

(NFDIN 2003:52-53). As per the clause, the number is likely to increase in the near future as the list has been further updated to 81 groups by a recently formed Technical Committee of the Government of Nepal in 2010 (Dahal forthcoming).

The population size of identified Janajati groups in the 2001 census was 8,473,429. Also 5,259 people were placed under unidentified Janajati groups. If both the numbers are added, the total population of Janajati groups comes to 36.6 percent of the total population of Nepal. Of this, 24 per cent belongs to Tarai, and the rest to the Hills. Tharu alone comprise 58.8 percent of the Tarai Janajati population, and six Janajati groups, i.e., Magar, Tamang, Newar, Rai, Gurung and Limbu together comprise 65.5 percent of total hill Janajati population. In addition, there are 23 small Janajati groups, such as Kusunda (164), Yehlmo (579), Raute (658), Munda (660), etc., whose combined population size is less than 0.1 percent of the total population of Nepal (Dahal forthcoming). It is also stated that the identified 59 groups are not in similar status in terms of their socio-economic conditions . Having realized this, the 59 groups have been classified and put into the following five categories.

Table 1:   Indigenous groups /nationalities with their process of marginalization

	Classification of Janajatis				
Region	**Endan-gered**	**Highly mar-ginalized**	**Marginal-ized**	**Disadvantaged**	**Advan-taged**
Moun-tain		Siya, Shingsa-wa (Lhomi), Thudam	Bhote, Dolpo, Lar-ke, Lhopa , Mugali, Topkego-la, Walung	Bara Gaunle, By-anshi, Chhairotan, Marpahali-Thakali, Sherpa, Tangbe, Tin-gaule Thakali	Thakali

Hill	Ban-kariya, Hayu, Kush-badiya, Lepcha, Surel	Baramu, Thami, Chepang	Bhujel, Dura, Pahari Phree,, Sunuwar, Tamang	Chantyal, Gurung,Jhirel, Limbu, Magar, Rai, Yakha , Hyolmo	Newar
Inner Tarai	Raji, Raute	Bote, Danu-war, Majhi	Darai, Kumhal		
Tarai	Kisan, Meche	Dhanuk, Jhangad, Satar	Dhimal, Gangai, Rajbanshi, Tajpuriya Tharu		
Total	**10**	**12**	**20**	**15**	**2**

Source: Tamang 2004; see also NEFIN 2005 cited in Dahal (forhcoming)

They are: (1) endangered groups; (2) highly marginalized groups; (3) marginalized groups; (4) disadvantaged groups; and (5) advanced groups. As per the classifications, 10 janajatis are listed in the first category whereas 12 are in the second, 20 are in the third, 15 are in the forth, and only two are in the fifth category. As far as regional (geographical) strength of the 59 identified Janajatis is concerned, some 18 are from mountain, 24 are from hill, 7 are from inner Tarai and 10 are from Tarai.

If we go through the history of Nepal, the Shah rulers used to pamper the ethnic groups to grab their support for the unification project, by saying that it is the 'homeland' of this and that ethnic groups. But once the 'unified' Nepal came into existence in 1769, the process of Hinduisation[2] (making Hinduism as a "state religion") and Nepalisation[3] (Nepali as the 'official language', and thereby marginalizing other linguistic and religious groups) have become the major aim of the same rulers.

Let me first discuss the overall political scenario related to conflict of interest between the state and ethnic groups of Nepal before and after unification. In other words, I will focus on the ethnic groups and their access to power and other social domains in different political era. In

---

2 For details about the term, see Uddhab Pd. Pyakurel, Maoist Movement in Nepal: A Sociological Perspectives (New Delhi: Adroit Publishers, 2007).

3 For details about the term, see *Ibid.*

doing so, this paper discusses the paradigm shift of state policy under five different periods - pre-unification, Shah Regime 1769-1846, Rana Regime 1846-1951, Pseudo-Democratic Period 1951-60, Panchayat regime 1960-1990, and Democratic System after 1990.

Pre-Unification: Background to the Process of Hinduisation and Nepalisation

Nepal's present international boundaries are of recent origin. In its present form, the boundaries were fixed after the Sugauli Treaty of 1816, which the government of Nepal and British East India Company had signed. Prior to that, Nepal's territory was unstable and unclear. In fact, it covered the whole of the sub-Himalayan hill area; its boundary extended from the border of Bhutan in the east, to Kangra in the west (Joshi and Rose 1966:3). Before 1769, only the Kathmandu valley with three Malla rulers was known as Nepal. At least 56 small princely states, which were outside the valley, were not referred to as Nepal. In fact, even after the unification until 1909, 'Nepal was referred only to the Kathmandu valley. Today's Nepal were referred to as various 'countries' (desa) all subject to the house of Gorkha' (Burghart 1984 cited in Gellner et el. 1997:5). Ranas were credited to have given a single name 'Nepal' to avoid varied and ambiguity complex names. It is said that the Ranas, for the first time, began to define the country (Nepal) 'as a nation-state' (Ibid). Kathmandu valley was a great lake prior to human settlement. It was known as Naghdaha (lake of snakes) and Naga tribes inhabited its surroundings. They survived on fish, animals, and birds available in the lake and its surrounding areas. When the lake dried up, it became a valley with fertile land. Later, the Nagas along with Gopalas (cow-herders) and Mahispalas (buffalo-herders) moved into this valley and made it their dwelling place. At that time, king or ruler of the valley was appointed through election (ISRSC 2004). 'A sage (muni) called Ne appeared on the scene as the protector (pala) of the land and the founder of the first ruling dynasty. Thus, the chronicles explain the origin of the name of the country Ne-pala, the land protected by Ne'. Gopalavamsi Guptas replaced Ne Dynasty and ruled for 491 years (Shah 1992:7). Gopalvamsis dynasty was replaced by Mahispalvamsa regime (buffalo-herder dynasty) which lasted for a period of eleven years and seven months. Later, the Kirats of the Mongolian stock entered the valley and became the ruling dynasty by replacing the Gopalas and Mahespalas. The Kiratas who ruled for a period of 1,581 year and one month (cited in Shah 1992:7) were replaced by Lichhavis who entered Nepal around the middle of the 5th century B.C. from the republic of Vaishali in the present northern Bihar of India. Lichhavi dynasty was based on some kind of divine right: justice and morality were associated with the religion of the time. The judges of civil and criminal courts were termed 'religious authority' (Dharmadhikari) at that time. There was a provision for a state minister for religious affairs or religious activities. Lichhavis are thus considered the first Hindu rulers of Nepal. Before the Licchhavis, the indigenous peoples, who were originally Saiva and Vaishnava non-Hindu and casteless community (Shah 1992: 28), were subjected to influences. However, some ambitious Lichhavi kings like Amsuvarma tried their best to impose occupation-based caste system among the people (Ibid). Also, it is said that the Lichhavis made Sanskrit the official and literary language of Nepal, and extended it to the field of architecture and sculpture. These were hallmarks of the process of Hinduization and Nepalization by the Nepali rulers. On these counts, the Licchhavi period has been described as the golden age of the Nepali history by 'mainstream historians' and subaltern historians see it as 'a set-back to indigenous rights of people'. However, religious antagonism was not evident in the Lichhavi period. Rather, there was 'religious harmony' within the society. Everyone was free to worship any of the deities they chose according to their personal preference. All the temples and monasteries of Saiva, Vaishnava and Buddhist sects made during the Lichhavi period were subsidized by the rulers without discrimination (Shah 1992:29-31).

The Malla Dynasty replaced the Lichhavi dynasty. When Jayasthiti Malla came into power, he restored order and stability, and managed a century-long anarchy of Kathmandu valley. He brought many Karnat priests from Mithila, and started social reforms by initiating many social rules and regulations (ISRSC 2004:4). Jayasthiti Malla started a long-term policy for consolidation of the Nepali society with the help of five Brahmans, who hailed from North and South India. He introduced a Civil Code, and classified people into 64 sub-castes, and introduced detailed rules with regard to their social activities and social behavior. Although Jayasthiti Malla's reformist activities aimed at consolidating the Nepali society within the orthodox Hindu religious framework, he is considered 'liberal' in the matter of religion because of his belief in polytheism and especially his devotion to Shiva and Vishnu (Shah 1992:57). In the Malla period, it is said that the two religions—Buddhism and Hinduism—were developed harmoniously and simultaneously. To summarize, prior to the unification, many principalities [states] had their existence in the present territory of Nepal. As many as 46 kingdoms were in the western part. Makawanpur, Vijaypur and Chaudani kingdoms existed as prominent states under the Sen Dynasty of Palpa in the southern and South-eastern part of modern Nepal. Kathmandu, Patan, Bhaktapur (also colloquially known as Bhadgaon) and even sometimes Nuwakot and Banepa kingdoms,   were located in the middle and surrounding areas of the Kathmandu valley. There is still some debate about the Baise and Chaubise and other principalities and their territory being under medieval Nepal. Shaha (1992), referring to Francis Buchanan-Hamilton, considers Gorkha as one of the Chaubise states ,but Joshi and Rose (1966) contest this argument and write that Gorkha was never under the Chaubise states.

In terms of linguistic/social features of Nepal, at least three major racial trends are visible. These are: -

(a) Indo-Aryans, who migrated to Nepal from the plains or from the hill areas of India several hundred years ago in the wake of Muslim invasions of Northern India.

(b) The people of Mongolian origin inhabit the higher hill areas in the east and west including Kirat tribal communities like Rais and Limbus.

(c) A number of tribal communities may be remnants of indigenous communities whose habitation of Nepal predates the advent of Indo-Aryan and Mongolian elements. Among the three, the third one had gradually been driven back into the more isolated sections of Tarai jungles and the humid, malarial river valleys in the hill areas during the course of the Indo-Aryan and Mongolian incursions (Joshi and Rose 1966:10).

Although there is not enough literature about religious affiliations of the above-mentioned groups, there are indications that they were practicing different religions like Buddhism and Shamanism. Buddhism came to Nepal in its Mahayan form from Tibet and had tremendous influence on the Nepalese society up to the 7th century A.D. The Hindu Lichhavi rulers imposed Hinduism on various tribal groups of Nepal. The Indian impact had also helped the growth of Hinduism in Nepal during the Lichhavi rule. Before the Hinduism got ascendancy in India, the old form of Hinduism and Buddhism continued to survive, but later on, a majority of Nepalese reverted to the Hindu religion (Chauhan 1989:1). Rose and Schulz assume that during the Lichhavi period, a number of ethnic communities such as the Rais and Limbus in eastern Nepal, various Tibetan groups (Sherpa, Tamang, etc.) in the north, the Magars and Gurungs in the central-western hills, and the Khas in the far west, established themselves in areas of what is now Nepal. Those communities, except Chaubise states, had tribal culture, and culturally and economically, they were more dependent on the Buddhism in the north rather than on India or Kathmandu valley (Rose and Scholz 1980:12). It is important to note that Buddhism was not only dominant among the Newars of Kathmandu valley but also in other Mongolian, and tribal and indigenous communities. Shaha has a different view. He writes that the Kirats, who are considered as ethnic groups with remarkable skill in archery and warfare, also used to celebrate the well-known Hindu epic, the Mahabharata, and the Puranas (Shaha 1992:8). There is a saying that Buddhism co-existed with Vaishnavism and Saivism. Such a situation continued till the rule of Manadeva in Nepal. Manadeva seemed dedicated to both Buddhism and Hinduism, although he was a Hindu ruler. The Buddhist monastery, which is situated at Swayambhu, Kathmandu, is thought to have been built on Mandeva's order. It is said that the Vihar is named as Mana Vihar because it was constructed on Manadeva's initiation (Shah 1992: 14).

Jayasthiti Malla of Kathmandu (1382-95), and Ram Shah of Gorkha (1606-33) were the orthodox Hindus who, before unification, attempted to codify the structure of Nepali society—both Hindus and non-Hindus—within an orthodox Hindu framework. The former imposed the social code on the Newars of Kathmandu valley. For this task, he received guidance or advice from the Indian Brahmans. The latter did the same thing to the non-Hindu tribal community of Gorkha. Jayasthiti Malla divided the Newars of Kathmandu valley into 64 sub-groups and imposed on them the essential characteristics of Jatis (caste) applicable in the context of the Hindu caste system. These two incidents were considered as a setback to religious freedom so far enjoyed in Nepal. These incidents played a critical role in the ongoing 'Nepalization' and 'Hinduization' process among the Newars and other low-caste groups. The impact of the process was that the low-caste or non-Hindu communities gradually adopted the rituals and ideologies of high-caste Hindus. Another notable thing of Jayasthiti Malla's reform was that it had given similar status to the Buddhist Newars and Hindus. Such a social code was retained throughout the Malla period, which helped Newars to become closer to the Hindu religion (Joshi and Rose 1966: 11-12).

Post Unification : Hinduisation and Nepalisation

Dravya Shah, younger brother of the king of Lamjung (Lamjung is about 30 miles north-west of Gorkha), conquered Gorkha, in the middle of 1559. After assuming the position of the king of Gorkha, Dravya Shah began conquering the neighbouring states. Invocation of the Rajput heritage was the driving force behind it. However, he succeeded in conquering only two small states—Siranchock and Ajirgarh—during his rule (Gyawali 1935 : 3,31). Evidence shows that the newly established Shah dynasty, with the exception of Ram Shah, had made continuous plans to expand the state territory. Nara Bhupal Shah, descendant of Ram Shah and father of Prithvi Narayan Shah, unsuccessfully tried to defeat the neighbouring state of Nuwakot in 1737. His son Prithvi Narayan Shah ultimately conquered Nuwakot in the fall of 1744 (Gyawali 1935: 3, 83).

The credit of unification goes to Prithvi Narayan Shah, who brought about the 'Central Himalayas' into a single state. Apart from his personal contribution, he used many strategies to make the unification process easy. He strategically maintained marital relations with the powerful Sen Dynasty of Palpa, and had *Miteri* relation (ritual friendship within the same gender) with other principalities. Because of such affection based on relation, religion, culture and traditions with the Gorkha principality, several other neighbouring principalities accepted Prithvi Narayan Shah's request to help him in his dream to make a unified and great Nepal. Some weak neighbours helped Shah by submitting their states to Gorkha . There was an open declaration by the Gorkha regime that if a state accepted the offer to submit its sovereignty into the Gorkha regime, the rulers of the state could enjoy a broad degree of autonomous control over their 'subjects' on internal matters. Those local rulers and elites who surrendered to Gorkha continued to enjoy 'a fully autonomous status with a tenuous political authority' (Joshi and Rose 1966:4-5).

In terms of strategies enforced by the Gorkha ruler to unify Nepal, there are many stories. The ruler used religion, relation, etc., as weapons to unify other states. Before unification, most of the rulers were Hindus in those small states. In the central parts of Nepal, there were some autonomous indigenous tribal areas under the Rajput-ruled principalities; however, they were under the domination of the high-caste Hindu elites. They started establishing socio-cultural relations among the neighboring kingdoms through marriage and Miteri relation as they belonged to the same religion and culture. This helped to promote the concept of 'we feeling', and led to a psychological bond of togetherness. Ultimately, this nearness helped in the 'integration into a unified nation-state system.' Ram Shah's 'first written legal code in the hill area' also brought the hill principalities closer to each other as the 'legal code evoked positive responses from other hill principalities.' The legal code was based upon the orthodox Hindu religion but 'suitably modified to accommodate the social and political traditions of the non-Hindu subject of the principality in the 17th century' (Rose and Scholz 1980:15). There is a popular saying, 'if you are deprived of justice, then go to Gorkha.' It is presumed that the saying might become a reality after Ram Shah's legal code was applied to Gorkha.

Prithvi Narayan Shah could not capture Kathmandu valley easily. He was successful only after his third attempt because of the powerful presence of Malla rulers and Newars who defied the 'unification' process. However, when he captured the valley, he ordered that the ears and nose of the people of Kirtipur (the gateway to Kathmandu valley), should be slashed, which weighed 18 *dharnies* (equivalent to 42 kg) when collected (Bhattachan 2000: 140, cited in Pyakurel 2006a:115). There is a debate as to whether Prithvi Narayan Shah's policy of a united Nepal was 'unification' or a 'conquest'. After all, he used not only diplomacy and consensus but also military force in the name of unification of the state. Not only the rulers but also the people of the other states, which declined the offer of the Gorkha states, faced lots of violence and brutality by Gorkha soldiers. That is why the process was termed 'based on the right of sword' (Hachhethu 2003:281).

In fact, it was the Gorkha regime which killed all the adult males and young boys of Khumbu-Kirat community of eastern Nepal, who had not accepted or surrendered to the proposal of the regime. Data collected by Hudson indicated that pregnant women, due to fear of giving birth to a male offspring, were compelled to go for abortion, and the fetuses were also snatched away and destroyed by putting them into an *Okhal* (mortar in which rice is husked). Such brutal behavior of the Gorkha ruler compelled all other people either to surrender to the ruler of Gorkha, or to leave their birthplace and enter the Indian territory (Dhungel 2006). Another example of such brutality was seen in Jumla. Jumla was one of the powerful principalities before unification, which is situated in mid-western Nepal. When it defied surrendering to the Gorkha ruler in 1794, the Gorkhalis ordered its local authority to 'kill all rebels above the age of 12 years.' They warned Jumla people by using very arrogant terms. The Gorkhalis threatened that if anyone engaged in rebellion or intrigue, the Jumla regime would degrade the 'culprit' into a lower caste, even if he were a Brahman. However, if the 'guilty party' belonged to other lower castes, enslave or behead him according to his caste. Chauhan termed it as 'obedieance elicited through reign of terror' (Chauhan 1989:111). People of different regions were not considered as citizens but as 'subjects' of unified Nepal. With the unification of the country, it was hoped that the people could do business at the place of their choice, but the government imposed religion, caste, and social code and wanted the people to adhere to the regime and their traditional professions of their respective places. The royal order of 1846 banning Jumla from visiting other places for trade (Chauhan 1989:112-13) was an example of such an imposition, which made people frustrated in the so-called unified Nepal and became the major cause of the marginalization of the region.

However, there are several sayings about Gorkha states and its rulers' flexibility or liberality towards the policy related to the ethnic and tribal community. Bista presents Prithvi Narayan Shah as an egalitarian who regarded Brahmans, Khas and Magars simply as different ethnic groups with none of them superior or inferior to the others (Bista 1991:45). Sharma agrees with Bista's argument and writes that Prithvi Narayan Shah 'was able to rally a broad cross-section of Gorkhali society, including the Brahmans, the Khas, the Gurungs, the Magars and others to his cause.' According to Sharma (1997:477) there was social harmony among the different caste groups. Whelpton writes that the two ethnic groups, Magar and Gurung were found among the ruling elite of Gorkha house (Whelpton 1997:43) when there was the practice of *Chha Thar Ghar* (six family linage) system to support the king for policy making. Even, one can assume such a feeling when one reads the famous quotation by Prithvi Narayan Shah. The quotation reads as, 'Nepal is a garden of four Varnas and thirty-six Jatis or castes'. There are many evidences that prove this quotation. Prithvi Narayan Shah himself says, 'I (Prithvi Narayan Shah) am king of Magars' (Gurung 1997:501). Being the then king of Gorkha, Shah's expression should be considered as a radical expression in the society. It is because the Magars were considered as lower caste people by the society and high-caste-dominated society still treats the Magars not as citizens but as subjects.

To substantiate the above argument, Yogi and Acharya state that the king of Gorkha, prior to unification, used to listen to the voice of people before taking action. The Kings' hearing would be based on 'the local populace with its composition and function'. 'When the king had to choose the minister, he obtained a consensus of his court and subject' (Yogi and Acharya 1953:5-9). Shah rulers, in the name of hearing the 'local populace' before taking action, used to take the consensus of six elite families (*Chha Thar Ghar)*. These families, belonging to different castes and ethnic groups, were prominent in the social and political life of Gorkha (Joshi and Rose 1966:26). However, after having a look at Prithvi Narayan Shah's long-term policy of Hinduization and Gorkhaization, one is inclined to conclude that his quotation was more of a slogan to draw the different groups for the 'unification process.' There is another quotation by Prithvi Narayan Shah, which was contradictory to the above mentioned quotations. The quotation says, '*Yo Asali Hindustan ho* (this is the pure land of Hindus)' (Gurung 1997:501). This statement enlightened us about his actual position on the religion. After this quotation, one can easily argue that his earlier mentioned statements were only a strategy for getting support from the non-Hindu and lower caste people. In addition, his real position is reflected in his later statement. To Gellner, his role was neither as a wisher 'of becoming a garden of every sort of people' nor 'really a nationalist,' but he was 'very far from being a multiculturalist celebrating cultural diversity for his own sake (Gellner 1997:25)

After he had successfully conquered the Kathmandu valley, he reduced the *Chha Thar Ghar*, his consultative body, into *Char Thar Ghar* (four family linage) by excluding the two ethnic groups, the Magars and Gurungs. This exclusion also indicates his actual position on non-Hindus and lower caste people. The position was later converted into a state policy. The policy was the process of Hinduization (concept of Asali Hindustan) and Gorkhaization. The state tried to establish the Gorkhali peoples' hegemony over all the Gorkha defeated states. Prithvi Narayan Shah launched such a policy when he declared that Nepal was an ideal garden for flourishing of Hinduism along with its four Varna and 36 caste systems. For fulfilment of these objectives, the state began the process of granting new Guthis (the land donated to priests for performing daily Pooja to deities and for managing food, shelter etc., for the pilgrims during religious festivals) to the Brahmans. Most of the fertile lands were granted as Guthi. Such a practice was accelerated 'particularly in those areas where the Hinduism was nominal, i.e., towards the eastern region.' The settling of 28 Brahman families simultaneously in July 1811 in the Hattigisa of Morang, a part of eastern Nepal (Chauhan 1989:89) was an example of such a policy initiated by the state.

Upon the emergence of Nepal as a nation-state in 1769 under the leadership of Prithvi Narayan Shah, the participation of two high-caste Hindu groups—Brahmans who were considered as the intellectual elite and spiritual preceptors, and Kshatriyas who were considered the warrior caste—started ruling the state where 'participation in the political process became virtually their exclusive prerogative' (Joshi and Rose 1966:23). The state enforced the ancient Hindu scriptural requirement where 'the ruler of the state should always be recruited from the Kshatriyas and that they should exercise their political function with the advice and consent of the Brahmans'. Brahmans were given the role of priests, lawgivers, astrologers, and diplomatic emissaries. Other governing and administrating posts were given to the Kshatriyas. Among the Kshatriyas, especially the members of four prominent families—the Shah, Pandeys, Thapas and Basnyats, enjoyed such privileges. This system continued until the emergence of the Rana Family in 1846 (Joshi and Rose 1966:11-12). For making Brahmans a respectable group, the then government implemented the royal order wherein the people were urged 'to respect Brahmans and not to take the flesh of dead cattle.' The government further ordered that 'only the Brahmans could perform religious ceremonies in the house of individuals and none else,' and 'Brahmans would not be put to death throughout the kingdom howsoever heinous his crime might be.' Although the death penalty systems was operative, Brahmans were exempt from such a penalty; 'he could be degraded from his caste and imprisoned, but he could never be executed' (Chauhan 1989: 93). Caste discrimination was also extensively practiced. For example, the government employed 65 postmen during the year of 1825-26 and each one was allotted rice land on *adhiya* tenure as a repayment for their service. However, the high-caste postmen were allotted lands measuring between 95 to 105 *Murris*, the (one *Muri* is equivalent to 45 kg paddy and 50 kg corn), and the low-castes were allotted only 35 to 45 *Muris* (cited in Chauhan 1989:97) as emoluments for doing the same work.

In the later Shah rule, the state policy became more rigid. The Shah rule started recruiting military and civil stalwarts only from one region of the country—the Gorkha, the name of 'the trusted' people. Gorkha was the dynasty's native land. Further, even from Gorkha, the dynasty was chosen exclusively from the high-caste Brahman and Kshatriya families. Regmi (1995) states that despite the phenomenal growth of the Gorkha kingdom, its leadership until the mid-19th century continued to come from a small set of families from the heartland of Gorkha. And, as the class was completely dependent upon the king for its economic security, modern Nepal, under the absolute control of the king, also functioned as a socially hierarchical Hindu polity with no legal or constitutional recognition of ideas related to the concept of equality until the mid-19th century (Onta 2006: 305).

On account of such an established practice of the Shah dynasty, Chauhan defined the term 'Gorkha' 'as those progeny of Brahmans and Kshatriyas who had migrated from the southern plains and had come into contact with the Khas and Magars of this region, and who had accepted the Hindu religion, including diet and deity' (Chauhan, 1989:79). Chauhan mentioned seven imbibed characters as the basic criteria to be considered as Gorkha people by the ruler. These were: (a) they had contempt against the elite of other religions; (b) they abhorred all religions except Hinduism;

(c) they did not hold high opinion about the low castes; (d) they had no respect for the vanquished; (e) they did not regard trade, commerce and other business activities as respectable professions; (f) they had no esteem for art, literature and architecture; and (g) possession of land and military post was their prized holding. Examining the 'Gorkha' culture, Chauhan writes, 'in Gorkha there was no Gorkha in the sense that it was populated by the *Matwalis'* (Chauhan 1989:79). The Khas Magars, who had not accepted Hindu religion and its dietary restrictions, were not known as Gorkhas by that criterion. For general information, there is a trend in Nepal to classify people into *Tagadhari* and *Matwali* group on the basis of wearing the scared thread. Those who wear the sacred thread are called *Tagadharis* and the others *Matwalis*. Taking note of those seven characters, one can conclude that such a policy was introduced to ban other native and indigenous groups to be state elites to preserve the posts only for high-caste Hindus. There were Newars of Kathmandu valley, the Tamangs in the surrounding area of Kathmandu with good knowledge as entrepreneurs, skilful in arts, architecture and traders, but they got fewer chances to be in state mechanism.

Rana Regime, 1846-1951: Acceleration of the Hinduisation and Nepalisation along with new initiatives of Ranaisation

In the history of Nepal, the Rana hereditary system came to power in 1846 as a result of 'intrigues, counter-intrigues and conspiracies' within the members of four prominent Kshatriya families. Janga Bahadur Kunwar, backed by the then younger queen Lakshmi Devi, organized a massacre and 'established virtually dictatorial control over the government' (Joshi and Rose 1966:29). The massacre was named *Kot Parva* (Kot Massacre) and Janga Bahadur is considered as an initiator of the Rana regime. In the 'Kot Parva most of the prominent Kshatriya elites were either assassinated or compelled to leave the country. According to Acharya, 30 were killed, 60 fled the country, and 26 others were banished from prominent four Kshatriya families. Again, one-and-half-months later on October 13, 1846, at least 23 Basnyat prominent nobles of Kshatriya caste, were killed by Janga Bahadur. They were accused of being organizers of the *Bhandarkhal Parva* or 'Basnyat conspiracy' (Acharya 2005: 107, 115)

After establishing himself in power, Janga Bahadur combined in himself the roles of the chief of army, the prime minister and the *'Maharaja'* (His Majesty) of Kaski and Lamjung, two small principalities of Nepal. Then, the third title *'Maharaja'* was made as an inheritable title of the

Rana family. Within 10 years in power, the Ranas ruled the country by their hereditary premiership system. The system was termed as the 'Rana oligarchy' in the history of Nepal.

With the coming of Janga Bahadur to power, a seven-decade long rule of four Kshatriya nobles disintegrated. However, the change did not move towards the inclusive and democratic system of government. Indeed, the Rana system had been more repressive towards the people. The regime sought to perpetuate backwardness and ignorance among the people by discouraging opening up of the education institutions. The system imposed orthodox and discretionary social rule. The regime not only tried to ban people from getting education but also banned travel abroad. Further, it controlled the people by intensifying communal disputes and rivalries through the social controls exercised by the royal priests. In the name of religion or *dharmashastra*, the priests were vested with the authority to punish any attempt on the part of the people to modify social, ethnic, and caste inequalities. As a political system, it was observed:

> 'The Rana political system was an undisguised military despotism of the ruling faction within the Rana family over the king and the people of the country. The government functioned as instrument to carry out the personal wishes and interests of the ruling Rana prime minister; its main domestic preoccupation was the exploitation of the country's resources in order to enhance the personal wealth of Rana ruler and his family. No distinction was made between the personal treasury of the Rana ruler and the treasury of the government; the Rana ruler, as private income, pocketed any government revenue in excess of administrative expenses. No budget of the government's expenditures and revenues were ever made public. As a system accountable neither to the king nor to the people, the Rana regime functioned as an autonomous system, divorced from the needs of the people and even from the historical traditions of the country, and served only the interests of a handful of Ranas and their ubiquitous non-Rana adherents (Joshi and Rose 1966:38-39).'

The Rana regime, initially, promoted the process of 'Ranaization' or their hegemony over the society where, for assuming power and getting privilege, one required to be from the Rana family. For other people there was no opportunity; they were even banned from getting education. In the army, which was the key to the survival of the system, generals and colonels were appointed from Rana families soon after their birth, and sometimes even before their birth. Ordinary people were restricted from wearing clothes, ornaments, making houses, etc. For such a societal sanction, they used the orthodox Hinduism as a weapon. For middle and lower level job opportunities in the military and bureaucratic cadre, Brahmans and the earlier discussed noble family were selected. The selection itself was a strategy to win the support of those families (Joshi and Rose 1966:40).

The Rana regime introduced the first Muluki Ain (Civil Code) in 1854. It was not new in the strict sense, because it was practiced earlier as a 'legal code' during the period of Jayasthiti Malla (1382-95) from late 14th century in Kathmandu valley, and during the period of Ram Shah (1603-36) in Gorkha from first half of the 17th century. What was new was that the regime put it in a nationwide legal framework. Before being declared as a law, it was practiced as a tradition. By promulgating it as a civil code, the Rana regime compelled all the 'subjects' to obey it. It was part of their strategic policy to continue their regime for a long time. They were aware that they could control the people only by such religious code of conduct, which had already gained legitimacy as a tradition. The orthodox Hindus accepted it and even claimed it as a vital step for promoting the Hinduism as a national religion. The code had revised caste categories from the four Varna classical Vedic models into six categories. It had provisioned a different type of punishment system on the basis of caste; to the higher caste, there was one type of punishment, and to the lower caste people for was applied the same crime. In other words, the system did not break the continuation of discrimination between the people of higher and lower castes. Another characteristic of the code was that it tried to accommodate the ethnic identities into Hindu Varna system, which 'translated diversity into inequality.'

Comparing the Shah rule and Rana oligarchy in Nepal, Chauhan termed Rana administration as 'less cruel and not that exploitative' (Chauhan 1989:119). However, no one is of the view that the system was not exploitative. The classification of Rana family into 'A', 'B' and 'C' classes on the basis of their purity of blood itself was a saleable example of the regime's exploitive nature. Later on, the classification was also made on the basis of caste of their mothers and kind of marriage (whether she was a concubine or formally married). Such a classification led the Ranas to divide themselves into three groups as noted above. The three groups started fighting amongst each other for power and position. In fact, the struggle within the Rana family became the most important cause for disintegration of their 104-year long rule.

Hinduism was practiced in a very orthodox manner in this period. Travelling abroad was termed as a 'violation of religious and social tradition' by conservative Ranas. Even Janga Bahadur, the initiator of the Rana regime, was accused of being a violator of the code. He was told that he had lost his caste by dining and socializing with Europeans when he visited Europe in 1850-51. After his return to Nepal, he visited important Hindu pilgrimage centers of India to be purified. Another intention of his visit to pilgrimage centers might have been to close the mouth of conservative people. Another example of the Rana's religious orthodoxy was that they were not even ready to reform Hinduism and when some Nepalese started reforming the movement of Hinduism in the name of Arya Samaj, they were socially disgraced, paraded through the street, beaten and sentenced to jail.

Ranas were more concerned about the impact of education and exposure. They knew that education and exposure would have helped in people's freedom and creating awareness. In this context, they seriously observed the returnees of 'Gorkha' army and western education holders. One of the threats to the Rana regime from those people was that they might bring modern ideas of freedom into their village and society. Therefore, the Ranas requested British authorities not to promote Gorkha recruits beyond the rank of sergeant and upon their return to the country rigidly enforced on them the rules of caste purification (Joshi and Rose 1966:52). Although the other religions were allowed   'except for doing acts prohibited in the code, including the slaughtering of cows', conversion of people from Hindu religion to others was prohibited. The permission to enjoy other religions was only for those who 'were already Muslims or Christians when they entered Nepal, and were born in Nepal from Muslim or Christian parents' (Gaborieau 1972:87).

Linguistically speaking, the Rana regime not only continued the process of Nepalization of the Shah regime, but also accelerated the process. For the first time in history, Khas Kura or Gorkhali Bhasa was declared as the official Nepali language in 1930. Chandra Shamsher was the prime minister. The regime in the process gave rise to the idea of a 'nation'. Prior to that, Nepal was referred only to the Kathmandu valley, and the rest of the country was known by the individual names of the places. The job of Ranas during their period was on the pretext of the 'nationalist objectives' (Whelpton 1997:45). In aspect of other religions and languages, the Ranas again followed the path of Shah Regime. The late Dharmaditya Dharmacharya, a brilliant Buddhist scholar, was expelled from Kathmandu Valley in the 1920s for the 'crime' of publishing and circulating Buddhist and other books in the Nepal Bhasa (Newari language). Buddhist monks Mahaprajna and Amritananda were imprisoned, and Tsering Narbu Lama was expelled in 1937. In 1925, another four monks, and in 1944, eight more monks were expelled from Kathmandu (Bajracharya and Khatry 2005:73-74). The state sponsored rampant migration of people from the west hill area to east hill area during this period. The main objective of such migration was to spread Nepali speaking and Hindu people with a view to promote and expand their cultural hegemony all over the territory, especially in the eastern hill area where Rais and Limbus—the non Hindu indigenous group—inhabited.

In regard to the ethnic issue, both the Shah and Rana regime played the same role of suppressing the indigenous people. Earlier the regime wooed the indigenous people by distributing land as kipat (land given to indigenous community for enjoying as common land of the community) to encourage them to support the unification process, but later the regime abolished the *kipat* system. Many indigenous groups including Bhote, Chepang, Danuwar, Garung, Pahari, Majhi, Rai, Limbus Thakali had customary occupation of land. All except the Limbus got alienated by the land under the regime. In case of the Limbus, the land got alienated only after 1964. The regime faced several revolts like Gurung revolt against Ranas in 1857 because of such policy (Joshi and Rose 1966:43).

Pseudo-Democratic Period (1951-60)

I have used the term 'pseudo' while examining the period of 1951-60 in the Nepali history. It is primarily because of the fact there it was the period, which had a character of both, democracy and autocracy. Another factor for using the term 'pseudo' has been that in democracy, government has been always elected by the people, but in this case, Nepalese could witness the elected government only for 18 months (May 27, 1959 to December 15, 1960) out of total of ten years.

During this period, Nepal became free from 'isolation' from the world, and it could witness a few constitutional and social changes along with people's movement in 1951. One of the significant changes was abolition of the 104-years-old Rana oligarchy. An interim government with the people's choice was constituted to change the existing system into a democratic system. The king, who was caged without rights in the palace by the Ranas, was also freed with the support of people. After the freedom, the king promised to let the democratic system run the country. The 1951 interim government made some important decisions in favour of democracy and the people.

It is well known that the NC was the only major political force which launched a nationwide protest against the Rana regime. Once the anti-Rana movement was over the NC got an opportunity to be the part of the Interim Government in 1951. The interim cabinet abolished many feudal practices 'at the initiative of the NC', such as monetary exactions in the form of mandatory gifts and presents, and forced labor to maintain public work which had been an integral part of the Rana political system. Birta (rent-free land), the traditional base of the Rana economic power was abolished. The monopoly of Ranas in the high position of the army was brought to an end by the government. Further, those positions were made accessible to other castes/ethnic communities. All government schools were directed to open the gates of their school for children of untouchable castes. Prior to that, only the 'male children of elite families' were permitted to go to the school and 'mainly Brahman boys were taught in the classical Sanskrit Pathshalas or school' (Hoftun et. al. 1999:4).

Also, the ethnic activism was first noticed with the dawn of democracy in 1951. NGOs and other organizations like Pichadieka-Barga Sangathan (the backward class organization) including Gurung Kalyan Sangh, Tharu Kalyankari Sabha, Kirat League and Dalit Sangh were established during this period. The Tarai Congress, the first regional party in Nepal, was established in 1951. However, after few months rule of the Interim Government, the king tried to be active by making/sacking the government. And interestingly, the king-nominated government constituted a committee called Nepal National Education Planning Commission, 1955 which recommended the use of Nepali language in such a manner that other languages were gradually wiped out with an expectation 'to provide greater national strength and unity' (Whelpton 1997:49).

Though the primary objective of the NC of 1950s was to make a constitution through the election of the Constituent Assembly, it was never materialized. Rather King Mahendra, after mounting pressure from major political parties, decided to held first general election in 1959. Then, the first elected government was formed under the premiership of B.P. Koirala, who himself was reported to have 'antagonized orthodox Hindus and the conservatives' (Joshi and Rose 1966:308). Once he formed his cabinet, he resumed the goal of strengthening democracy and Nepal prosperous.. He started implementing the programs promised in the election manifesto. The main slogan of the party was to 'end the very roots of the traditional social and economic inequalities.' The highlights of the Nepali Congress (NC) manifesto included: abolition of the proprietor system, abolition of Rajyas (small principalities which enjoyed the semi-autonomy), a ceiling

on landholding and redistribution of the excess landholdings, forests'
nationalization, promotion of co-operative farming, etc. Respect for
religion and a guarantee of the right of any citizen to practice the religion of
his/her choice and encouragement of the development of regional and local
languages were other important highlights of the election manifesto of NC.
In fact, the first elected government of B. P. Koirala tried to deconstruct the
very notion of language policy recommended and implemented in 1955;
the government, in doing so, had also given the status of national language
to other languages like Newari, Hindi and Maithali. Again, for the first
time in 1959, news was broadcast in languages other than Nepali. The
motive behind such a decision was the promotion and appreciation of other
languages (Gellner 1997:29). Hindi was accepted for use in Parliament
discussions in 1959.

Unfortunately, the first democratically elected government of NC,
which was set up 'as the champion of the poor and indebted peasantry,'
started facing disturbances shortly after its formation. It was assumed
that the Gorkha Parishad, a political party that represented the 'feudal
exploiters, cruel moneylenders, and profiteers,' backed such disturbances
(Joshi and Rose 1966:357). Also, the orthodox Hindu advocates and
royalists like Yogi Narahari Nath backed those disturbances. Ultimately,
the king dismissed the 19-month-old government and imprisoned all the
political leaders on December 15, 1960 which led to a complete halt of the
entire reformist program.

Panchayat Regime (1960-1990): Extreme Face of Hinduisation and Nepalisation

This period could be seen as a resumption of the early Shah dynasty. The
Shah family ruled over the people absolutely. The only difference during
the period was that the king started his rule by a system called 'Panchayat'.
It was a party-less system made out to be 'suitable to the soil and climate
of Nepal. The system was innovated by the king after the dismissal of the
elected prime minister and the democratic system.

The Panchayati ethos—*Euta Bhashsa Euta bhesh (one language ,
one dress)*-- was a perfect example for examining policies and programs
of the period in respect of the plural identity of the country. The process
of Nepalization and Hinduization continued vigorously with the state
declaring a Hindu state and making the King as the symbol of religion
and politics. The Constitution of Nepal has more clearly enunciated
this doctrine along with making Nepali as the only national language. It

was declared by the King that "Nepalis were Panchas, all Panchas were Nepalis" thus making people and Panchayat system synonymous. It is said that the 1962 Constitution was written in accordance with the King's Interest. The king was considered as "symbol of national unity and source of political authority in accordance with the Hindu tradition and custom (Baral, 2006 , p. 3). Once the constitution was promulgated along with the party-less Panchayat as system of governance, Nepali state tempo the Nepalization process also. For maintaining the hegemony of Nepali languages in society, the regime stopped the news broadcasting service in Newari and Hindi from Radio Nepal in 1964. The program was started by the first elected government in 1951 (Gellner 1997:29).

The state accelerated the process of Hinduization and Nepalization through internal migration. In the name of cultural assimilation, and to avoid the demand for autonomy raised by Tarai people since 1950, the regime supported the migration of hill Nepali speaking people to the Tarai. Indian penetration into the Tarai was singled out for encouraging people of the hills to migrate so that a balanced could be made *vis-a-vis* Indian domination. People of the Tarai were generally branded as Madhese or Indian origin. King Mahendra too followed the role of both his ancestors and of the Ranas for weaning away the support of the indigenous community to the regime. The differences between the roles played by the two kings were the strategies of Prithvi Narayan Shah that was based on community and King Mahendra's effort to enlist the support of various communities on individual basis. He took some elites individually from the indigenous community and vested some roles in them. The elites got privileges and power in the name of ethnic and regional representation. For such an opportunity, the elite had to support the Panchayat and surrender activism based on his/her community. As a strategy, Bedananda Jha, president of the Tarai Congress, was appointed as minister by the king in 1963. But it was made possible only after Jha dissolved his party. In the name of accommodation to diverse groups, some middle and higher class elites from indigenous communities were given state power and facility by the king, but the groups, as such, remained excluded. Panchayat policies towards other religions and ethnicity can be illustrated through some examples. To make Hinduism influential within other communities and to achieve its primary goal of Nepalization, the Panchayat officially declared Buddhism as a branch of Hinduism (Raeper and Hoftun 1992:154-63). Gopal Gurung's book, the first blueprint for ethnic resentment, was banned by the regime for 'its allegedly communal overtones and for inciting mutual hatred between different cultural groups' (Sharma 1997:487). Likewise, Limbu's traditional customary rights over the land, which was called *kipat* system, was abolished by the Panchayat regime. It is said that, because of the abolition of this customary right, the Limbus now face severe economy related deprivations and problems. In fact, 71 percent among them live below the poverty line.

National symbols and the national anthem are other examples which exposed the regime. In respect of set of national symbols—the crown, scepter, royal crest, royal standard, coat-of-arms, cow, national flag, pheasant, rhododendron, and the red simrik (Tika) invented by the Panchayat system, seven out of ten were related to 'monarchy and Hinduism' (Gurung 1997:505). The national anthem that was used for a long time copied the British pattern as if the British constitutional monarchy and Nepal's absolute monarchy shared the same values. Although King Birendra was considered more democratic than other Kings, he also followed his father's path in the process of Nepalization and Hinduization. He tried to reform the Panchayat system after the referendum in 1980 but was not willing to change his father's policies. Indicating his belief in 'ethical code,' Birendra once said, 'the king cannot change the value system' of Hinduism. He further said, 'the monarch and his subjects have been governed by Dharma, a system drawn from Hindu religion' (*Newsweek,* September 10, 1973 cited in Shaha 1990:9). This statement pointed to the fact that he was also in favour of orthodox Hinduism to legitimize his rule. No fundamental change had occurred on ethnic, gender, regional and religious issues during his two-decades -long rule in Nepal.

Democratic System 1990-2002: An Era of New Ethnic Awakening

After 30 years of imposed autocratic Panchayat system, Nepal reinstated the democratic system as a consequence of the successful mass movement. In the wake of democratic upsurge , ethnic, lingual, and cultural issues once again surfaced in the public sphere.. This was obvious because the dominant issue in the pre-1990s was to restore the 'multi-party democracy' rather than the caste, ethnic, religious, linguistic and gender questions. Any autocratic regime does not allow such trends that purport to destroy the established ethos of the absolutist regime.

After the end of the Panchayat System, different groups started raising their own slogans and making demands on the state. When the new constitution making process began, the issues of language, religion and ethnic conflict came to public attention. During the six month transitional period, the above agenda was very influential compared to that of the power game. In the debate on secularism vs. Hinduism, not only the minority religious groups—Buddhists, Muslims and Christians—but also the Hindu fundamentalists became visible in public life and started to articulate their ideology. Although all the indigenous groups, including the civil society, were in favour of secular state, the constitution came out with the status quo provision of its earlier version of 1962 as the 'Hindu kingdom'. Several rallies and even demonstrations were organized for making a secular status of Nepali state. It is said that it was the largest one with 150,000 protestors was held in Kathmandu. Gellner mentioned this was the largest protest 'ever held in Kathmandu' (cited in Gellner 1997:178). Their demand to declare Nepal as a secular state was sidelined because of the neutral position of two main political parties--- NC and CPN(UML), and 'the influential intervention' of the king backed by in-service and ex-service army officers, Hindu fundamentalist groups of Nepal and India (Pyakurel 2005:6; Pyakurel 2006:110). It is said that King Birendra had a desire to retain Nepal as a Hindu state. This was proved when the King recommend Achut Raj Regmi, who went on hunger strike until death in order to continue Nepal as a Hindu state and not to change the religious status of Nepal, to be in the cabinet as minister.

Although the phrase 'Hindu kingdom' remained unchanged, the Constitution of the Kingdom of Nepal 1990 accepted Nepal's 'multi-ethnic, multilingual' character. It recognized orphans, women, the aged, the disabled and incapacitated persons, as well as socially and economically backward groups and communities as marginalized groups, who deserved special treatment from the state in education, health, employment, and social security. The Directive Principles and Policies of the State of the Constitution of the Kingdom of Nepal, 1990 says, 'the social objective of the state shall be to establish and develop, on the foundation of justice and morality, a healthy social life, by eliminating all types of economic and social inequalities and by establishing harmony amongst the various castes, tribes, religions, languages, races and communities'. In the state policy, the constitution provisioned that 'the state shall, while maintaining the cultural diversity of the country, pursue a policy of strengthening the national unity by promoting healthy and cordial social relations amongst the various religions, castes, tribes, communities and linguistic groups, and by helping in the promotion of their languages, literature, scripts, arts and cultures" Freedom of press, organization and expression, which the constitution guaranteed, were also better provisions provided to the people. It helped them to organize and to raise their common voices against the state. Many caste/ethnic and religious organizations sprang up during this period. The government identified 59 caste/ethnic groups and announced some affirmative programs for them. On the language issue, although Nepali was declared as the official language, all other languages spoken as the mother tongue in Nepal were also declared as 'national languages'. In addition, government committed itself to provide education in the language of the mother tongue till primary level, following the recommendation of the Rastriya Sanskritik Samiti, 1992.

In 1992, the government formed a committee called Rastriya Sanskritik Samiti to formulate programs for a national cultural policy. The committee recommended the formation of a national coordination committee. Recognizing the multilingual character of the state, Nepal for the first time started news broadcasting in eight minority languages. These were Rai, Gurung, Magar, Limbu, Bhojpuri, Awadhi, Tharu, and Tamang. Earlier, news was broadcast only in three languages—Hindi, Newari and Maithali. The government offered several scholarships for school going girls and boys of deprived and under privileged groups.

Although a lot was done by several democratically elected governments in Nepal from 1990-2002, the governments also showed some shortcomings, especially with regard to enforcing the spirit of the constitution, i.e., abolition of all kinds of gender, religion, region, caste and ethnicity related disparities and discriminations. Inclusion of Sanskrit as a compulsory part in lower-secondary and secondary level curriculum, as well as the decision of broadcasting news in Sanskrit from Radio Nepal are, according to the ethnic elites, other negative aspects of the democratic government. In fact, Sanskrit is termed as 'a dead language' by ethnic elites in Nepal. The NC and UML have been accused of giving space to Brahmanism by making Sanskrit compulsory in secondary schools and introducing newscast in Sanskrit in 1995. Both the decisions are criticized as a ploy 'to create government jobs for unemployed Brahman boys' (Malla 1992 cited in Gellner 1997) . More than that, the structure of Nepali elites and their continued domination in polity, society and economy do not allow Nepali state to be progressive and participatory both in form and substance (Baral 2006:18). In fact, all earlier marginalized groups, including ethnic groups did not show any change in the pattern of representation during the three parliamentary elections after 1990. On the one hand, the number of Brahmin in the House of Representative (HOR) increased from 39 per cent in the HOR in 1991-94 to 44.4 per cent in the second (1994-1999), and 43.6 per cent in the third (1999-2002). Chhetri, another dominant caste group of Nepal, had similar record as they 17.1 per cent in 1991, 18.5 per cent in 1994 and 17.1 per cent in 1999. On the other, the representation of other hill ethnic groups declined from 16 per cent in 1991 to 11.7 percent in 1994, and 12.2 per cent in 1999. There had been a similar trends in Madhes as the representation decreased from 20 per cent to 18 percent to 17 per cent in 1994, 1996 and 1999 respectively (Ibid: 19).

Also, the Supreme Court's verdict of 1 June 1999 against the use of local language as the official language along with Nepali has been criticized as a continuation of Nepalization process in the recent democratic period. The Court invalidated the announcement of Kathmandu Metropolitan city, Dhanusa District Development Committee and Rajbiraj Municipality to use their respective dominant languages as the official languages in addition to Nepali. Most of the people under these three local bodies speak their own language (*Nepal Bhasa* or Newari language in Kathmandu, and Maithili in Dhanusa district and Rajbiraj municipality) rather than the Nepali. The court's decision has been criticized as 'a clear case of linguistic discrimination' by the state. Apart from that, inability to get equal development of all the regions by allocating adequate budget and deploying sufficient manpower, lack of attention to prevent caste-based discrimination and untouchability in society, especially in public spheres, such as denial of access to the public drinking water trap, temples etc., are other grievances raised against the governments.

In the meantime, it seems quite relevant to discuss on how the Maoist party became instrumental in popularizing the agenda of ethnic autonomy and federalism and what were the lacunae of political parties to address this very issue raised by the ethnic groups and other marginalized communities. Initially, the Maoist movement was confined to controlling anti-social activities such as anti-alcohol and anti-gambling campaign; it campaigned against polygamy, wife-beating culture, etc. The Maoist raised the issues related to caste/ethnicity, gender, region, religion, and language. They demanded ethnic autonomy, regional autonomy, inclusion of all marginalized groups, freedom for the promotion of own language and religion, declaration of Nepal as a secular state, etc.

In fact the communists in Nepal had attempted to take up arms twice before the Maoist started "people's war" in 1996. The first, in Jhapa district in 1971 was an attempt to replicate Indian Naxalite movement; the second was on the eve of 1990s Mass Movement. However, both these attempts failed, and its cause can be attributed to the exclusive focus on 'class' by Nepali Communists following the conventional script of Marxist ideology (Pyakurel 2007). It seems that the Maoist party had a great realization from the past, and they had assumed potential power of identity politics.

That is why, the Maoist party took up an identity-related popular agenda in the 1990. To attract people from ethnic communities towards the 'people's war', the Maoist party formed All Nepal Nationalities Association in 1994 and adopted Ethnic Policy in 1995. In fact, ethnic groups mobilized themselves in 1991 around the twin agenda of secular state and linguistic/ethnic equality. However, the Maoists decided to take up the cause of ethnic right to self-determination in 1997, just to sell ethnic agenda to the people.

It is also witnessed that the 'people's war' seemed to be expanding relatively slowly during the first two years. It may be because of people's indifference towards the Maoist's political agenda, which the people had perceived as being not substantially different from those of other parties. However, when they started taking up the ethnic agenda in 1997, the support base of the Maoist expanded dramatically. Interestingly the influence of the Maoist got further expanded once it established Ethnic Department at the central level and formed 11 ethnic/regional fronts. Out of 24 districts, where the Maoist formed District Janasarkars (people's governments) during December 2000 to June 2001, 18 districts had 33 to 68 per cent ethnic/Dalit population. Having a look at such a scenario, one can conclude that the Maoist have gained appreciative support from the ethnic/Dalit population. Once the Maoist leadership knew the fact, the Maoist formed about a dozen ethnic/regional front organizations between 1998 and 2000. These fronts were formed on the basis of nationalities and religions. Among 11 front organizations, only two (Madhesh and Karnali) were based on region, and the rest were formed on the basis of the different nationalities. The Maoist nominated all the heads of the front from the same identity. Needless to say that the Maoist applied the policy to lure support of 'marginalized' groups.

As we all know, Nepal's democratic system again went into 'coma' on October 4, 2002, when the king 'unconstitutionally' dismissed the elected government. During the period, the political parties were sidelined, people's rights provided in the constitution were made inoperative by the king. Such a situation ended on April 24, 2006 after the king was compelled to restore the parliament and give up all powers. For the change, millions of Nepali people came to the streets, protested against the four-year- long 'regressive and repressive action' of the king. During the democratic movement, approximately some 21 people lost their lives, hundreds were injured, and thousands of people were imprisoned and tortured.

Actually, the February 1, 2005 coup was the fourth invasion of monarchy against democracy. The first was by King Tribhuvan in 1952, the second by King Mahendra in 1960, and the third by King Gyanendra on October 4, 2002. Because of such interventions by the monarchy against democracy, people in general joined hands against it. The agenda of inclusive democracy was another attaraction of people, especially the marginalized community. According to them, only inclusive and substantive democracy could solve the identity issues arising out of disparities existing in the society. So all political parties were under pressure to include the agenda of inclusion. In April 2005, the Seven Party Alliance (SPA) of parliamentary parties reached an agreement on the issue. It focused on the democratic and progressive restructuring of the state to lay a solid foundation for social, political, and economic inclusion. Admitting their mistakes, they resolved that such a thing would not recur. On November 26, 2005, the SPA and the Maoist reached a 12-point understanding to end the king's absolute rule and to restructure the Nepali state. The SPA, with the backing of the underground Maoists, called for a four-day general strike as a protest against the king's autocratic regime in April. The strike continued for 19 days and the king finally agreed to reinstate the parliament, and to hand over power to the people. The reinstated parliament unanimously resolved to go to the Constituent Assembly (CA) to make the new constitution, and declared Nepal as a secular state. Also, while addressing the demands put forward by Madhes Andolan 2007, Nepal decided to amend the Interim Constitution 2007 to go for federal set-up. Today, all the ethnic communities, including Madhesis believe that the decision for the federal set-up will transform Nepal into an inclusive country. Keeping this in mind, the political forces, civil society, and other activists have been working together to restructure the state for transforming Nepal into a democratic state based on inclusion and empowerment of all sections of society.

In summing up, the ethnic movement has been one of the most influential social movements that Nepal has ever seen in the post 1990 era (Onta 2006). The movement, which was initially launched by individual activists during the late years of the king-led Panchayat system, was strengthened after 1990 when some of those individuals and activists started to organise themselves under various ethnic institutions. Concerning the demands, the ethnic movement has been able to achieve a lot, especially after *Janaandolan* -II. For example, they are well represented in the CA. They are also being benefited by each and every government's steps in order to change its old structure from exclusive to inclusive one. Yet, their inclusion now needs to be qualitatively better along with the figures of increased representation.

Today, the following two issues are important from ethnic point of view:

i) Nepali state should be restructured along federal, and it must also be based on the principle of caste/ethnicity. While doing so, they started claiming their ethnic territory within the federal set up with which they could safeguard their identity;

ii) Social inclusion for the *Janajati* groups in every sector of Nepali society.

One can see a paradigm shift of Nepali ethnic movement along with these recently added demands. The shift seems to be more complicated and challenging, which may invite further conflict inside Nepal. In fact, it seems that the demand of having 'federalism based on ethnicity' is likely to bring much more complication not only in the Nepali political discourse but also inside the ethnic movement as a whole. Here it is appropriate to quote Thapa (2012), who rightly states:

> …Nepali scholarship has evolved over the years; "ethnic groups" are now identified as those that are known by the generic term "Janajati". But ethnicity, and its Nepali equivalence *jati,* is surely more than that, and can also be defined by particularistic traits such as language (making Maithili-speakers within Nepal as well as Nepali-speakers in the UK ethnic groups), religion (Muslims), place of residence (Madhesis) and even caste (Chhetri). Any province that identifies with any of the above or similar characteristics is an "ethnic province".

It is because of the fact that all ethnic/caste groups are inter-mingled in any village or district throughout Nepal. It is therefore hard to find the concentration of the population of one Janajati group to be more than 20 per cent in the districts, except for a few districts. In this the obvious fact is that more than one ethnic group would   claim to a particular territory as its traditional territory triggering off territorial clash resulting in disputes and violence over the ownership of the territory. As a result, the ethnic movement which has been, in a way, united movement of all ethnic communities till today, is likely to be fragmented into many movements. Also, the claims of more than one ethnic group over the ownership of the territory are likely to shift their violent activities to other areas,

The following table provides a basic feature of the recommendation by majority members of the High Level State Restructuring Commission (HLSRC).

Table 2: Population Composition (in percentage) of Major Caste/ Ethnic Groups in the Majority HLSRC Proposed 10 Territorial Provinces.

Name of Provinces	Brahmin	Chhetri	Gurung	Limbu	Magar	Newar	Rai	Tamang	Madeshi	Dalit
Karnali-Khaptad	11.47	48.04	0.65	0.01	6.42	0.33	0.05	0.12	1.14	19.50
Kirat	7.66	18.98	1.63	0.47	6.89	5.35	34.68	6.27	0.75	10.29
Limbuwan	12.18	15.06	2.79	27.38	4.55	3.07	13.30	6.64	0.49	7.27
Madesh-Awadh-Tharuwan	11.17	12.54	1.13	0.09	5.13	1.02	0.08	0.37	54.54	12.68
Madesh-Mithila-Bhojpura	7.51	5.44	0.44	1.25	1.53	2.19	1.67	2.09	69.31	14.83
Magrat	16.83	17.81	2.82	0.01	35.37	2.33	0.04	0.19	1.36	15.99
Narayani	30.60	14.45	7.20	0.02	10.67	6.92	0.34	2.86	3.52	14.23
Newa	17.54	19.36	2.09	0.45	2.94	35.63	1.74	8.46	3.94	2.98
Tamsaling	13.56	16.26	1.35	0.04	5.96	7.61	1.29	34.75	0.96	7.10
Tamuwan	19.70	13.12	32.22	0.06	4.97	4.49	0.65	4.25	1.27	13.56

Source: Census 2001, computed by the author as per HLSRC Report Submitted to the Prime Minister, 2012.

If one follows the modus operandi of state apparatus in order to handle ethnic aspiration in Nepal, he/she finds that the political parties including responsible state authorities perform in very immature manners which have been providing quite a lot ground for such violent future of Nepali ethnic movement. For example, the ruling Maoist party, which was initially advocating for 11 provinces, all of a sudden comes up with a proposal to have 14 providences. Similarly, the state restructuring committee of the CA puts forward a proposal to have 14 provinces with names and boundaries of those provinces. But, another constitutional body formed by the government in consultation with major political parties-- the High Level State Restructuring Commission (HLSRC)-comes up with recommendation to delete some of the provinces from the list. Then, some of the ethnic groups took to the street to oppose the recommendation of the Commission saying that it had no right to delete names of the provinces decided by the CA committee.

Generally, being an elected body, the CA should be the final authority to decide what kind of state structure Nepal needs today. Before deciding those serious issues, the CA had to ask expert's opinions on those matters. And the HLSRC was provisioned in the constitution for providing expert's feedback to the CA. But, on the contrary, Nepal practiced differently. As the issue of state restructuring was first debated in the State Restructuring Committee (SRC) formed by CA, and once it came up with a proposal, then again the parties decided to form the HLSRC in order to seek experts' views on the matter. Unfortunately, the Commission also could not bring a unanimous recommendation. Rather, it submitted two separate recommendations to the Prime Minister. Coincidently, the commission members divided along ethnic lines--- three members belonging to Brahmin and Chhetri group; took a position, and the rest six (five ethnic community members and a Dalit) took another position. The fact was that the stake holders were already divided when the SRC under the CA put forward its proposal. And, though the commission was termed as expert's commission, it was indeed a partisan Commission because all members were recommended by the four major parties and the Madhese Front. When the Commission itself was divided, there was no point of accepting its' recommendation by all stake holders. Thus, it was natural that, there was a widespread criticism after the report was made known to the public. Two members of the Maoist party including Lekh Raj Bhatta and Top Bahadur Rayamajhi have been opposing the delineation of boundary as recommended by the Commission. Bhatta is against the division of Far West into Khaptad-Karnali and Tharuwan, and Raymajhi has demanded a state called "Khasan" where Brahmins and Chhetris make majority of the population. He is in favour of calling Chhetris as *adibasi/janajati.* Also leaders of all three major parties, including Maoist supremo Pushpa Kamal Dahal opposed the division of Chitwan district as suggested by the Commission's majority report.

Finally, we could already see signals of a divided ethnic movement in which one Janajati group fights against another. In fact, the Tharu movement of 2009 has already set an example which by-and-large was the clash of two ethnic groups—the Tharus and Madhesi communities—in order to claim the Western and mid-and Far Western parts of Tarai as their traditional territory. Major party leaders of Far-Western region, in almost unanimous manner, are claiming Kailali and Kanchanpur districts for their "undivided Far West" province. Along with these assertions, we could see multiple ethnic groups which put their claim for a particular territory. Lately, the religious minority-the Muslim community has also demanded that they be recognised as a separate minority group — not under ethnic Madhesis. Till today, the Muslims of Nepal are demanding a separate status. But eventually they are likely to assert their self rule based on identity. It is because the Muslim organisations already say that the government's move to include Muslims in the Madhesi is a ploy to ignore the identity of Muslims[4].

These are major visible complications, for the Madhes. But, such opposing claims over the territory can also be made in many other areas as no single ethnic group commands a majority. Only a matured state apparatus can handle such a complexity. The State should bring all stake holders on board while deciding the division of provincial territory. And the solution should a comprehensive one through an intense discussion of all stake holders. **But the modus operandi of Nepali state till today is just opposite. It acts on an ad-hoc basis** or in **compulsion without seeing long-term impact of any of its decisions.** That makes the situation more complicated. That is why, Nepali state should change its working style while dealing with such new aspirations various ethnic and regional groups. Once state starts dealing with them with the backing of major political parties, Nepali ethnic movement would be moderate. Any failure on the side of the state would only invite more violent, scattered and ethnic movements in the country which may eventually invite even a foreign intervention.

References

Acharya, Baburam (2005), *Aba Yesto Kahilyi Nahos* (Let such things never happen), Kathmandu: Prof. Sri Krishna Acharya (in Nepali language).

Bajracharya, Ranjana and Prem Kumar Khatry, (2005), 'Inter-Religious Dialogue: An Unbreakable Thread to Unite the Diverse Cultures of

---

4 For details, see "Muslims Demand Separate Status", *The Himalayan Times*, February 1, 2012; also "Muslims demand separate identity", *The Republica*, March 22, 2012.

Nepal' in R.D. Bajracharya, K.B. Bhattachan, D.R. Dahal and P.K. Khatri (eds.) *Cultural and Religious Diversity: Dialogue and Development* (Monographs and Working Papers: No. 6) Kathmandu: UNESCO.

Baral Lok R. (2006) "Participatory Democracy: Concept and Context", in Lok Raj Baral (ed.) *Nepal: Quest for Participatory Democracy*, New Delhi: Adroit Publishers

Baral, Lok R. (2006). *Opposition Politics in Nepal*. Kathmandu: Himal Books, (second edition).

Bhattachan, K.B. (2000). "Possible Ethnic Revolution or Insurgency in a Predatory Unitary Hindu State, Nepal". In Kumar, D. (ed) *Domestic Conflict and Crisis of Governability in Nepal*. CNAS. Kathmandu.

Burghart, R. (1984), "The Formation of the Concept of Nation-State in Nepal" *Journal of Asian Studies* 44(1): 101-125.

Chauhan, R.S. (1971), *The Political Development in Nepal 1950-70: Conflict Between Tradition and Modernity*, New Delhi: Associate Publishing House.

Chauhan, R.S. (1989), *Society and State Building in Nepal: From Ancient Times to Mid-Twentieth Century*, New Delhi: Sterling.

Dahal, Dilli Ram (1979), " Tribalism as an incongruous Concept in Modern Nepal" *Asie Du Sud: Traditions et Changements*. Paris : CNRS

Dahal, Dilli Ram (1979), "Adibasi/Janajati(Indigenous/Nationalities) of Nepal: Socioeconomic Situations and Some Questions on Change and Development" In B.C. Upreti and Uddhab Pyakurel (eds.) CONTEMPORARY NEPAL: Reflections on Emerging Political and Social Issues and Trends, Delhi: Kalinga Publications

David N.Gellner, Joanna Pfaff-Czarnecka, and John Whelpton (eds.) (1997), *Nationalism and Ethnicity in a Hindu Kingdom: The Politics of Culture in Contemporary Nepal*, Amsterdam: Harwood Academic Publishers.

Dhungel, Ramesh (2006), "Limbuka 'Sampriti' Ra 'Niti' Samuha: Gorkha Sasan Ko Den (Sampriti and Niti Groups of Limbus: Contribution of Gorkha Rule)", in *Himal Khabarpatrika* 28 February-13 March (in Nepali language)

Gaborieau, Marc (1972), "Muslims in the Hindu Kingdom of Nepal",

Contribution to Indian Sociology, New Series, No. VI, December, pp. 84-105

Gurung, Harka (1997), "State and Society in Nepal". in David N. Gellner, Joanna Pfaff-Czarnecka, and John Whelpton (eds.), *Nationalism and Ethnicity in a Hindu Kingdom: The Politics of Culture in Contemporary Nepal.* Amsterdam: Harwood Academic Publishers.

Gyawali, S.B. (1935), *Prithvinarayan Shah,* Darjeeling: Gyawali (in Nepali).

Hachhethu, Krishna (2003), "Democracy and Nationalism Interface between State and Ethnicity in Nepal". *Contributions to Nepalese Studies* 30(2) July.

Hachhethu, Krishna (2002), *Party Building in Nepal: Organization, Leadership and People,* Kathmandu: Mandala Book Point.

Hoftun, Martin, Raeper, William and Whelpton, John (1999), *People Politics and Ideology: Democracy and Social Change in Nepal,* Kathmandu: Mandala Book Point.

ISRSC (2004), *District Development Profile of Nepal,* Kathmandu: Informal Sector Research and Study Center

Joshi, Bhuwan Lal and Rose Leo E. (1966), *Democratic Innovations in Nepal: A Case Study of Political Acculturation,* Berkeley and Los Angeles: University of California Press.

Malla, K.P. (1992) "Bahunbada's Myth and Reality', *Himal* 5(3).

NEFIN (2004), Classified Schedule of Indigenous Nationalities of Nepal prepared by the Janajati Classification Task Force and approved by the Federal Council of NEFIN, 1 March

NFDIN (2003), National Foundation for Development of Indigenous Nationalities (NFDIN), An Introduction, Kathmandu: NFDIN

Onta, Pratyoush (2006), The Growth of the Adivasi Janajati Movement in Nepal After 1990: The Non-Political Institutional Agents, *Studies in Nepali History and Society,* Vol. 11 (2), December.

Pyakurel Uddhab Pd. (2007), *Maoist Movement in Nepal: A Sociological Perspectives.* New Delhi: Adroit Publishers

Pyakurel, Uddhab (2005), *2046 Ko Paribartan ra Nyayapalika* (1990

Change and Judiciary), Kathmandu: Nepal Center for Contemporary Studies.

Pyakurel, Uddhab (2006), "Identity Politics in Nepal", *Research Journal* Vol. 1 (1), January-July.

Reaper, William and Hoftun, Martin (1992), *Spring Awakening: An Account of the 1990 Revolution in Nepal,* New Delhi: VikingRegmi, Mahesh C. (1995) Kings and Political Leaders of the Gorkhali Empire 1768-1814. Hyderabad: Orient Longman

Rose, Leo E. and Scholz, John T. (1980), *Nepal: Profile of a Himalayan Kingdom,* Boulder: Westview Press

Shah, Rishikesh   (1992), *Ancient and Medieval Nepal,* New Delhi: Manohar.

Shah, Rishikesh (1990), Modern Nepal: A Political History, 1769-1955, 2 Vols. New Delhi: Manohar. (check- not cited)

Sharma, Prayag Raj (1997), "Nation-Building, Multi-Ethnicity, and the Hindu State" in David N. Gellner, Joanna Pfaff-Czarnecka, and John Whelpton (eds.), *Nationalism and Ethnicity in a Hindu Kingdom: The Politics of Culture in Contemporary Nepal,* Amsterdam: Harwood Academic Publishers.

Tamang, Mukta S. (2004), Nepal Federation of Indigenous Nationalities (NEFIM): Policy Reform Appeals for Social Inclusion. Case Study Draft, GSEA Research

Thapa, Deepak   (2012) "Generalised precision", *The Kathmandu Post,* March 1.

Whelpton, John (1997), "Political Identity in Nepal: State, Nation and Community" in David N. Gellner, Joanna Pfaff-Czarnecka and John Whelpton (eds.), Nationalism and Ethnicity in a Hindu Kingdom: The Politics of Culture in Contemporary Nepal, Amsterdam: Harwood Academic Publishers.

Chapter VII

Women in Conflict: The Gender Perspective in Maoist Insurgency

Indra Adhikari

About The People's War

The Communist Party of Nepal-Maoist (CPN-Maoist) has been waging the 'People's War' (PW) since 1996 for establishing a communist republican state in Nepal instead of constitutional monarchy and the western model of parliamentary democracy. On parliamentary democracy, the Maoists have, of late, changed their strategy by accepting it as a route to the ultimate objective, i.e. establishment of the so-called "people's democracy". Analysts see it as a Maoist attempt to contextualize their ideology as the fulfillment of people's democracy would not be possible in the existing national and international settings.

Yet, the Maoist War does not show any sign of abatement. Nepal has now been facing the problem created by the conflict between the Maoist and the government. The Maoist insurgency has been one of the main political problems of Nepal for the last seven years. Demanding a constituent assembly and round table conference through an all-party government, they have been putting pressure on the government by killing the people suspected by them to be informers. They attack security personnel, abduct, torture, extort and harass people and attack army camps, police posts and the administration offices and bomb the public places. Similarly, the security forces also use some of these methods for harassing and torturing the people. [1]

---

1 Adhikari, Indra, "Beni Attack and After", The Kathmandu Post, 9 November 2004. For other information of the Maoist war, see also her "Nepal: The Maoist War and Prospect of Peace", Agni (Delhi), 6:4: January-April, 2003, pp.13-22.

The Maoist insurgency, over the last ten years, has spread all over the country, except two districts-Manang and Mustang- out of the 75 districts of the country. Altogether more than 10,000 persons have already lost their lives since 13 February 1996.[2] The cost of reconstruction of development infrastructure that was destroyed by the Maoists is estimated at NRs 200 billion[3] . A question raised here is: why do the Maoists thrive? Different people argue the cause of the Maoist insurgency differently. Generally, it is argued that social injustice, underdevelopment, unemployment, problems of exclusion, lack of good governance, corruption, poverty etc. are contributing to the escalation of the Maoists' insurgency is the basic of their disciplinary background. Developmentalists argue that the Maoist insurgency "is basically a social and economic issue and is produced and sustained by failed development[4] . It is true that the epicenter and heartland of the Maoists' insurgency is mid-west hill districts-Rolpa, Rukum, Salyan, Dailekhg, Jajarkot, etc. -to which the Human Development index categorizes as the lowest rank districts of the country[5] .

Social and ethnic activists analyze it mainly from the ethnic angle. Thirty five percent hill-high-caste-Hindus-Brahmin, Chhetri and Newar- have control over the power structure of the country. Others- hill ethnic groups Tarai caste and tribal groups, and Dalits are generally excluded as marginalized groups. Analyzing the Maoists' insurgency, a social anthropologist argues, "People's War has blended class-based and cast/ ethnic-based insurgency in the country[6]. In addition, other parts of the Nepali society based on religion, caste and sex-Muslim, Sheikh, Christian, Buddhists etc; Dalits of Tarai and hill, Tharus of Tarai and women- all over the country are also marginalized. So the Maoists have tried to involve those marginalized groups in the party, which have their own ethnic and region based organization by proposing a project of restructuring the state.

Political scientists analyze that the failed governance is the main reason for weakening the state and strengthening the Maoist insurgency. The "ambiguity of constitution", King's assertion for power against

2 Informal Sector Service Centre, Vol. 5, No. 2, April 2003, p. 41.

3 Space Time, 27 May 2003.

4 Pandey, Devendra Raj, Nepal's Failed Development: Reflections on the mission and the Maladies, (Kathmandu, Nepal South Asia Study Centre, 1999), p.12.

5 NESAC, Nepal Human Development Report, (Kathmandu: Nepal South Asia Study Centre, 1998). Pp.264-65.

6 Bhattachan, Krishna Bahadur, "Possible Ethnic Revolution for Insurgency in a Predatory Unitary Hindu State" in Dhurba Kumar (ed.) Democratic Conflict and Crisis of Governability in Nepal, (Kathmandu: Centre for Nepal and Asia Studies, 2000), p.159.

the spirit of constitutional monarchy, lack of effective and charismatic leadership, power-centric intra and inter-party faction and conflict, political instability, lack of institutionalization of party and parliament, pervasive corruption, etc, have impeded the task of democratic consolation in Nepal[7] .

All the above factors are supplementary and are not enough to answer why the Maoists took the path of armed struggle. The question is related to the political and ideological aspects of communist philosophy. Adopting the saying of Mao Tse-tung of China, "Russian history has created the Russian system.... Chinese history will create Chinese system"[8], the Maoists also want to establish "People's Democracy" in Nepal for addressing the Nepali reality applying the theory of "Prachanda Path" on the basic of communist philosophy such as Maoism in China.

One important dimension added to the Maoist insurgency in the participation of women who constitute about fifty percent of the guerilla force. Even if the figures might have been exaggerated on the basis of some heavy recruitment of women in some sectors, the nature of participation of women is not low. The motivating factors and others reasons are different, but the guerilla force has experienced that the women are no less ferocious and courageous in combat operations. These various dimensions have to be analyzed while addressing the conflict in Nepal.

Conflict as a Means for Change

The "People's War" (PW) of Nepal is conveniently interpreted both as insurgency and terrorism by both the native and foreign governments and other organizations. The Nepali governments used "terrorism" much later when the Maoists withdrew from the negotiation. Other countries-United States, the United Kingdom and India -too have used it according to their convenience.

Nevertheless, conflict is loosely used here in relation to terrorism/ insurgency or to other forms of struggles. Generally the term 'conflict'

---

7 Hachhethu, Krishna "The Maoist Uprising in Nepal from Insurgency to Negotiation", an unpublished paper presented to a regional workshop on "Strengthening Security and Cooperation in South Asia" 1-3 July 2003 in Dhaka, organized by Bangaladesh Enterprise Institution. See Lok Raj Baral, Nepal: The Problems of Governance (New Delhi: Konark Publishers Pvt. Ltd, 1993); Lok Raj Baral, Krishna Hachhethu and Hari Sharma Leadership in Nepal, (New Delhi: Adoit Publishers, 2001).

8 "On Coalition Government", a report submitted by Mao Tse-tung to the Seventh Party Congress, Selected Workers, Vol.3, (Peking: Foreign Language Press, 1945), 283-84.

has been interpreted as the opposite of peace[9] that occurs in all societies manifesting within an individual, within and between the family and community. Conflict is spread among caste and ethnic groups, political parties and countries. People understand conflict differently. Many people think of it as an undesirable and destructive phenomenon of society and it should be avoided or eliminated.

Warner states that conflict can refer to a debate or contest a disagreement, argument, dispute, quarrel, a struggle, battle confrontation, or a state of unrest, turmoil, chaos and violence[10]. Similarly, Buckles says that conflict is an active stage of disagreement between people with opposing opinions, principle and practices manifested in different forms such as grievance, conflict, dispute and war. When they clash among the different social groups and individual based on culture, social norms and values, economic and political interests create antagonism that lead to conflict in the society. So, sometimes conflict can create social disorder. But at other times, it is a means of positive change of society.

Are terrorism and conflict compatible terms? For, the intensified conflict also takes the form of terrorism, though the methods and missions might be different. And because of the violence as a means of change and revolution, it is difficult to define what terrorism actually is. Many studies have highlighted the existence of innumerable definition of terrorism. According to the oxford dictionary, the world "terrorism" means extreme fear. If the meaning is accepted, then a terrorist is one who attempts to instill extreme fear among the target audience. Terrorism is defined "as an act or threat of violence against non combatants with the objecting of exacting revenge, intimidating or otherwise influencing an audience[11]". The meaning of this definition is adaption of violent methods in order to create fear and influence. The target that may be a government, community, or particular individual. It is also said that:

> Terrorism is most cases, essentially a political act. It is meant
> to inflict dramatic and deadly injury on civilians and to create an
> atmosphere of fear, generally for a political or ideological (where

---

9 Warner, M., (2000) Conflict Management in Community Based Natural Resources Project: Experiences from Fiji and Papua New Guinea, IDI working Paper, London: Overseas Development Institution.

10 Warner, M., (2001) Complex Problem-Negotiated solutions: Strategies and Tools for Reducing Conflict as an obstacle to Sustainable Rural Livelihood, London: Overseas Development Institute.

11 Stern, Jessica, The Ultimate Terrorist (Cambridge: Harverd University Press, 1999), p. 11.

secular or religious) purpose, terrorism is a criminal act, but is more than mere criminality. To overcome the problem of terrorism it is necessary to understand political nature as well as its basic criminality and psychology[12].

Many researcher have tried to define the term "terrorism", but no one is able to provide a comprehensive definition that world cover all of its aspects. Emphasis on these statements such as "Today's terrorist is tomorrow's freedom fighter", "Terrorism on some is heroism to others", "One man's terrorist is another man's freedom fighter" make further difficulties in the task of defining the term.

The word "terrorism" or "terrorist" is used depending upon the situation and mission of the various opponent groups. For many, the heroic needs, and sense of sacrifice that is often manifested by "suicide squads" is taken as means of realizing the mission. For other people, such people including in killing, extortion and carrying out destruction of both people and material of enemies are criminals or terrorists. They are called militants an in Kashmir and different names have been given in other different countries.

On the basis of our own observations and conflicting interpretations, this paper would like to use the Maoist war as "Insurgency" launched for specific political objectives, despite some methods used by the Maoists being similar to those of other groups called "terrorism".

General Causes of Insurgency and Gender Perspective

In March 1995, at the Third Plenum of the Central Committee, the Unity Centre changed its name to the Communist Party of Nepal (Maoist) and adopted 'The Strategy and Tactics of Armed Struggle in Nepal'. The document states that 'the conscious peasant class struggle developed in the western hill districts, particularly in Rolpa and Rukum, represents the high level of anti-feudal and anti-imperialist revolutionary struggle. That struggle has given birth to some new tendencies in the Nepali Communist Movement which have inspired us to be more serious about the business of armed struggle'.[13]

---

12 "Report of the policy Working Group on the United Nations and Terrorism", p. 5 Annex to a/57/273; s/2002/875, http:/www.un.org/terrorism/a57273.hmt accessed on 12 October 2002.

13 CPN (Maoist) Strategy and tactics of armed struggle in Nepal, A document adopted by third plenum of the central committee of the CPN (Maoist) in March 1995, The worker, No. 3, February 1997.

It is very difficult to explain the actual causes of the Maoist insurgency in Nepal. The Maoist and some other Left analysts believe that it is the ideological factor that has been the principal force for genesis, growth and intensity of the insurgency. Nevertheless, other aspects cannot be totally ruled out on the basis of Nepal's socio-economic and political situations. The following general causes of insurgency can therefore be identified as other contributing factors.

1. Socio-political injustice, persistence of extreme poverty and accompanying deprivations such as unemployment, low levels of literacy, extreme poverty and limited access to health services, especially in the context of Nepal, have fuelled the rural-centered insurgency.

2. Malfunctioning of democracy is another cause of insurgency.

3. Brutal suppression of human rights over an unlimited period of time.

4. Historical humiliation created by *de facto* discrimination in jobs and other opportunities of different socio-cultural and ethnic groups is continuing the insurgency. Those who have been victimized and oppressed by the structure can only break free of their chains by using violence.

5. Marginalization of a large section of population from the social development activities carried by the state.

Such general causes notwithstanding, women have, as it has come to light through interviews and opinion, also joined the Maoist War for "fun, revenge, and mission". Some of the guerrillas have stated that they would enjoy more freedoms than they did in their homes. Similarly, unbearable life conditions, atrocities committed by the state force drove them to be rebels who could take revenge for the murders of their relatives.

As violence is perceived as the only means of bringing about the structural transformation of society and polity in the country, the high degree of indoctrination along this line is also responsible for motivation to join the insurgency. During the liberation movements, most developing countries used violence as a weapon against colonialism, imperialism, neo-colonialism, and racism. In Nepal too, the NC, a moderate democratic party that believed in Gandhian non-violence, used violence thrice (1950, 1961-1962, 1971-1974) for achieving democracy. But today, in addition to it, violence is used against socio-economic and political exploitation of the state and of different traditional elite groups based on caste hierarchy, class disparity, language, culture, etc. so the violent activities carried out by different insurgent groups are increasingly becoming intractable in ideological, organizational and psychological terms, notwithstanding its use as a means of bargaining with the adversary or for achieving a mission such as a separate homeland, democracy, autonomy, etc.

Such common causes of violent conflict are not new to the Maoist insurgency. And the wretched conditions of women in the country which can be observed in the following tables and narrative plus the immediate reasons have motivated girls to join the insurgency.

Faulty Structure of Nepali Society

The construction of Nepali society is primarily based on social stratification and disparity between the rulers and the ruled. Its developed traditions throughout history continue even today. If we try to understand legitimacy as the basis of power, caste, feudalistic economic structure and other forms of discriminations were the bases of power. Thus, inequality of various forms was the hallmark of the state. The past rulers, especially Jayasthiti Malla of Kathmandu (1382-95), Ram Shah of Gorkha (1606-33), and founder of the Rana oligarchy, Janga Bahadur Kunwar (1846-77) reinforced the tradition of discrimination. Before the beginning of the Rana rule, the founder of modern Nepal, King Prithvi Narayan Shah (1768-77) had started the tradition of stratification along Hindu caste and religious lines[14]. By clearing the construction of Nepali society and state, as a Nepali sociologist remarks, that since the expansion of "Gorkha Imperialism" in 1768 under the leadership of King Prithvi Narayan Shah, predatory Nepali state coercively tried to make the country "Asali Hindustan" through various cultural instruments such as Hinduization, Sanskritization, Nepalization and the Bahunbad synchronized with centralization of power and authority[15].

Such caste-ridden political tradition in which the domination of Brahmans as the preceptor and adviser of the rulers and the Chhetries as

---

14 Cited in Lok Raj Baral, Conflict generation or conflict resolution? Education and Social Disparity in Nepal (unpublished paper, 2001) p. 1 as cited in Bhuwan Lal Joshi and Leo E. Rose, Democratic Innovation in Nepal: A case study of political acculturation, (Berkeley: University of California press, 1996) p.5.

15 Bhattachan, Krishna Bahadur, Social perspectives on gender issues in changing Nepalese Society, (eds.), Laxmi Kashari Manandhar and Krishan Bahadur BHattachan, Gender and Democracy in Nepal, (Kathmandu: Women Studies Programme and FES, 2001) p. 77.

both the core power cliques and other influential factions of the state have contributed to create social disparity. Now some other social members of various ethnic communities have used the ladder of upward mobility of what is popularly called Sanskritization that prompts the lower caste people to accept the ethos of upper caste groups. As a result, during the 104 year old autocratic Rana rule, 30- year Panchayat rule and even 13-year democratic exercises, both women and indigenous ethnic groups have been continuingly discriminating legally and practically. Women continue to be discriminated against by the law as well. "In the last two centuries, women have been suppressed, oppressed and exploited not only by the families and communities but also by the state controlled by the so-called "high caste" Hindu men[16]. Dalits in general are treated inhumanly. Similarly, the people belonging to indigenous ethnic groups continue to be neglected by the predatory state by denying them exercise of their basic human rights, including minority rights, rights of indigenous peoples and right to educate in their mother tongue[17]. The people belonging to various nationalities, Madhesis and Muslims who speak their own mother languages are discriminated (against) by the state in the use of their language in local bodies, government-owned media, and educational institutions. Subsequently, many people from these castes remain illiterate, uneducated and others who speak "Khas Nepali" language are in a more advantageous position because of the constitutional provision of it being the only official language.

Religion also affects people directly. Hindus are more privileged than non- Hindus such as Animists, Bon, Buddhists, Lamaists, Islam and Christians. Regional variations also affect people because of centralization of power and development. People living in the far-western and mid-western regions are more disadvantaged than in western, central and eastern development regions.

Economically, the elite structure is narrow. Internal and external opportunities are available only for the privileged people. Non-Bramin/Cheetri people of Nepal belonging to the lower caste hierarchy were given other kinds of jobs of a non-governing nature. The hill ethnic communities were enlisted in the Gorkhali army which in the modern sense not only constituted the military elite[18] but also developed a Lahure (military) culture. The male members of hill ethnic groups also came into contact

---

16 Ibid

17 Ibid

18 Baral, Lok Raj, Conflict Generation or Conflict Resolution? Education and Social disparity in Nepal (unpublished paper, 2001) p.1.

with the outside world after they joined the British-Indian army following the Treaty of Sugauli (1816). Yet, the Lahure did not change the power structure after their return from foreign army.

In accordance with the national census of Nepal of 2001, the social composition is formed (on the basis of geography and caste) by 99 castes and ethnic groups. To compare the distribution of population with the existing reality, it is proved that the minority, so-called high caste Hindu that is near about 35 per cent (Chhetri 15.80%, Bahun 12.74%, Thakuri 1.74% and Newar 4.64%) population has been ruling over the majority among whom women have hardly participated in the process. And they have access to and control over the resources of the country.

Table 1:
Status of Women

S.N.	Particulars	Male%	Female%
1	Population	49.96	50.4
2	Average age	59.3	59.8
3	Literacy	65.08	42.49
4	Labor force	73.3	71.3
5	Council of Minister	94	6
6	House of Representatives (1956-59)	94.14	5.86
7	National Council	85	13.34
8	Civil service	91.45	8.55
9	Policy making grade	96	4
10	Judges	97.92	2.08
11	Legal Professionals	95.03	4.97
12	DDC (2054-59)	93.3	6.7
13	Municipality (2054-59)	81.5	19.5
14	VDC (2054-59)	92.3	7.7
15	Chief District officers	100	0
16	Ambassadors	100	0
17	Head/Member of Constitution body	100	0
18	Communication Sector	88	12
19	Teachers	86.3	13.7
20	Primary Enrollment	79.4	64.4
21	Lower Secondary Enrollment	36.9	25.5

22	Secondary Enrollment	25.3	16.3
23	TU Enrollment	75.1	24.9
24	Agriculture	66.8	85.2
25	Arable Land Ownership	89.16	10.64
26	House Ownership	94.49	5.51
27	Livestock Ownership	92.26	7.24
28	Head of the Household	85%	15%

Source: CBS Census, 2001.

Table 2:
Some Indicators Showing Women's Position in Nepal

S.N.	Subject	Male%	Female%
1	Population	49.96	50.03
2	Life expectancy (average)	61.8	62.2
3	Literacy (above 15 yrs in age)	62.2	34.6
4	Participation of Cabinet	94.45	5.55
5	MP/Lower House	94.15	5.85
6	MP/Upper House	86.67	13.33
7	Civil servants	91.45	8.55
8	Judges	97.96	2.04
9	Teachers	74	26
10	Information sector	88	12
11	Foreign employment	89.15	10.85
12	Ownership over land	89.16	10.83
13	Ownership over house	94.49	5.51
14	Contribution in agriculture	39.5	60.5

Source: Informal, Vol. 16, No. 4, December 2003.

Table 3:
Women's Participation in local bodies (1997 election)

Bodies	Total No.	Male	Female	Female Ratio
DDCs	1117	1047	70	6.8
District Assembly	10000	9850	150	1.5
VDCs	50857	46944	3913	7.7
Municipalities	146	3340	806	19.5
VD Assembly	183865	179952	3913	2.1
Ward Committees	173031	137823	35208	20

Source: Informal, Vol. 16, No. 4, December 2003.

According to an observer, "the invocation of the faction of the Nepali Mahila (women) submerges the dimensions of class, cast, ethnicity, religion and age fundamental in the constructions of different realities of different women, within that of single, collective Nepali female really engineered/invented by an elite"[19].

Table 4:
Major political parties' candidates for election to House of Representative, 1999

Political Party	Candidacy for Election of House of Representative, 1999			
	Female	Male	Total	%
NC	14	196	205	6.82
ML	11	187	198	5.55
UML	12	183	195	6.15
RPP	14	183	197	7.10
RPP(C)	13	171	184	7.06
NSP	5	63	68	7.35
Others	66	1099	1165	6.00
Total	135	2077	2212	6.10

Source: Data collected and analyzed by FWLD.

---

19 Tamang, Seria, Gender sensitive planning what, why and how in Nepal (Kathmandu: Women Awareness Center Nepal (WACN), 1994.

Question of Women's Empowerment

Socio-economic and political oppression against women create a gender gap and compel women to be dependent on men due to lack of property right of women. The patriarchal social structure of the Nepali society, which treats women as second-class citizens and compels them to accept a low and subordinate status in society, has a lot of negative aspects inhibiting women's mobility. Thus the social values of Nepali society have a direct bearing on gender discrimination. Nepali proverbs such as "let it be late, let it be a son" provides the importance of the birth of a son in family. According to it, only a son paves the way for parents to heaven. If a son is born it is celebrated by sacrificing a goat, if it is a daughter, a pumpkin is enough; it is a sin if the groom kills the bride. A society based on son preference has perennially belittled the status of women in Nepal. So, the social, economic, educational and political status of women is comparatively much lower than their male counterparts. Hindu society thinks of the daughter as a burden created for the other person. They do not get parental property and are tortured by traditions such as Daijoo, Tilak, etc. that create domestic violence. Most women are married in childhood. Polygamy, mismatched marriage, lesbianism and untouchability torture them. Deuki, Jhuma and Kumari customs have also culturally exploited women. Women are further exploited by the Badi custom, bonded labour, prostitution and trafficking.

So, "women can't participate in politics on equal footing with men because of both social constraints, lack of mobility and access to resources. Her access to resource is conditional by her sexuality"[20]. That is why women still remain confined to their traditionally prescribed and socially acceptable roles, lower status and subordinate to men within the patriarchal socio-cultural, economic, political and legal framework.

Economy related to land and property is a major factor in developing career of the people, which creates a vicious circle of poverty in every sector. Limited access to productive assets such as land, property and credit, lack of modern of knowledge about information and technology, lack of opportunity in training and education, concentration of women in low agricultural productivity and increasing work burden without increasing access to resources, child labour, poorly paid informal jobs, risk to personal security and sexual harassment in the informal sectors, limited market access to women entrepreneurs, lack of economic resource,

20 Acharya, Mina, "political participation of women in Nepal", In women and politics Worldwide, (eds.) Brabara Nelson and Nazma Chaudhari (New Haven, USA: Yale University Press, 1994).

low marketing opportunity, etc. are the main hurdles in the development of Nepali women. These factors are responsible for making women poorest of the poor.

Women have less support of the family because of growing criminalization in politics, rampant corruption, derailment of democratic norms, values, rising cost of electioneering, etc. Weak civil society, isolationist as well as divisive tendencies among women groups, loss of credibility for most women groups due to the tendency to distance from the political process and obsession with the NGO type project-oriented activities of women groups make it difficult for women to participate actively in political and social activities.

Political participation of women has not increased significantly after the restoration of democracy. In the last general election in May 1999, out of 2238 candidates for 205 seats, only 135 were women and 11 (5 per cent) women – five from NC, five from CPN-UML and one from RPP – won the election. As many as 133 constituencies did not give even five per cent women candidates, which is the constitutional provision. Even major political parties didn't have more than six per cent women candidates. The percentage of women candidacy is lowest from the big parties and the percentage of women members in the party working committee is not more than nine. After 1990, three governments – 1992/4/27 – 1995/12/12, 1994/9/6 – 1994/12/2, and 1998/12/25-... 2001 – had remained without women. If women got a chance to participate in the government, they hardly got the post of state minister.

All women politicians feel bypassed, ignored and insecure. Very few women politicians projected by political parties have an independent identity of their own. "Their political background has been usually characterized b the inscriptive dynastic patronage of a powerful leader or non-merit factor"[21] because of the dependence of woman politician on the patronage and support of the senior male politicians in the party. A decade-long experience of women in the legislature shows that they have not been able to develop sufficient confidence or capacity to raise their voice on behalf of women and pass a bill in favour of women. For example, they could not pass two important bills, "Women's Inheritance Bill" or "Reproduction Rights Bill" related to women rights, due to weakness of women members to convince their male counterparts and change the

---

21 Shrestha, Kapil, "Reconsidering the issue of Women's Human Rights and Political Right", Laxmi Kashari Manandhar and Krishna Bahadur Bhattachan (eds.) Gender and Democracy in Nepal, (Kathmandu: Women Studies Programme and FES, 2001) p.150.

patriarchal traditional thinking of other male members of parliament.

The promulgation of the Local Bodies Act, 1999 required the election of at least one woman from each ward committee (20 per cent in ward label) of the VDC and municipalities. However, according to the Election Commotion's report of 1992, the number of candidates in the VDCs was 102,502 out of whom the number of women candidates was 956 (0.9) percent. The number of elected members was 0.55 per cent out of 44,662 members.

Maoist Attraction

The involvement of women in the PW lacks reliable data to determine the actual percentage of women in different roles within the organization. However, it is the most attractive part of the whole exercise. As has been pointed out, "Women and children are generally used as human shields when attacking police posts and military garrisons. Women are often used to carry heavy loads of arms, food and other war materials[22].

Women are easily convinced by the revolutionary slogans of the Maoists in the hope of all kinds of emancipation and participated in the organization. Hisila Yami says that since the new democratic revolution (NDR) is anti-feudalistic, it will at once remove feudal Brahmanical Hindu rule, which sees women in relationship to men. It (NDR) is saving women from sweatshops of anti-imperialist and anti-expansionist forces for exploitation sexually and economically. The Maoist raised the issues of inheritance of property right of women, and autonomous government for the oppressed nationalities. They have opposed discrimination against the downtrodden and the practice of untouchability. As for women, they are "subject to class, gender, national and regional oppression simultaneously these agendas of the Maoist prompted women to join the Maoist movement"[23].

In a practice sense, the Maoist struggle at the local level has given space to an anti-alcohol campaign, anti-sexual violence and anti-women exploitation. An incident of Surkhet district - an all-women guerrilla unit with area commander came to a village at 10 p.m. to hold court. On trial

---

22 Mahat, Ram Sharan, in Defence of Democracy: Dynamics and fault lines of Nepal's Political Economy (Delhi: Adroit, 2005), p.321.

23 The Worker, February 1999. For a good account of the motivation of women to join the Maoist Insurgency, see Mandhira Sharma and Dinesh Prasain "Gender Dimensions of the People's War" in Michael Hutt, (ed.), Himalayan People's War. Nepal's Maoist Rebellion (London: Hurst & Co, 2004), pp.154-56.

was a husband who was habitually drunk and mercilessly beat his wife. The unit warned him, telling everyone to bring out their bottles of raksi (local wine). The bottle was to be returned to the shop. The Maoists would warn the shopkeeper. The home-brewed alcohol was destroyed after keeping some aside for medicinal and ritualistic purposes. A lecture was delivered on the ill effects of alcohol, and the linkage between alcohol, wife beating and illiteracy. After holding an adult literacy class, they left[24]. It express that women's participation in the Maoist movement has increased due to the social reform activities of the Maoist.

The Maoist ban on local gambling as well as punishment given to professional card players are also appreciated by the people. In some areas the Maoist administrators have imposed sanction of polygamy. It has been more strictly enforced then by the government. They have been dispensing justice immediately for the victim (first wife of the criminal). The Maoists also punish the person who exploits women sexually. Explaining the case of polygamy and the sexual exploitation of women, Com. Parbati says:

> At village area and district levels, women have been mobilized under women's mass organizations. In revolutionary stronghold areas, people's courts have been established, in which, along with other cases, cases against women's exploitation have been brought to trail by the combined efforts of the Village Defence Committees, women's mass organization and the people as a whole. Many cases of land usurpation of widows or of single women have been brought and their land restored to them brought and their land restored to them through such courts. Many defaulting husbands, who have taken to drinking and beating of their wives or practicing polygamy, and sexual exploiting women, have been disciplined through such courts. One interesting case in Parbat district is worth mentioning. A school teacher was known to exploit women sexually while promising to help them find matches for their marriage. He was brought before the people's court and was to stand up and sit down, holding his ears, for several minutes, and was made to apologize for his crime, eventually he was let off, after a warning of more serious consequences, should he continue with his criminal behavior[25].

---

24   Gautam, Shobha, Amrita Banskota and Rita Manchanda, "Where There are no men: Women in the Maoist Insurgency in Nepal", in Deepak Thapa (ed.) understanding the Maoist Movement of Nepal, (Kathmandu: Martin Chautari, 2003) p. 107.

25   Com. Parvati, "Women's Participation in People's War", in Arjun Karki and David Seddon (eds.) The People's war in Nepal: Left Perspective, (Delhi Adroid Publishers, 2003) p. 172.

Maoist provide justice through community activities, collective farming and redistribution of grain 'looted' from the labour of the people by the local feudal. By burning the office of the Agriculture Development Bank, the symbol of rural debt, they destroyed the records, and attacking and looting the bank distributed debt bonds to the poor farmers. They used the looted money for people's war. In the initial phase of the Maoists' movement, the Maoist punished the local feudal who invested money in the poor and took unnecessary money as interest from them. Being the poorest of the poor, women are further attracted by the activities of the Maoists.

Ethnic and oppressed groups, especially women, have experienced disparity in school attendance and in other sectors thus further widening the social divided. Their deprivation of opportunities, entrenched class and caste system and its overall impact on continuing the vicious circle of disparity have worked as breeding grounds for participation of women in the Maoist movement. In the total national average of literacy rate, 65 per cent is male. Only 30 per cent children of Dalit and disadvantaged ethnic groups attend school. Though the attendance in urban areas is better, in the national average such figure lags behind. Moreover, the elitist bias of education is so pervasive and strong that public school and colleges are increasingly becoming irrelevant to the context of national development and employment. The privileged sections of society including politicians, bureaucrats and other elites send their children either to foreign countries or private institutions where they get quality education. So, on the one hand, women's literacy rate does not represent the women's education, because most rural women are taught the adult literacy class that can make women literacy but not educate them. Their parents also marginalize most girls who are educated in the public schools. They cannot compete with the products of private schools. What is more problematic in that either the girls get low quality education or are totally deprived of opportunities even in the village schools. So, marginalization and unemployment are also other causes of women's participation in the Maoist movement.

In addition, the Maoist launched their programme in the public schools where most girls study. They are convinced that a "progressive education system" is practical and the "bourgeois education" is meaningless. If students are not positive towards them, they compel girls forcefully to participate in the Maoist movement. Sancharika Samuha, A Nepali women's organisation, claims that 50 per cent students are girls in Gorkha district village schools. Its main reason may be that parents are sending their sons outside. They fear that their sons will get politicized in schools and campuses under the Maoists' influence. Also, boys will be the first choice to send to other place while the girl students are left behind. There is therefore the possibility of coming under the influence of the Maoists[26].

Some narratives from the women guerillas are interesting. Some of them are reproduced below for a better understanding of the motivation of women for joining the Maoist war.

Women are also attracted towards the Maoist movement due to social division and artificial hierarchy created on the basis of capacity and skill. Such hierarchy and discrimination are not evident as males and females are sitting, working and eating together with the leaders and other guerillas. They like to join the guerrilla as they can walk and work together with other people. Kabita, who recently reached the age of 18, joined the second Lisnegam battalion six months ago. Having been educated not above the fifth class, Kabita says in Maobadi style: "A person who had not come out of home has now got the opportunity of seeing a new world".

Some women are engaged for humanitarian work such as nursing and caring of the injured, and some are related to arts such as singing, dancing and anchoring. Sangita of Kalikot, aged 19, is platoon commander of Seti-Mahakali Cultural Company. Having gone underground at the age of 14, she says that for class struggle she has chosen the present path. Sangita conducts Jana Sangit (people's song) and "women liberation" programmes over Maoist Radio. They claim that there are about 30,000 militias in Lisnegam that command the Seti-Mahakali area, among whom five hundred are women, says Platoon commander Raksya. Similarly, Usha Bam – Apekshya – of Baitadi, who joined the Maoist force in 2001 while studying in class nine, is now platoon assistant commander in Lisnegam Third Brigade. Having just reached 19, Apekshy says that she alone had nursed 36 wounded persons during the Myagdi attack.

Rakhya, who joined the Maoist force in 1999, is now platoon commander in Lisnegam second battalion. Her name figures among those women who reached a high position within the Maoist force. Rakshya, who hails from Kailali has 46 militias under her command. Rakshya feels that there are fewer women guerrillas in the Maoist force was on maternity leave. Married in people's style (Janabadi bibaha), Rakshys thinks of sex as natural. She adds, "Struggle is today's mission, others are secondary".

---

26   Gautam, Sobha, Amrita B. Anskota and Rita Manchanda, "Where there are no men: Women in the Maoist Insurgency in Nepal", in Deepak Thapa (eds.) Understanding the Maoist Movement of Nepal, (Kathmandu: Martin Chautari, 20030 P.22

Denied school, Karishma of Kalikot joined the movement in 2003 and participated in big operations. Karishma, who wears GPMG, says that after realizing that a woman should never be slave to anyone, went underground. Married in 1996, she went underground with her husband.

But, on the basis of statements of five-Sangita, Apekshya, Rakshya, Krishma and Kabita – it is felt that the guerrillas are more dominated by superficial factors (Bhool Bhulaiya) than deep knowledge and understanding. These women guerrillas who say they have taken up arms form women's liberation cannot give logical and analytical views expect their readymade statements. Those who have not understood subjects such as state affairs, political process, gender exploitation, women's rights, cannot understand who has or has not exploited them. Even then, the politburo member and Seti-Mahakali in charge, Janardan Sharma, shays: "They have taken up arms after knowing the ideas"[27].

Due to the opportunity for open love, women are stated to be tempted to join the Maoist war. For, the Nepali society and law can't allow girls to contact on their own to choose their boys. The age of a girl must reach 18 if she wants to decide her marriage[28]. She is not permitted to consummate marriage by her independent decision[29]. The process of divorce is also difficult. That is why most women involved in Maoist movement enjoy freedom of contact.

Atrocities by security forces also prompted young girls to join the militia either for their security or for taking revenge. Twenty-year-old Jharana has been working in the Maoist militia for the last three years. During this three-year period, she has become a section commander of the Maoists and is now entangled in a love marriage.

Ranju too is a young girl of the same age as Jharana. She was also recruited into the Maoist militia three years ago. Now she is a section commander. She has also had a love marriage. Thus, the number of rural young girls in the east joining the Maoist militia is increasing suddenly after having simplified love and marriage in the Maoist militia. The women have become stable in the militia after having the opportunity to love with the consent of the party. Jharana says that they are allowed to love by informing the party. But the love must be converted into marriage

---

27 Dhami, Ravim "Bachal Bandaichhan Mahila Chhapamar", Himal Khabar Patrika, August 17-31, 2004, p.16.

28 Section on Marriage, Muluki Ain.

29 Section on Husband and Wife, Muluki Ain.

soon. The number of such youth is large in the Maoist militia.

Especially during the last three years, the militia is significantly on the rise. Ranju, an inhabitant at Khejenim of Taplejung district, says that when she was studying in class nine, she had to join the Maoist guerrilla after the Royal Nepal Army (RNA) harassed her repeatedly without any cause. She has collected enough experiences of war even during this short period. She said that she has participated in eight wars including Lahan, Rumjatar, Bhiman, Chinpur and Banduke of Ilam district. In the beginning the cause of her joining the cause of her joining the Maoist war was the atrocity of the army. But she says that now she is fighting for the nation and society. She has become politically aware. Even Jharana says that after developing rebellious thinking in her fresh young mind due to the atrocity of security force and repression of government against women in the village, she joined the Maoist organization. She says, "The security personnel started coming and raping the women in the village. Therefore, I joined the Maoist organization after I didn't have any alternative." A single statement of most of the women who have joined the guerrilla is- 'cruel excesses against women.'

Almost all the women militia found at Gufapokhari said that they joined the Maoist organization due to the state repression. It has become a good opportunity to develop the Maoist guerillas after having found the opportunity to enter into the Maoist organization at a budding and young age and also a good opportunity for open love within the organization.

According to section commander Ranju, there is no meeting with her husband in three to six months due to the party's work. It is especially so during preparation of attack. 'We must walk up to three months to attack in the east and west. She said, "I have walked three months continuously in the preparation phase of attack. Since we have gotten necessary pocket money, we can also spend it. Normally, we can spend 200 rupees pocket money. Eleven militants are under a section commander.'

Almost all, young girls above class ten joining the Maoist organization are seldom found. According to a central member of CPN Maoist, Parbhat (Ganga Shrestha), three military brigades are functioning in the east. From one thousand and two hundred to two thousand and one hundred guerrillas are in brigade. Bethan Smriti, Soul-Sallery and Mechi-Koshi are fifth, sixth and seven brigades. There are only about one thousand and two hundred guerrillas. According to the Maoists, 40 per cent women are in the Maoist guerrilla. Most of them are the Kirati women in the east. A central member of the Maoists' organization, Tanka Prasad Angabuhang, claims that the attraction of the Kirats towards the Maoist guerrillas is increasing due to the exploitation by the state for years[30].

Being revengeful after the murder of their relatives by the security forces, women have participated in the Maoist organization. In an effort to mobilize women for the Maoist movement, widows of martyrs are helped and their 'sacrifice' for the revolution is publicly lauded. Nanda Kumari Shrestha refused to mourn when the security force killed her husband. She said, "I was not to cry if he was killed by the enemy and I should not go into ritual mourning, for a revolutionary never dies." Nanda stresses in true Maoist style, "I am ready to lift a gun to fellow my husband beliefs. I will make his dream come true." Similarly Sabita, a widow, believes that her husband was not a political person but the security forces killed him as well as other five persons when they were digging out potatoes in the field. She is committed to joining the Maoist party as a party worker and says, "Who would have created if my husband had died falling off a cliff or a tree? But because the police killed him, the society honors him as a martyr. They help me too".

The gender perspective can also found in the following tables that indicate the victims killed by the state and the Maoists.

---

30 Nepal Samacharpatra, 9 June 2004.

Table 5
Victims killed by the state and the Maoists
(Based on occupation)
1 January-31 December 2003

Type of Victim	By non-state or Maoists					By State				
	No. of Events	Male	Female	N/A M/F	Total	No. of Events	Male	Female	N/A M/F	Total
Agriculture	107	134	5		139	100	141	12	-	153
Business	12	13	1	-	14	9	11	1	-	12
Civil/Private Service	15	14	2	-	16	-	9	-	-	9
Dacoits	1	1	-	-	1	-	-	-	-	-
Engineer	1	1	-	-	1	-	-	-	-	-
Health Assistant	1	1	-	-	1	-	-	-	-	-
House Wife	1	-	1	-	1	1	-	1	-	1
Human Rights Activist	-	-	-	-	-	-	-	-	-	-
Indian Civilian Journalist	1	1	-	-	1	1	1	-	-	1
Labour	6	7	1	-	8	13	16	3	-	19
Law Professional	1	1	-	-	1	-	-	-	-	-
Military	46	109	-	-	109	1	2	-	-	2
Photographer	1	2	-	-	2	-	-	-	-	-
Police	93	212	-	-	212	6	6	-	-	6
Political Worker	46	65	2	-	67	286	616	95	142	854
Prisoner	-	-	-	-	-	1	1	-	-	1
Social Worker	2	2	-	-	2	1	1	-	-	1
Student	14	18	3	-	21	29	34	9	-	43
Teacher	13	12	1	-	13	2	2	-	-	2
Unavailable	30	32	4	1	37	71	84	17	12	113
Total	391	624	21	1	646	521	925	138	154	1217

Sources: Human Rights Situation Reports (INSEC), Year 12, No. 1, 9 April 2003.

According to INSEC tabulation, The Persons killed by state and the Maoists between 16 February 1996 and 31 May 2004, Reached 9729 of whom 6460 and 3269 were respectively killed the state and the Maoist. Now such figures have already crossed 10,000 with the increasing rise of death figures in the PW.

Table 6
Nature of events committed by State and Maoists

Type of Events	By Non-state				By state	
	By others		By Maoist			
	No. of Events	Total	No. of Events	Total	No. of Events	Total
Killings	103	119	17	21	70	138
Injured	18	22	23	42	18	28
Arrest & Torture					75	389
Disappearance	1	2			26	39
Beatings	66	88	19	27	15	36
Threats	5	7	10	18	4	6
Right to Assembly					2	6
Racial discrimination	18	21	1	1		
Right to prompt, fair trial and hearing					1	1
Landless and Squatters' problem	1	1				
Economic and social rights	3	3	3	3	4	5
Forced prostitution	3	4				
For practicing witchcraft	54	66	1	1		
Rape	55	68			7	9

Rape attempt	43	44			5	8
Polygamy	76	80				
Torture due to being women	15	21				
Women trafficking	20	29				
Jari (compensation to elope with other's wife)	8	9				
Attempt to traffic	14	20				
Domestic family violence	99	104	1	1		
Sexual abuse	126	131	2	2	1	3
Abortion	6	6				
Child rights	3	3				
Child trafficking	19	31				
Child marriage	8	9				
Killing of newborn baby	2	2				
Deprived from various opportunity	1	1			1	1
Deprived from education	1	1	1	1	1	1
Attempt to kill					1	1
Inhuman behavior						
Rubbing soot on face	2	3	2	5		
Abduction	12	13	43	69		
Other	2	2	1	1		
Total	784	910	124	192	231	671

Sources: Human Rights Situation Reports (INSEC), Year 12, No. 1, 9 April 2003.

Women have become double victims due to the People's War. First, they are direct victims of the security forces as relatives, wife, daughter and mother of the rebels. Security forces have been threatening, torturing and harassing in the name of inquiry as well as rapping, killing and disappearing women as suspects, rebels and also relatives of rebels. The first-hand data, as a case study, put in writing by Manjushree Thapa about the atrocities of the army against the women in the highly conflictual Dailekh district, after the Maoists' attack at Mangalsen - the district headquarter of neighboring district Achham, state that "[The] army had come searching for the Maoists who had waged the attack on Achham.... They told us - you are all Maoists ..they beat anyone they met on their patrols - men and women ....[my] since, a child of six, was shot near the stomach, when she run into the house in fear...[my] mother was shoot in the knee. All because my child of six had run from them....one woman, 22, had been raped there. Sometime later, another, 24 and a third, 25, had also been raped. They were all married; with little children.....the army raped them when they came to search their house"[31].

Second, the Maoists also demand lodging, food, money and sex from women any time and any day. Rapes have been frequently reported in the press and field works conducted by individual visitors and human rights groups. They also can abduct torture and killed by suspecting people as informers, opponents and class enemies. Third, they are suffering from their widowhood and sorrow due to the killing of their husbands and family members from both security force and the Maoists. Last, they are compelled to bear the double burden because of absence of their male members, somewhere, especially in the highly Maoist-affected areas; the male members of the families are compelled to leave their homes their wives and children.

Perspective

The Maoist started the 'People War' on 13 February 1996 with the declared objective of achieving a 'New People's Democracy". But the question can be raised there: is the Maoist movement in Nepal really driven by the ideology of Marxism-Leninism and Maoism? The ideology of Maoism, of course, is tactically used as a means to achieve its goal. The Maoist has been rejecting the system of monarchy as well as parliamentary democracy ideologically. They have also believed in the Mao's dictum that "Power comes from the barrel of a gun". That is why the Maoist party

---

31 Ibid. See also, Manjushree Thapa, An Elegy for Democracy: forget Kathmandu (New Delhi: Penguin Viking, 2005), pp. 212-13.

has mobilized its armed guerrillas. The people's war is not only confined to the western backward hill districts, they are also present all over the country including the capital, Kathmandu. The combination of all caste, class and gender is a major characteristic of People's War as middle and lower class people, ethnic and caste groups and women are involved in it.

The Maoist movement has definitely empowered women, sometimes knowingly and sometimes unknowingly. In reality, most men in the conflict zones have either field to the capital Kathmandu or to India to escape the atrocities of both security forces and the Maoists. Many have also gone to the jungle to join the Maoist guerrillas. Women have thus been compelled to take responsibly of running household works. They have been to plough the field to feed their family members. Women are engaged more in public life than ever before. They have become more vocal in community activities. As for the women participating in the Maoist organizations, they have gradually impressed the party with their leadership quality as being "formidable, fighting, committed, disciplined, reliable, tolerant, courageous and honest militant and cadres" as stated by the Maoist leaders. The active involvement of women in both political and military organizations of the Maoist party has boosted the confidence of the Nepali women as a whole. This has indeed produced a wide-ranging impact on the Nepali state. The first of its kind can be seen in prompting the government to recruit women into the Royal Nepal Army itself. It shows that the "new regime", i.e. the Maoists, has taught enough lessons to the "old regime" to recognize the power of women. The parliamentary force also might have realized the increasing role of women in the parliamentary exercise.

With the Royal cup in Nepal on 1st February 2005, no substantive change in women's activities in the Maoist movement has been seen. But some dead bodies of young women guerillas have been found on the battlefield. It is reportedly said that approximately 40 per cent women constitute the Maoist force. The strength of the Maoist force that ran over Beni Bazaar the Headquarter of Myagdi district located in the hill of the Western Region of the country, was believed to have equal sharing of women as militants. But the number of women at the centre and in the region is comparably insignificant as no women member in the Standing Committee of the party. Only two women members - Hisila Yami and Pampha Bhusal - are among the 27 Politburo members. The same women members of the Politburo are also in the 39 -members Central Committee.

In the military wing, there is no single woman in the division command because of absence of woman members in the Politburo. In addition, all nine brigades under three divisions - East, Mid and West divisions - have no woman commissar and commander. It means that the CPN (M), like other parties has also accommodated fewer women at the central level of organization and in the military where most decisions are made. Many reason apart, this reflects the structure of Nepali society to which the Maoist party is no exception. It is a hard fact that majority of women in different Maoist organizations are illiterate, neo-literate, have less exposure, and are subjected for a long time. They have obviously less capacity to develop leadership quality. The Maoist party and its various sister organizations are also dominated by the "High Caste Hindu Males". Neither males nor females from Dalit and Tarai communities are in the top leadership or in the standing committee, the highest body of the party. Both the chairman of the party, Pushpa Kamal Dahal (Prachanda) and another influential leader in the five member standing committee of the party, Dr. Babu Ram Bhattarai, have come from a Brahmin family, which controls the party except Ram Bahadur Thapa (Badal), a Magar from Gulmi. In the case of female leaders, only two women - Pampha Bhusal and Hisila Yami - among the 40 per cent women representation in the Maoist movement - have represented at the politburo and central level. During the 10 years of people's war, no women leader except the two has been in the forefront. Moreover, Prachanda is also a chief of the women and Dalit wings in the name of "leadership centralization" at the critical "offensive state" of the party.

Similarly, the attitude to women is not much different in the Maoist party from the feudal traditional culture and value that is deep-rooted in the Nepali society. The radical organization, CPN (M), is also not able to accept the individual identity of a woman. Being the wife of an influential leader of the party, Dr. Babu Ram Bhattarai, Hisila Yami - chief of women's wings and vice-chairperson of foreign division - had been punished "without any charge sheet" and dismissed from responsibility by the party accusing her of "supporting" and "promoting" Dr. Bhattarai's activities against the "party discipline". She was also affected by the personality clash between two party leaders - Prachanda and Babu Ram.

It can be said that after the Nala Pani war against the colonial East India Company, Nepali women have participated in the Maoist movement from the grass roots level. The issue of gender is highlighted more by the Maoists than by other parties. It is certain that the human rights of women would be more prominently raised in the future in Nepal. All the exploited subordinated, subjugated and marginalized women can no longer be included under the patriarchal social structure because the women have participated as rebels in the Maoist movement for taking revenge or for compensation to all kind of exploitation, and for emancipation from the subjugation and suppression. The Maoists have at least been responsible for sensitizing the Nepali political elites about gender disparity in the Nepali society.

Chapter VIII

Women in Armed Conflict: Lessons to Be Learnt From Telangana People's Struggle

Uddhab P. Pyakurel

This essay elaborates and compares the role of women in two political movements - the Maoist movement in Nepal and the Telangana people's struggle in India. The first is an ongoing struggle, while the latter is a struggle which started in the middle of 1946 and lasted for five years until it was called off in October 1951 after the involvement of the Indian army. This paper is confined to the scenario of women's participation, their feelings and some push and pull factors for joining the struggles. Apart from the above this paper explores the participants' views on the movement, their leaders, policy, and the programme of their parties for favouring their participation. The women's condition at the end of Telangana movement after the party forgot its earlier promise, has also tried to bring it out as a matter of concern for discussion. This paper concludes by bringing out some bitter experiences of the women participants of Telangana movement, and tries to make the Maoists aware of the harassing experiences. Before going on to examine both the struggles, let me briefly introduce both the struggles.

Telangana People's Struggle

Under the British Raj, India was ruled basically by two types of rulers: (a) the British administered provinces of India known as British India, and (b) 'princely India' or those states governed by princes, *maharajas, rajas,* and nawabs. Among them, Hyderabad was the largest state, which was under the *Nizam* prince, and Telengana is one out of three linguistic regions - Telugu, Marathwada and Kannada - of Hyderabad. The Telangana revolt began in mid - 1946 and lasted for five years. It was an armed resistance of women and men to the feudal oppression or against the princely state in Telangana. It was a struggle against the autocratic rule of the *Nizam* and the *zamindari* system.

(i) There were three types of land holding systems - sarf-e-khas (the land controlled by the *Nizam* and his family from where revenue collected was used for meeting their personal expenses), and

(ii) jagirs (the land which was given to *Jagirdars*), and

(iii) *diwani* or government land.

Jagirdars were those who were loyal to the *Nizam* enjoying their own police, revenue, civil and criminal systems. They had received jagirs and became revenue officers or generals in the army. They also had the right over forests and fisheries, and exercised police and judicial functions. Having all the power, they coerced people for various illegal extortions and forced labour. The peoples' conditions of *jagir* areas were far more oppressed than in the *sarf-e-khas* lands; the *jagirdars* and their agents were free to collect a variety of illegal taxes from the actual cultivators. *Jagir* lands were excluded from the jurisdiction of civil courts. There was also the vetti (free services to the proprietors) system. Every peasant was compelled to contribute vetti to the zamindar. Only after completing tasks on the landlord's fields, peasants and labourers could work for themselves. If the tenants and their families were having their meals and the landlord called them, they were expected to leave their food and immediately attend to the demands of the landlord.

Women were more suppressed under this rule. They were not allowed to feed their babies while working in the landlord's field. Women were repressed, not only in the field of free work or vetti, but were also sexually harassed and exploited. There were many instances of such suppression; if the landlord fancied a woman, she was taken as a consort. Sleeping with the landlord on the first night was a compulsion to newly married women. It was the landlords' prerogative. Hence, peasant women, along with men, came into the Andhra Maha Sabha (AMS) and started an armed struggle against the 'oppressive feudal system and the fundamentalist militia of the Nizam - the Razkars".

In 1928, people established AMS converting it from the Andhra Jana Sangam, which was established in 1921 with the objectives of social and cultural upliftment of the Telugu people. It changed not only the name but also the objectives from socio-cultural to political activity. Earlier, it was a common organization to all parties - the RSS, Congress and even to the nonpolitical - who wanted change in society. In 1930, the Mahila Navjivan Mandal was formed in co-ordination with AMS. These organizations are accredited with bringing women into the movement. During 1940-42, some important leaders of the AMS joined the communist leadership and assumed AMS into the character of a mass organization. AMS went into an armed struggle against the decision made in November 1946. The struggle was an extended form of grassroot level resistance, using local weapons to resist the regime. The movement was also considered as one in which "the Mao's thought was first put into practice out of China" (Louis 2002:49). Local arms like lathis, slings, stones were used in the first struggle took place to support Ailimma (a woman who was threatened by the landlord's goondas); women used sticks and chilly powder. Later, volunteer squads were not only formed, but were also skillfully trained in the usage of these kinds of weapons. They started making local weapons professionally and even used modern weapons. Several struggles took place between the squads and Nizam's supporters. The rebels seized arms 'raiding police stations and landlord's houses'. But women did not give up their strategy of using local means to defend themselves against the police. Women used to attack the police with packets full of chilly powder.

Ruler's oppression was not a single cause of women's participation in the revolt. Women-oriented programmes of Sanghams were other reasons; when women's issues like wife-beating and early age marriage came up, the Sangham immediately called the authorities concerned, held debates and resolved the matter. The act of misbehaving with women was severely punished. These rules were practiced even in their organization which attracted women to join the Shangham. For instance, Shankar, a member of the organization who was accused of raping women and mismanaging the party funds, faced the firing squad. According to them, these punishments were declared by the people themselves as the correct line of action.

"Large number of peasants spontaneously participated in the struggle directed against the government, landlords and their agents. The insurgents had neither firearms nor official training, but were required to use them. A few volunteers' corps had come into existence, which were not well organized guerrilla squads, but formed on ad hoc basis in response to the situation. Initially the revolt was spasmodic (Dhanaghare 1983: 195), but later it became frequently and regular, and usually between the people and state security forces when the rebellion received support from all, especially the women. With such enthusiastic participation by both men and women, they were able to carry out some social transformation in the society. They ousted several police stations from the village, vetti was abolished and thousands of acres of land distributed and debts to be repaid were dismissed. However, the movement started facing a lot of trouble when the Indian Union Army was deployed against the Nizam. After the Nizam surrendered in September 1948 to the Indian Army, the communists and the movement became the target of the Indian Union Army and the party and its cadre were compelled to leave the villages. The party tried to organize the tribal people for fighting against the local governmental institutions, e.g., forest officials and moneylenders "who subjected them to exploitation". However, it was not an alternative to continue emergency. Finally, the politburo of the party, took the decision on 21 October 1951 to call off the struggle, citing it due to "the increased repression by the Indian Union Army".

The Maoists Movement in Nepal

The Maoist insurgency during the last ten years has spread all over the country. Some 15,000 people have already lost their lives since 13 February 1996. The cost of reconstruction of development infrastructure, until 2003, which was destroyed by the Maoist, is estimated to be NRs. 200 billion[1]. Developmentalists argue that the Maoist insurgency 'is basically a social and economic issue and is produced and sustained by failed development' (Panday 1999:12). It is true that the epicenter and heartland of the Maoist insurgency are mid-west hill districts - Rolpa, Rukum, Salyan, Dailekh, Jajarkot, etc.,which the Human Development Index categorizes as the lowest rank districts of the country (NESAC 1998: 264-65). Not only this, but some political exclusions and brutal human rights violations are also fostering factors for the insurgency.

The involvement of women in the People's War (PW) lacks reliable data to determine the actual percentage of women in different roles within the organization. Even statistics given by the Maoists vary from leader to leader. Hisila Yami, the Central Committee member of the Maoists, has given tentative data by writing, "the participation of the women in People's Liberation Army are from 30 to 40 per cent" (Yami 2006: 66). For Sapana, company commander, more than 40 per cent are women in the People's Liberation Army (Mulyankan, Bhadra 2061: 14), and for Uma Bhujel, a central member who broke and fled from Gorkha jail and came back under the open sky, the ratio is approximately 40 per cent in the army and more than 50 per cent in other fields (Ibid: 16). The number of women

---

1 See Space Times, May 27, 2003

in the party and militia is approximately 40 per cent, and in autonomous government and in industries, the number is above 50 per cent (Janadesh 2006: 8).

Here, a question arises about the causes, which inspired or compelled Nepali women to join the movement. It is said that some women are forced to join the Maoist movement by the Maoist themselves and some are compelled to join them due to misbehaviour by the security forces. For example, Ganga and Sobha Thapa (16 years old and studying in grade nine in Satakhana School of Surkhet district), were abducted by the Maoist on 29 September, 2005.[2] Shanti 16, Resmi 16 and Binita 15 are examples of how the security personnel irritated the students and general public.[3] Brutal suppression of security forces have also encouraged young girls to join the militia either for their own security or for taking revenge. Being revengeful due to the murder of their relatives by the security forces, women have participated in the Maoist organization. Sarita is a perfect example in support of the argument. She took to guns after her innocent brother was killed by the army (Paudel, 2004:14). For the sake of revenge, she joined the movement. Low success rate in School Leaving Certificate examination and lack of training options for engaging students who failed in their school level examination, is another factor for their joining the Maoist movement in order to escape idleness and frustration (Karki and Bhattarai 2003:5).

Apart from that, propaganda of women's liberation, equality in the Maoist organization in opportunity, in award and promotion, the hope of all kinds of emancipation, and on-going women - related social reform programmes like anti-alcohol, anti-gambling campaigns, anti-sexual violence programmes, and anti-women exploitation programmes are the main attractions for women to participate and support the movement. Some are there only for "romance, pleasure, and luxury". But, there is a consensus that the credit has to be given to the Maoist for "widespread women's awareness in the Nepalese history" (Mulyankan, August-September 2004: 13).

Slogans on 'progressive education' rather than 'bourgeois education' and love/ courtship are also a vital factor for women's attraction. Orthodox

---

2 For detail see Times special.nepali times.com/issue268/ceasefireroundup-lhtp

3 They are the students of Rolpa district and were taken to the army camp, and then their names were in the list of Krantikari student wing. They were threatened by the army that there was apossibility of killing. Them then they were freed, but were required to report to the army camp at two or three days interval (see Karki and Bhattarai, 2003).

social system towards widows is another cause for compelling women to join the movement. In Nepal, generally, girls are not allowed to choose their own life partners and to find their marriage; and the society does not accept love marriages easily. If the love affair is inter-caste, acceptance is difficult by both, the parents and the society. Increase in the number of widow population and the unchanged social perception on widow marriage seems another factor, which led women to join the movement. After the Maoist movement, 15,000 people were killed; most of them were male leaving behind young widows in the society. However, the society does not accept a widow-marriage easily. In a patriarchal society in Nepal, if people are involved in these activities, females have to face social degradation in comparison to their male counterparts. In such a situation, the Maoist movement became accommodative to socially mistreated women. It is said that a majority of women in the movement are "influenced by superficial factors (*bhool bhulaiya*) than deep knowledge and understanding of state affairs, political process, gender exploitation, women rights, etc" Adhikari 2006. Denying these factors, Hisila Yami, a senior woman Maoist leader, said that the women are not recruited for party's "contemporary advantages" but hired because of "their double resistance capacity than man" (Mulyankan, August-September, 2004: 12-18).

To sum up, the social reality, which promoted women to join the Maoist movement, we can agree with the argument made by a political scientist Kapil Shrestha. He argues, "after democracy in 1990 some positive changes towards women participation in politics has appeared, but sociologically speaking, most of the Nepalese women politicians belong to 'the small upper strata of urban, middle class, upper caste and educated elite background, not from the rural, grassroots or low caste background" (Shrestha 2001).

Comparison

We can compare both struggles based on its objectives, goals and achievements. Apart from that, the paper tried to examine validities and reliabilities by observing available narratives, and data of both the movement.

Firstly, the Telangana movement was declared against the Nizam's oppression. The Telengana struggle supported abolishment of the Nizam feudalism from Telangana. It seemed that the Telangana struggle was more focused on democracy and freedom. However, the Maoist movement in Nepal was launched after the restoration of democracy in 1990, which provisioned, at least, freedom to the people. Abolishing the monarchy and establishing the "Democratic Republic" were the said specific objectives of the Maoist of Nepal.

Secondly, the Telengana movement had supported the independent struggle of India from British *raj*. If such a disturbance had not occurred in several parts of India, Britain could have taken the independent struggle at face value and they could have tried to use more force against the struggle. People were able to raise slogans against the feudal and brutal regime and able to abolish not only local principality, but also its backbone - the colonial power. Ultimately, the Nizam principality was abolished after the departure of the British from India.

Although the Maoist have shown their eagerness to join the "competitive democracy" and signed different agreements (12-point agreement in November 2005 and 8-point agreement in June 2005) with Seven Party Alliance (SPA), their earlier targets were SPA cadres in the villages undermining democracy. The Maoist killed, injured and compelled people to leave the village, who were believed to be at least progressive compared to feudal regimes. The SPA cadres were not only tortured but also banned from launching political activities in the Maoist-influenced-areas. Apart from such 'undemocratic' behaviour against the democratic forces, the Maoist claimed that they had a "tacit understanding" with King Birendra. These activities of the Maoist compelled the people to be skeptical. The doubt of the people was 'the objective of the Maoist movement was not to strengthen the freedom and democracy but to support the undemocratic and feudal regime'. The feeling of suspicion of the people about the Maoist was obvious because the monarchy itself has been considered as "the main obstacle for strengthening the democracy in Nepal".

The doubt of the people over the Maoist increased, when both Maoist and the king trapped democratic forces or parliamentary parties in Nepal. On the one hand, as mentioned earlier, the Maoist banned the movements of the parliamentary parties in the countryside, which made the government unfit for holding the parliamentary and local elections. On the otherhand, the king started ruling the country blaming the democratic government for its 'incompetence' to hold the election and for maintaining the peace and security in the country. It is said that the democratic process was initially disturbed by rampant violent activities of the Maoist; even the democratically elected government was triggered to impose the state of emergency and termed the Maoists as 'terrorists'. The Maoist activities became the major 'trump card' for the king to be used in asking support for his autocratic regime.

As a consequence, more than 40,000 women's representation in different democratic agencies was directly hit antagonizing them. However, the Maoist defended such antagonism as the initial compulsion when they were weak. Prachanda, in an interview, defended it and said such a strategy was there only for "extended political disclose to establish the ideology and to preserve the power when the party was overall weak in ideology, politics, organization and physical power". According to him, they are trying to bring all possible forces together because they are now "strong and reached near the strategic aim" (Prachanda in Janadesh 2006: 15-16).

Thirdly, both the struggles, the Maoist movement and Telangana movement, have definitely empowered women, sometimes knowingly and sometimes unknowingly. Although the Telangana struggle was called off without success, it has has brought some qualitative changes in women and in their life. After 40 years of the unsuccessful struggle, women still have no guilty feeling for the struggle but they take pride in it. Somaka of Vimpati who participated in the Telangana struggle says, "In those days, could we sit and talk to you like this? Today we can do that. If we dressed up well, if we put *kumkum* they used to say, what does she think of herself?" (Stree Shakti Sangathana 1989: 16). For her, that sort of empowerment was gained by the struggle, although the entire problems were not solved. Another woman participant, Kausila, was also satisfied by the things were achieved. She says, "We didn't know what was behind this wall. We could never go out. Now we go out and look at our agricultural work (Ibid: 16)."

One question may be raised about how the women are empowered by the Maoist movement. Some direct and indirect factors created by the movement, however, have led the women to be empowered. The Maoist's conflict compelled majority of the male members to leave their homes and go into urban area or escape to the jungle to join the Maoist guerrilla force. Women have thus been 'compelled' to take the responsibility of running households. They have had compulsion to go and take part to express their opinion in front of the masses, etc. Women were compelled even to plough the field to feed their family members, which was restricted to the menfolk earlier. Engaging more in the public life than ever before, they have become more vocal in community activities.

On the other hand, the active involvement of women in both political and military organizations of the Maoist party has boosted the confidence of the Nepali women as a whole. This has indeed produced a wide-ranging impact on the Nepali state. Now, the government itself has started to recruit women into the Royal Nepal Army. The parliamentary forces also have realized the need to launch more progressive and reformist programmes to increase the role of women in political participation.

Taking all these factors into consideration, we can conclude that women were sensitized and made aware about their role in society. On the other hand, they are affected badly by the ongoing conflict. Women have become double victims due to the People's War. First, they are the direct victims of the security force as they are participants, relatives, wives, daughters and mothers of the rebels. They are continuously threatened, tortured and harassed in the name of inquiry as well as raped and killed, and they disappear as suspects, rebellions and also relatives of rebels. Second, the Maoist also demand lodging, food, money and sex from women at any time and on any day. Rapes by the Maoist have been frequently reported in the press and fieldwork reports conducted by individual visitors and human rights groups. The Maoists are also following the security forces' footstep to torture people suspecting them as informers, opponents and class enemies. Third, women are compelled to bear the double burden because of absence of their male members who are either killed or are compelled to flee from their domicile.

Although, the Maoist claims itself as a radical party, it is also not far from being feudal towards the issue of women. Only two women members - Hisila Yami and Pampha Bhusal - are among the 27 politburo members. The same women members of the politburo are also in the 39 - member Central Committee. In the case of female leaders, only two women-- Pampha Bhusal and Hisila Yami - among the 40% women representation in the Maoist movement - have been represented in the politburo and central level. In the military wing, there is no single woman in the division commander where most decisions are made. But we have to say that the issue of gender is highlighted and sensitized in the Nepali society.

After having a look at Latchampas elaboration, we can conclude that the women in Telangana struggle faced the same problems that Nepali women are facing now - the fear of rape, sexual harassment, torture, etc. They kept secrets and protected the other party workers, especially the males, by facing all the troubles of the state security.[4] But they blamed

---

4 She says, 'my husband was scared, but I did not listen to him. I joined the Sangham. After all what could we do alone? Amin was terror. He used to make the men run on their knees. Many women were raped. In fact, we used to stay together and escape together – or the pretext that an old woman was dead, someone had delivered a baby or a girl had matured. We never revealed to the police or Razakar the whereabouts of the Sangham'

the party for not being able to evolve any policy regarding the women. The charges over the party by women is not only about its policy towards women in the organization, their main grievances are that the party initially appreciated and welcomed women's support in the movement by wooing them, and later it distressed them in the way without any alternatives. Some of them left their husbands, kids and home in the name of 'emancipation'; however, they got nothing but more trouble. Reminding Party's promise to women thwarted their involvement in the struggle, Mallu Swaraj, who commanded a guerrilla squad and was a legend in Telangana, says:

> In the party, they will see only what the movement needs... So when struggle was withdrawn they told us to go and marry ... we fought with them. We said that even if the forms of struggle had changed we should be given some work (Stree Shakti Sangathana 1989: 271-272).

But when the movement was called off, the party had not fulfilled its promise by giving work to women. They themselves, who spent their entire active life in the movement, often felt suppressed when the party withdrew the struggle and asked the women to go back and marry. Women are mentally tortured by such an immature decision of the party. Priyamvada who spent years in the struggle said, "she often felt like committing suicide" (Stree Shakti Sangathana 1989:272)". Sugunamma's observation is an example how they got frustrated after the party's order to women "go back and marry". She says:

> They have used us so long and now they say go stay at home. How could they even understand what the situation was at home? What mental torture - I was really upset. That was my first taste of suffering (ibid).

Kamalama and Salama are examples of exploitation by the party where Kamalama, now, is begging in her village to feed her children and is carrying "liquor and worked as a wage labor to bring up her sons" (Ibid). They themselves are in doubt whether they were able to make some achievements or not because, according to Pesara Sattemma (Stree Shakti Sangathana 1989: 221-227), the struggle's initial aim was for land ownership and against the *vetti*. *Vetti* was abolished, but women were not successful in getting land in their own name. Women considered that situation as a big blow and insult to them. Priyamvada, another woman participant in the struggle, explained the struggle as a failure to address the

---

(cited in Sanghatana, 1989: 16).

agenda of women. She says, "After the parliamentary election and police action, these dreams were - smashed-crushed like an egg. What a blow it was, after the elections, do we know where we were? Like a proverbial rug ... lying exactly where it was thrown" (Stree Shakti Sangathana 1989). Ultimately, when the movement ended, women neither got land, nor enjoyed other sort of settlement. The slogan 'all sorts of emancipation' remained a fantasy.

Everyone who is aware of the situation of women after calling off the Telangana struggle, has always raised the question, fearing whether the Maoist movement will also go the same way as that of the Telangana struggle? The fear is real because there were no women participantly at the decision-making level in the Telangana movement. The condition remains the same in the Maoist movement because only two women members - Hisila Yami and Pampha Bhusal - were among the 27 politburo members. No women are there in the Standing Committee, which is the supreme body of the party. And, only three (two representing in politburo also, and another was Uma Bhujel) members are in the 39 - Member Central Committee. Now, the Maoist party has dissolved the Standing Committee and the politburo; all the power has been centralized, which according to them, is because of their forth-coming general convention. In the military wing, there is only a single woman, Sapana who is the company commander, where they claim 40-50 per cent women's are working under them. The party and its women are still eager to revive the agenda of women participation in all the sectors.

After the Janaandolan II (peoples' movement), the reinstated parliament has unanimously provisioned 33 per cent reservation to women in Nepal. The concern of the people is how this decision of the parliament would be implemented. The decision of 33 per cent reservation to the women seems unique and progressive in South Asia. People are having a doubt over its implementation because of the traditional thinking of all the political forces dominating women in Nepal; till date, every party has offered opportunities to women for fulfilling the quotas. Recently, after the Janaandolan II also, the position of the parties on the issues of women remained unchanged. Only a state ministerial portfolio has been given to the women; neither the Maoists nor the SPA sent any women in their dialogue teams, and in the interim constitution drafting committee.

After reading the narratives of the participants of the Telangana struggle, the research has concluded that radical agendas would be harmful for society, if the agendas were raised just to woo the people.

It will not only be harmful to the organizer, but also to the individual or participants, making them frustrated. Such frustration may possibly direct another revolt. The Telangana movement should be taken as a guide in which the CPI called off the movement in 1951 but the party was not able to control its activists to join another revolt. Those who were not satisfied by both, the achievement and the party's decision to end the struggle, tried to reorganize such a struggle. After being unable to resume revolt by the same party, they tried to form an alternate party. Ultimately, in 1964, the split took place in the CPI and CPI(M) was created in the initiation of those dissatisfied members, which again continued armed struggle against the Andhra rulers in 1969 demanding a "separate Telangana state" (Mohanty 2005:11-15). Hence, one can conclude that if someone takes a weapon, s/he rarely will quit the weapons until s/he has accomplished his target. Experiences show that all revolutionary parties and their accountable leaders can analyze the entire situation and decide to compromise by suspending and even giving up the armed struggle, but applying such a theory in cadres and followers, who took to weapons after a suppressed and marginalized feeling, has not succeed properly. For them, 'do continue the revolt and die in the battlefield' is better than being back without getting something. The leader of the Maoist must think of preventing such a possibility, and hopefully that may be the signal of thinking over it by the Maoists supreme commander when he realized that "whatever has supported for successful development of the people's war, it is both, the main possibility and main threat."

It is the desperate need of time to Nepali Maoist leaders to think and rethink about those hindrances felt long before by Priyamvada, Sugunamma, Kamalama and Sattemma, and that group which split and re-organized the revolt after the wind-up of the Telangana people's struggle. Every top-level leader of the groups, including the Maoist, which raised the radical agendas, must learn a lesson from Telangana before they take any step forward.

References

Adhikari, Indra K. 2006. "The Maoist Movement in Nepal: Gender Perspectives". (Unpublished paper)

Chakravarty, Renu. 1980. *Communists in Indian Women's Movement 1940-50*. New Delhi: PPH.

Chatterjee, P. 1989. "The Nationalist Resolution of the Women's Question". In K. Sanghar and S. Vaid (eds.), *Recasting Women: Essays in Colonial History*, New Delhi: Kali for Women.

Denzin, N.K. 1970. *A Sociological Method: A Source Book*. Chicago: Aldine.

Dhami, Ravi. 2004. "Bachal Bandaichhan Mahila Chhapamar". Himal Khabarpatrika, August 17-31.

Dhanaghare, D.N. 1983. "Social Origins of the Peasantinsurrection in Telangana, 1946-51". In D. N. Dhanaghare (ed.), *Peasant Movement in India 1920-50*. Oxford: Oxford University Press.

Gautam, Shobha. 2001. "Women & Children in the Periphery of People's War". Institute of Human Rights Commission of Nepal: IHRICON.

Gautam, Shobha, Amrita Baskota and Rita Manchanda. 2003. "Where There are no Men: Women in the Maoist Insurgency in Nepal". In Deepak Thapa (ed.), *Understanding the Maoist Movement of Nepal.* Kathmandu: Martin Chautari.

Hassaim S. 1993. Family, Motherhood and Zunu and Zunu Nationalism: *The Politics of the Inkatha Women's Brigade*. Fem. Rev. 43:1-25.

Immon-kenah, S. 1983. *Narratives Fiction: Contemporary Politics.* Longman: Methuen.

INSEC Informal Sector Service Centre. 2003 April. Vol. 5, No.2.

Janadesh, Special Issue 2006.p.8

Josiane, Racine and Jean-Luc Recine. 2004. "Beyond Silence: A Dalit-Life History in South India". In A. David and B. Stuart (eds.), *Telling Indian Lives*. New Delhi: Permanent Black.

Kakar, S. 1989. *Intimate Relations: Exploring Indian Sexuality*. New Delhi: Viking.

Karki, A. and B. Bhattarai (ed.). 2003. *Whose War? Economic and Socio-Cultural Impacts of Nepal's Maoist-Government Conflict.* Kathmandu: NGO Federation of Nepal.

Karki, A. and D. Seddon D. 2003. *The People's War in Nepal: Left Perspectives*. New Delhi: Adroit.

Kumar, Krishna. 2002. *Prejudice and Pride*. New Delhi: Penguin Books.

Labov, W. 1972. *Language in the Inner City*. Philadelphia: Philadelphia University Press.

Leijeune, Philippe. 1975. *Le pacte autobiographique*. Paris: Seuil.

Luintel, Samira. 2001a. "The Social World Of Nepalese Women", An Occasional Paper in Sociology And Anthropology, Vol. VII, Kathmandu.

Luintel, Youberaj. 200lb. "Exclusion, the Politics of Location and Women's Property Rights Debates in Nepal". An Occasional Paper in Sociology and Anthropology, Vol. VII, Kathmandu.

Mahat, Ram Sharan. 2005. *In Defence of Democracy: Dynamics and Faultlines of Nepal's Political Economy*. Delhi: Adroit.

Maithereyi, Krishnaraj. 2005. "Research in Women Studies: Need for a Critical Appraisal". *Economic and Political Weekly, July 9*.

Mohantay, C.T. 1991. "Under Western Yes: Feminist Scholarship and Colonial Discourses". In C.T. Mohanty, A Russo, L Torres, *Third World Women and Politics of Feminism* (eds.), as cited in loomington/indianapolis: Ind.univ.press.

Moniot, H. 2004. "Lhistorie des peoples sans histoire". In Le Golf and Nora (eds.), Faire de L'Histoire, 1:106-23. Cited in Josiance Racine and Jean-luc Racine.

Mulyankan, Bhadra 2061, p.14.

NESAC, 1998. *Nepal Human Development Report*. Kathmandu. Kath mandu: Nepal South Asia Study Centre, pp. 264-65.

Panday, Devendra Raj. 1999. *Nepal's Failed Development: Reflections on the Mission and the Maladies*. Kathmandu: Nepal South Asia Study Centre.

Pradhan-Malla, Sapana. 2001. "Women Inherent Right". In L. K. Manandhar and K.B. Bhattachan (eds.), *Gender and Democracy in Nepal*. Kathmandu: Central Dept. of Home science-women studies programme.

Sharma, Mandira and Dinesh Prasain. 2004. "Gender Dimensions of The People's War". In Michael Hutt (ed.), *Himalayan People's War: Nepal's Maoist Rebellion*. London: Hurst & Co.

Space Times. May 27, 2003.

Stree Shakti Sanghatana. 1989. *We are Making History: Women in the Tilngana Struggles*. New Delhi: Kali for women.

Thapa, Manjushree. 2005. *An Elegy for Democracy: Forget Kathmandu*. New Delhi: Penguin Viking.

The Worker, February 1999. For detail see Times special.nepali times. com/issue268/ceasefireroundup-lhtp

Yami Hisila, 2006, People's War and Women's Liberation in Nepal Chhattisgarh: Purvaiya Prakashan

Notes:-

(1) The biggest owners of land who claimed and enjoyed propriety rights over the peasants.

Chapter IX

The Vision of the *Jana Andolan*-II for the Future of Nepal

Uddhab Pd. Pyakurel

As the political situation in Nepal has been in turmoil for a long time, some scholars used to say that Nepal is in a permanent transition. Even 55 years after the end of the Rana hereditary prime ministerial system in 1951, the political situation has neither been stable nor improved. Prior to the Rana regime, Nepal was isolated from the rest of the world. The 1951 movement brought some change in the political sphere but this could not continue. Just two years later, the king started violating the constitutional provision and refused to hold elections. There was no election for almost a decade between 1951-59, but the power struggle continued between the king and the political parties. Even after paramount pressure of the political parties, the king did not agree to hold the election of the Constituent Assembly (CA), which was promised earlier, but declared the election for parliament later in 1959. The election paved the way for formation of the first elected government in the country. The king, however, dismissed the government on December 15, 1960 after one-and-half years of its formation.

After two years of the *coup d'état* in 1960, the then king Mahendra not only proclaimed a constitution, but also a new political system claiming that he is the source of the constitution and sovereignty also belonged to him. 'Panchayat' was the given name of the new ruling system, terming it as "suitable to the Nepali soil". During 30 years of Panchayat raj, the king ruled the country either directly or through his nominees. The system ended in 1990 when people launched a Mass Movement with the demands to restore the multi-party democracy in the country and to end the king's autocratic regime. The movement has been popularly known as

Janaandolan-I.

Nepal tried to enter into a new political era and improve the political system after *Janaandolan*-I. A new constitution was drafted and promulgated though it was a negotiated document of the major political forces, the Nepali Congress, the United Left Front and the monarchy. General and local elections were held, which helped democracy develop from the grassroots level. However, the "pseudo" democracy did not perform well in the country. The mid-term election in 1994, in which no party got majority, resulted not only in political instability, but also gave a bad image in terms of governance. Such weaknesses witnessed under the democratic system led to people's frustration at large and gave a pretext to those who were unhappy by the political change brought about by the 1990s *Janaandolan.* In other words, such shortcomings became a strong weapon for those who were in search of opportunities to attack the multi-party democracy to weaken and defame it.

Basically two political forces - ultra left groups led by the Nepali Maoist and the ultra right groups led by some royalists, were the forces which were not satisfied with the 1990s political change. The former had a dream to achieve a 'radical change', and the latter was angry due to the fact that the then king had to compromise with the political forces for electoral democracy, rule of law and human freedom. That is why several attempts along with non-cooperation activities were made against the 1990s political change from the very first day. The then king Birendra, whom most of the Nepalese respect as the democrat king, also became an instrument to weaken the achievement of *Janaandolan*-I, though the Maoist were in a leading position to disturb the system. As we all know, the Maoist "people's war", which began in 1996, had stated the infamous motto 'bourgeoisie democracy'. Along with the Maoist movement, brutal killings by the state agencies and the Maoist became rampant; torture, extortion, violation of human rights and destructive activities saw enormous increase; and the displacement rate from the villages roared. Ultimately, the political situation of the country became more fragile.

Talking about the Maoist movement and its impact on Nepal, it was not confined to the rural areas; the movement was able to draw the attention of the major political forces in the country. It was the Maoist movement which had a strong impact to define and redefine the intra and inter-party relationship. Several serious debates were held inside the parties and between the parties regarding the question of dealing with the Maoist movement. Again, a new conflict had emerged between the king and the

Prime Minister when the former became an obstacle for the implementation of the then Koirala's government's decision to deploy the army against the Maoist in July 2000. These conflicts obviously disturbed the schedule of the government, which was committed to solve people's problems related to livelihood. Interestingly, due to government's instabilities; conflicts and frustrations, the Maoist was the single beneficiary.

In between, the royal massacre which took place in June 2000, helped the then crown prince Gyanendra, emerge as an ambitious but undemocratic king of the country. As Gyanendra had a negative opinion about the 1990s political change from the beginning, he accelerated the conspiracy against the on-going multi-party democracy when he received the crown formally. Though he was, according to the 1990's constitution, a constitutional head of the country, his initial attempts were to destroy the elected bodies formed under the constitution and to weaken the main parties. He achieved great success when the parliament was dissolved on May 22, 2002 and Nepali Congress split in June 2002. It is said that it was due to the king's strong backing to the then Prime Minister Sher Bahadur Deuba that both the incidents became a success.

Having said that, what is argued is that the conspiracy against democracy was formally started by 22 May 2002, when the king, "on the recommendation of prime minister", dissolved the parliament. The next step against the democratization process was the postponement of the elections of local bodies, which had to be held by July 2002. As there was lack of constitutionally elected institutions at the local as well as at the central level, there was a political vacuum which helped king Gyanendra to interrupt the remaining democratic institutions. He dismissed the then Deuba government on 4 October 2002. The charge against the Deuba government was its incompetence in not holding the elections.

The move of the king to discharge the Deuba government gave birth to a new era of struggle. We can term it as the turning point from which Nepal shifted from two-party conflict - the mainstream vs. the rebellions - to three-party struggle between the Maoists, the monarchy backed by the security forces and the political parties. Arbitrary arrests, an increasing number of disappearances, violent activities, random searches all of which had a negative impact on the local communities. The daily killings reached from average 2.43 person per day before the king's take over to 6.26 (INSEC report 2005).

After dismissing the elected Prime Minister, the king maintained a distance with the major political parties which had more than 90 per cent seats in the dissolved parliaments and appointed two successive governments - the first under Lokendra Bahadur Chand (11 October, 2002), and the second under Surya Bahadur Thapa (4 June, 2003). Both of them were brought there as they had Panchayati background and were loyal to the monarchy. However, the king himself sacked both the governments on 30 May 2003 and 7 May 2004, respectively. The king charged the governments of being incapable of getting the support from the major political parties.

The tripartite conflict increased when major political parties announced their peaceful protest programs at the end of October 2002 against the king's move. On the one hand,   the violent conflict further worsened and human rights abuse increased during these days. The per day killing touched the ratio of 8.91 in August 2003, which was the highest during the year-long violent conflict witnessed by Nepal. On the other hand, the peaceful protest organized by parliamentary parties touched a new height when the civil society members, professional organizations, students' organizations, etc., were also involved in organizing several street protests against the 'autocratic' King with the demand for the restoration of democracy. At that time King Gyanendra attempted to get the political parties' support by the reappointment of Sher Bahadur Deuba as Prime Minister in 2 June 2004. Deuba tried to make an 'all-party' government as instructed by the king, but was able to get the support of the Communist Party of Nepal (CPN-UML)only, the second largest party which was part of the Five Parties Alliance (FPA) protesting against the king's move on the streets. Other major political parties, including the mainstream Nepali Congress (NC), decided not to join the government but to continue their protest on the streets for restoration of democracy. They termed the government as another conspiracy and the continuation of regressive action, and argued that the formation of the government was an alternative attempt to continue and to strengthen the king's autocratic regime.

The Deuba government was given the task of holding negotiations with the parties and the Maoist to settle the existing conflict. The government, as per the guidance, set mid-January 2005 as the deadline for the Maoist for the truce and negotiation. However, the Maoist declined Deuba's offer raising a question on the status of the government. The Maoist were inclined to negotiate with the king as they believed that the real power vested with the king. Here, some people raised the question about the intention of the Maoist; they doubted whether the Maoist actually wanted to accept the king's active role. One can have a debate on this issue also. However, the conclusion we can draw here is that all three attempts of the king to appoint puppet Prime Ministers and rule the country as *de facto* king failed when the political parties did not recognize the Prime Ministers as executive Prime Ministers as per the constitution. In fact, neither of the governments were able to convince the parliamentary political parties which were in peaceful protest against the king's October 4, 2002 move nor succeeded in ending/weaken the on-going Maoist Movement.

When the king Gyanendra attained only disappointment from all his attempts, and he was exposed more as violator of the 1990s constitutional provisions, he finally dismissed the Deuba government and declared a state of emergency in the country by a proclamation on 1 February 2005. It was the king's second dismissal of Deuba from the post of prime minister within 28 months. By the proclamation, the king declared that he would assume power for three years. He formed a Council of Ministers under his chairmanship. All the ministers appointed were supporters of the previous autocratic Panchayat system. He suspended all democratic rights and 'installed military rule' in the country. Immediately after this announcement, the army occupied the streets of Kathmandu; political leaders were put under house arrest or detention; media was strongly censored; telephone and Internet services were disconnected and the international airport was shut down. Fundamental rights, such as freedom of speech and assembly, were abrogated under the proclaimed state of emergency. However, the king defended himself by saying he was forced to take this step to defend multi-party democracy.

The king's move on February 1, 2005, again took a new shape of political polarization; the situation can be termed as king vs. all other people. The move not only affected the parliamentary parties, but also the civil society, professional organizations and the common people. Within 10 months of the king's direct rule (from February 1, 2005 to November 27, 2005), about 6,112 political activists and human rights defenders were arrested. At least 1,000 journalists and media personnel became jobless because of the restriction on broadcasting news from all the 47 FM radio stations. Thousands of political activists and human rights defenders were re-arrested by security forces and a total of 40 persons were restricted from leaving Kathmandu valley (INSEC 2005). Analyzing the severe situation of the country's democracy, all major political parties including those who were together with the king until February 1, 2005, assembled together, formed an alliance called the Seven Parties Alliance (SPA) and decided to begin a nation-wide protest against "the king's autocratic regime". The SPA was a new formation of the earlier mentioned Five Parties Alliance (FPA); Deuba headed Nepali Congress (democratic) and the United Left

Front were the new comers, and the UML had rejoined the alliance. When mainstream political parties showed their unity to go against the king's move, civil society, especially the lawyers, journalists, university teachers and students also gave a boost to their peaceful protest to restore the democratic system in the country. The SPA, after it got a positive response from civil society and other professional organizations, also announced a nationwide peaceful protest program calling it as *Janaandolan*. The joint movement commenced from May 22, 2005. After this, there were hardly any days when there was no protest rally and arrest until April 2006, though the number of the participants varied.

In between, the SPA had held several discussions with the Maoist when they were positive about the SPA's protest program. It should not be forgotten that there was a strong but internal debate in the Maoist party after the king's *coup d'état*; the topic of debate was whether the Maoist support the king to sideline the political parties. Initially, majority of the members of the Maoist party along with Prachanda were of the view to alienate the political parties and share the power under the king's regime. Baburam Bhattarai, his wife, Central Committee member Hisila Yami, and another Central Committee Member Dina Nath Sharma opposed the idea saying that it would be a suicidal decision. But the party had taken action against them. Reports say that Bhattarai was put under the Maoist's custody and the other two were suspended from party's membership[1].Later in April 2005, the Maoist corrected the decision by its Rolpa Plenum and decided to support the SPA and request them to organize a joint movement against the king's regime. There were several bilateral and multilateral meetings with the Maoist and other political parties. As a result, the parties accepted to go for the election of the Constituent Assembly (CA), and the Maoist decided to accept competitive democracy. The outcome of the discussion was disclosed through the 12-point agreement which was signed by both the parties only in November 2005. The main points of the agreement were to put forth a common front with a view to end the king's autocracy; to go for CA election; to allow SPA to mobilize the people in the rural area without hindrance; to return the confiscated property to the real owner, etc. Both the parties expressed that there was no alternative expect the peaceful Mass Movement to defeat the autocratic regime.

As the SPA and their cadres were the main sufferers of the Maoist movement, there was rivalry and suspicion in both sides especially at the cadre

---

1 Prachanda in a press statement issued on 12 April 2005 accepted that the party had taken action against Dr. Bhattarai. He, in several live interviews, argued that they had tacit understanding with the king.

level. Such antagonism in some ways started decreasing after the leadership signed a12-point agreement. Again, both the parties sat together in March 2006, and renewed their earlier commitments which helped reach an understanding of each other right from the grass roots level. The SPA announced a four-day general strike from April 6, 2005. The general strike was called at the time when the Maoist had already announced a nationwide program to block district headquarters and major highways. However, once the parties declared their general strike program and requested the Maoist to withdraw their announcement, the Maoist announced that they would support it and withdraw their unilateral action.

Actually, Kathmandu remained tense for many days prior to the formally announced dates of the general strike. Prohibition order against the peaceful protests, unlawful arrests, repression, etc., were like a continued phenomenon after the first joint protest of SPA started on May 22, 2005. The situation was more severe after January 2006 when people started protesting in opposition to the proposed Municipal Election. The government had issued a curfew order by April 4, 2006 to stop the people who were coming from outside the Kathmandu valley to take part in the peaceful street protest announced by the SPA. But such attempts of the royal regime did not stop the people from participating in the peaceful rally. Though the declared shutdown was only for four days, the general strike continued for 19 days and compelled the king to give up power. Millions of people from cities and the countryside of Nepal took part in the movement. The movement was totally peaceful although the king's regime tried to infiltrate its vigilantes in the movement with the motive of making the movement violent. Twenty-five people were killed who were later declared "martyrs"; 6,000 protestors were injured, fifteen lost their eyesight, sixteen received serious head injuries and 150 protestors in Kathmandu suffered broken arms and legs[2]. The government imposed "a shoot-at-sight 18-hour curfew" to diffuse the movement, but people defied the curfew and protested peacefully. It was because of patience of the SPA leaders who were very much committed to peaceful protests. They knew that if the movement took a violent mode, it would be difficult to get national and international support. When the SPA had publicly ruled out the violent nature of the movement and told that there will be "any formal relationship with the insurgents, unless and until the Maoist firmly renounce violence, put down their weapons, and commit to supporting the democratic process," India, the United States and other countries 'formally' welcomed the 12-point agreement which they said was "attempt by Nepal's political parties to

---

2 "House passes motion on probe commission", The Kathmandu Post, 5 May 2006.

convince the insurgents to rejoin the political mainstream"[3]. The SPA leaders did not care but dismissed the royal governments' threats to treat them like the Maoist terrorists.[4]

People from all walks of life participated in the movement. Not only the lawyers, journalists, doctors, poets, writers, teachers and other politically aware section of people, but also the generally apolitical people such as the laborers, farmers, rickshaw pullers, footpath traders, small hoteliers, etc., participated in the movement. Even taxi drivers and transport workers, normally the first to complain about a shutdown which affected their earnings, were universally supportive. The movement gained further momentum when government employees started participating; the first were employees of critical government corporations, such as the Nepal Telecommunications Corporation and Nepal Electricity Authority, and staff who shut down the national bank almost completely. Local administration officers in the districts stopped work; some palace-appointed regional and zonal administrators, as well as nominated District Development Committee chairmen, resigned in support of the *Janaandolan*. The families of security forces joined very public demonstration, as did retired soldiers and police officers. Security forces also distributed pamphlets in support of the movement in some places. Even senior civil servants in the Home Ministry went on strike to protest against the state violence for which they were theoretically responsible. The number of participants increased when the Maoist facilitated people from the villages to join the movement. Prior to the 12-point understanding, the Maoist used to bar people from taking part in activities announced by other political parties, especially the SPA.

Why did so many ordinary people join the movement? The answer was simple: they hoped the movement, if successful, would end the conflict which had adversely impacted their life for a decade. In rural areas, people were victimized by both the security forces and the Maoist during the "people's war"; people were forced to provide food and shelter to both the sides, but were then victimized by each side for helping their enemies. The security forces killed, raped, arrested, and tortured the villagers on the pretext of feeding and sheltering the Maoist, and the Maoist killed, extorted, kidnapped and compelled the people to leave their homes for the same charge. Villagers had lost their confidence to speak to strangers

---

3 "U.S. ambassador to Nepal, James F. Moriarty's statement to media in New Delhi", *American Embassy News Advisory*, Kathmandu, 17 November 2005; also see "US, India welcome new political development", *The Kathmandu Post,* 24 November 2005.

4 "Govt rejects constituent assembly; insists on holding election," *www.nepalnews.com,* 25 November 2005.

about polity and society due to fear created by both sides. On the other hand, people residing in the urban areas had relatively low impact from the Maoist conflict but they, especially transport workers, hoteliers and petty businessmen on the highway, had also faced hindrances due to the frequent and indefinite type of blockades, bandhs, extortion, coercion, etc., during the Maoist conflict.

But the moment the political parties came onto the streets after October 2002, there was no one who was not affected or disturbed by either of the movements; even those urban elites had to face traffic jams, inconvenience, etc., due to the frequent strikes, protest rallies etc., called by the SPA. As mentioned earlier, only on very few days the parliamentary political parties did not hold protest demonstrations, *dharnas,* general strikes, etc., in the urban area especially in Kathmandu and headquarters of the districts, between October 2002 and April 2006. People who were facing severe impact of the political conflict, spontaneously came out onto the street when they believed that the SPA and the Maoist reached in a 12-point agreement to bring peace and to get complete democracy in the country. During the movement, the people spoke out from the peaceful protest rally that they were ready to contribute more days to the movement if it would be able to end the entire conflict.

The second reason of the wide participation in the movement was the popular discontent caused by the repeated failure of the king's direct rule. In fact, the king's coup also helped to bring some positive outcomes to make Janaandolan-II a success, Some of which are:

- The kings' repressive actions against all political forces helped to understand the king's ultimate interest. The parties realised the importance of having a united front to fight not only for restoration of democracy in the country but also for their existence. The all-party meeting and the formation of SPA on May 8, 2005 was one of the outcomes of the king's coup. Otherwise, there would have been no unity but only competition to deal with the king to be in the power as they did earlier after the king's October move.

- The unity between the SPA and the Maoist is another outcome of the king's takeover. Earlier, there was strong rivalry between the parties and the Maoist as the main target of the Maoist was the local cadres of the parliamentary political parties. Parties and its leaders used to claim that the Maoist and the palace were in connivance to derail democracy. Maoist leaders also had accepted that they had a 'tacit understanding' with the king (Kantipur June 6, 2001; Nepal Samachar Patra, June 15, 2001; Singh 2003). But when the king took over the power, the Maoist must have realized the king's intention and decided, "to opt for competitive democracy" on August 2005 by its Party Plenum in Rolpa. When the Maoist came up with the decision, then only the 12-point agreement became possible which ignited the hope of ending the conflict and restoration of democracy in the country.

- The king's February 1, 2005 move helped people, mainly the elites, to realize the importance of freedom and democracy. Earlier they were quite critical and reluctant about democracy, political parties, etc. However, they knew the importance of freedom and democracy only after the king seized and censored all the means of communication, like telephone, mobile, print and electronic media, including movement of the people. Subsequently, they also directly and indirectly supported *Janaandolan*-II.

- Before February 1, 2005, the king used to condemn the political parties as being corrupt, self-centered, etc., which somehow triggered the people's frustration against the political parties. However, the charges not only became blunt but also acted as a setback to the king himself after he assumed power. People changed their negative mindset on political parties and its leaders when they found more notorious, corrupt culprit persons in the king's cabinet and advisory boards

Having said that, it can be argued that the success of the *Janaandolan* is in essence a victory of Nepali people at large, rather than purely of the party - or the Maoist. Here, it is appropriate right to quote some portions of the ICG report (2006) which rightly pointed out the pro-democracy movement as a victory for the Nepali people on four fronts. These are:-

- **Over the king.** Nepal witnessed changes in mood during the several weeks of protests and strikes in April but there had long been widespread discontent with the king and his direct rule. The mass defiance of curfews to march against the monarchy following the king's misjudged first offer on 21 April was a decisive popular verdict which – even in the face of the massed ranks of loyal security forces – left the king with no option but to surrender.

- **Over the parties.** People remained suspicious of the parties, both on the basis of their mixed record in government and their perceived willingness to do a deal with the king against the country's best interests. Nevertheless, most hoped sustained pressure would force the parties to provide representative political leadership in tune with public sentiment – an approach that has so far yielded concrete results.

- **Over the Maoist**. Maoist support, much as mainstream democrats are loath to admit it, was crucial to the movement's success. But people did not rally under the Maoist flag, even in rural areas where the insurgents had directly urged their participation. While most endorsed elements of the Maoist agenda, they did not heed calls for a revolutionary insurrection and sent a strong signal that people power is a constraint on the actions of the rebels as well as the palace and parties.

- **Over the international community**. Nepal is particularly exposed to external influence. Sandwiched between regional superpowers and long dependent on foreign aid, its leaders and people have often looked to outsiders at times of crisis. This time India, the U.S. and some European powers did help to create the environment for a democracy movement but were brushed off when they appeared to press for an unpopular solution to end the crisis (ICG report, 10 May 2006).

Talking of the vision of the *Janaandolan*-II for a future Nepal, one has to go through the reasons and causes which facilitated or somehow compelled the people to take part in the movement in large numbers. As discussed earlier, it was mainly due to two reasons; (1) the high hope for peace, democracy and prosperity in the country which came after the SPA and the Maoist signed the 12-point agreements for the purpose; (2) popular discontent caused by the repeated failure of the king's direct and indirect rules. If we go by the slogans raised on the streets during the *Janaandolan*, we cannot hide the people's aspiration to have a secular and federal republic with an equitable and inclusive democratic system in the country. Obviously, the election of the CA to write a new constitution was one of the prominent demands which emerged from the street protests through which people had a hope to write a suitable constitution for them. People, especially the marginalized communities, i.e., Dalits, Janajatis, women and those who were from deprived regions and religions had hopes of influencing the decision making process and compelling the concerned authority to make pro-people policies and programs if there was inclusive state structure.

Today, Nepal has already crossed almost 32 months after the success of *Janaandolan*-II. It has achieved an amazing social and political transformation during the period; it is no more a Hindu state now after the House Proclamation 2006 declared it as a secular state; it is no more the kingdom with any form of monarchy after the overwhelming majority of the first meeting of elected CA passed by the republican motion on May 28, 2008. By then Nepal had "entered into a new age" as the then Prime Minister Koirala rightly said while tabling the motion in the CA. Again, it became the first country in South Asia, and eighth country in the world, which assured at least 33 per cent representation of women at all levels of the state mechanism. The constitution also provisioned the reservation to the Dalits, Janajatis and Madhesis as per their proportional strength. Such progressive steps cannot be overlooked.

However, if we follow the implementation part, it is not so encouraging. Yes, there is 8.3 per cent representation of Dalits, 33.39 per cent of Janajatis and 34.09 per cent of Madhesis in the elected CA which is an amazing incremal over the past. But after observing the recent formation of the cabinet under the leadership of Prachanda, one can draw a conclusion that the parties have forgotten not only their earlier commitments but also the constitutional provision about the inclusive state. There is not even a single Dalit in the cabinet though Dalits comprise 15-20 per cent of the total population of Nepal; there are hardly 17 per cent women in the cabinet though the constitution secures 33 percent share for women in each and every structure. Talking about Janajatis' representation, there is a problem; no representation from Tamang community which is the second largest ethnic group with almost six per cent share of Nepal's population, and is considered as one of the most suppressed groups among the main ethnic groups in Nepal. If we analyze the background of those who are in the cabinet from the marginalized communities, it seems that they are also taken not on the basis of constitutional provision but on the basis of their 'merits', the past experience in the cabinet (Pyakurel 2008). Both the coalition partners of the present government remember the meaning of inclusive representation before sending their representatives in the cabinet. Again, if we follow the newly formulated team of the National Planning Commission and other political appointments, one finds it more ridiculous as it gives the best example of nepotism and approach rather than the respect of the concept of inclusion of the deprived community.

Observing the realities, all the marginalized communities are heavily critical about the government. They term it as a real betrayal for the Dalits, women, Janajatis and regional and religious minorities. It seems that they were hopeful that the Maoist may not do so. The reason behind the hopes was due to the fact that the Maoist became the single largest party by the Constituent Assembly for which, despite coercion and intimidation, marginalized communities also contributed a lot; Dalits, Janajatis and regional minorities were in the forefront during the Maoists' "people's war" as they were dreaming of liberation or a better life under the Maoist leadership. It was the Maoist who divided Nepal into 11 autonomous states and included some agenda to radicalize the marginalized section of the society.

Talking about the constitution making process, it seems that the parties have not taken it seriously. Though the CA has already completed its seven months, it spent the whole time in finalizing its rules and procedures. Before going into the debate of the new constitution, political parties have to settle many controversial issues like the integration and rehabilitation of the Maoists: People's Liberation Army, issue of reinstating the displaced civilians in their homes; issue to return all land, houses and property seized unjustly, etc. But none of the major political parties are taking initiatives to move these issues forward. Rather, they are now busy in blaming politics though the situation indicates that no one is in a position to proceed further unless there is all-party unity in the CA. However, even allies of the coalition government have their own but different views regarding the army, federal setup, etc. They promised to have a federal setup along with the restructured mechanism in the new constitution but the debate is it yet to be started. Even a commission to study the probable federal setup has yet to be announced despite the fact that it is one of the constitutional provisions. On the other hand, the Maoist party seems more disturbed from its internal conflict whether or not to go in for People's Republic.

Again, the Maoist could not control its cadres' involvement in the killing, extortion, coercion, etc., even after it is leading the government. Apart from this, the Young Communist League cadres which have been involved in various controversial activities, and who have been staying in commune, have not been allowed to go back home. Observing various activities of the Maoist in the rural areas, M.K. Nepal, a senior leader of the UML, which is the coalition partner of the government, spoke out that 'parallel administration by Maoist was still continuing' (see http://www. nepalnews.com/archive/2008/nov/nov14/news02.php).

Another sad part is that there is not even a talk or inkling about an alternative or relatively better development model than the World Bank, IMF accelerated development model. All parties including the Maoist are very much interested in having foreign direct investment for operating mega projects and big dams instead of having small and medium projects for sustainability. For months after being in the government, the Maoist leaders Prachanda and Dr. Baburam Bhattarai have been making it clear to business leaders and foreign governments that a Maoist-led government would guarantee private property and welcome foreign investment. In his first live TV speech on August 23, 2008 Prachanda pledged: "We will work to bring about a modern industrial economy for which the private-public partnership model will be followed..."

Recently, Finance Minister and the Maoist ideologue Dr. Bhattarai was pleading with the WB and IMF for more financial assistance. In a live interview with BBC Nepali Sewa, he said, "You cannot believe what kind of good relationship we have with the World Bank and IMF". Those efforts of the Maoist were to have more financial assistance from World Bank and IMF as they have declared their intention of turning Nepal into a "Singapore"—in other words, a regional investment hub and cheap labour platform. They also claimed that their government would deliver 20 per cent annual growth and US$3,000 per capita income by 2020. But it is witnessed from the experiences that such a World Bank and IMF model of growth does not necessarily help in the upliftment of the marginalized community; rather, it decrease the disparity of the rich and poor.

In conclusion, though Nepal witnessed a historical political transformation, there are still challenges ahead before ending the on-going political transition by drafting a new constitution. The post-election government led by Prachanda is not very old but it has been facing remarkable criticism from their cadres, sympathizers and frontier organizations today. The women wing of the Maoist party decided not to join the cabinet with state minister portfolio; Dalits are preparing to protest against their exclusion in the cabinet; Janajatis are also in a mood to have an agitation against the narrow natured and non-representative cabinet. It is due to this fact that the deliberation part from the government is very weak. It seems that the Maoists leadership which is in the government somehow sinks into the nepotism and personal interest. If so, they can neither deliver something good to the people, nor have the morale to share their difficulties with cadres. In this situation, a section of the marginalized groups which supported the Maoist, will again get frustrated. As a result, there is a possibility to form another morcha to fight against the state, which is totally against the spirit of the *Janaandolan*-II.

References

Adhikari, I. (2003), "Nepal: The Maoists War and Prospect of Peace", *Agni* (Delhi), Vol. 6 (4) January-April ICG report, May 10, 2006.

Baral Lok Raj (ed.). (2006) Nepal: *Facets of the Maoists Insurgency*, New Delhi: Adroit Publishers.

ICG Report (2006), "Nepal: From People Power to Peace? Asia Report No. 115 International Crisis Group: Brussels and Kathmandu, May 10.

Kantipur, June 6, 2001.

Nepal Samachar Patra, June 15, 2001.

Pyakurel, Uddhab (2005), 2046 *Ko Paribartan ra Nyayapalika* (1990 Change and Judiciary), Kathmandu: Nepal Center for Contemporary Studies.

--------(2007), *Maoists Movement in Nepal: A sociological Perspective*, New Delhi: Adroit Publishers.

---------(2006), "*Raya Ko Punarsamrachana Ra Pahichan Ko Prasna* (Restructuring of the State and the Question of Identity)" *Kantipur*, 16 November.

---------(2008), *Samabesi Dristhi ma Dahal Mantriparisad* (Dahal Cabinet: From the Eye of the Concept of Inclusion), *Kantipur*, September 10.

Singh, M.B. (2003) "The Royal Palace Massacre and the Maoists' Pro-King Line" in Arjun Karki and **Devid** Seddon (eds.), *The People's War in Nepal: Left Perspectives*, New Delhi: Adroit Publishers.

Used web links:

www.ekantipur.com
www.nepalnews.com
www.mysansar.com

Chapter X

Internal Conflict in Nepal after the Comprehensive Peace Agreement (CPA)

Indra Adhikari and Uddhab Pyakurel

Conflict is always a part of human life and is as ancient as human history itself. It can be seen as an essential aspect of social and political life of human beings, as it occurs within human relationship. In fact, conflict is an integral part of any society, from marriage to inter-state war. Since society is dynamic and has been transforming from a simple to a much complex direction, the nature of conflict also has been following the similar pattern of being more complex and complicated day-by-day. Everybody is aware of the fast moving global situation today in which the whole world system is in structural crisis and confronted by an age of transition.[1] In this situation, traditional states, which are formed on the basis of legitimate political forces, have been struggling to maintain their status quo. Contrary to this, the various deprived sections of the society, are struggling not only for their access to power and control over resources, but also their right to live with dignity and respect. Indeed, such traditional states mark a democratic deficit[2]. That is why, conflict is defined as "a struggle over values and claims to scarce status, power and resources in which the aims of the opponents are to neutralize, injure or eliminate their rivals"[3].

Conflict, as a part of human life, always brings a change—either positive or negative-in society. It is always neither undesirable nor destructive; rather it brings both the constructive and destructive results.

---

1 Immanuel Wallerstein. "New Revolts against the Systems," *New Left Review*, Vol. 18, November-December 2002. p. 37.

2 David E. Apter. Democracy, Violence and Emancipatory Movements: Notes for a Theory of Inversionary Discourse. Discussion Paper, No. 44, May 1999 p.38

3 Lewis Coser. *The Functions of Social Conflicts.* New York: The Free Press, 1964. p. 7.

Nepal's Maoist insurgency, which was almost a decade long conflict in the country, can be taken as an example that has brought positive changes also in the Nepali society. But, on the other hand, it has helped to expand the culture of intimidation and popularized the violent means of struggle in the country. It has more effectively promoted the anti-systemic ways rather than the systemic one using peaceful means, while opposing the existing socio-political, economic and legal system of the state or demanding for change. These are the major negative trends established by the Maoist insurgency.

Several studies show that the main contributors for boosting for the growth of conflicts are structural, political, socio-economic, and cultural perpetual factors[4]. Within the structural factor, there are three major components such as weak states; inter-state security concerns and ethnic geography. According to Brown, a weak state is one which lacks political legitimacy, politically sensible borders, and strong political institutions capable of exercising control over its territory, faces a vicious circle of crises to not only tackle but also resolve the conflict. The trend of weakening of the state structure often leads to the eruption of violent political conflicts. A weak state lacks the capacity to collect adequate tax revenue that helped undertake a self-sufficient state building project with required and justified distribution. Thus, social groups develop pre-national political solidarity and tend to be more able to assert themselves politically by claiming more power and autonomy to a higher extent like rights to self-determination. In addition, some powerful business and political groups develop an interest in the economy of violence through arms deals, perpetuation of illegitimate power circles or other strategies that fend off efforts towards reconciliation and peace process. A weak state may hardly deal with them. It can neither ensure the security of a particular individual nor groups. But all these groups affected and benefited from the conflict must then seek their own security[5]. The situation helps in further weakening the already weak state in the public eyes that leads hopelessness, insecurity and terror in the society. Encounter between political groups, while they try to be defensive, is the characteristic of conflict. The problem is that the political group within the system always counters the rival group by using the security agencies. Such a situation obviously creates a threat to the security of others[6], resulting in widespread violence in the society, if

---

4 Michael E. Brown (ed.) *The International Dimensions of Internal Conflict.* Cambridge: The MIT Press, 1996

5 *Ibid.*

6 Andreas Wimmer and Conrad Schetter. *State Formation: First Recommendation for*

the elites in government do not try to manage it responsibly and amicably in time.

What is CPA?

CPA is the agreement signed on January 6, 2007 by the Interim Government formed by the Seven Party Alliance (SPA) and the then CPN (Maoist) which has now been renamed and become the United Communist Party of Nepal-Maoist (UCPN-Maoist). It not only declared the "End of conflict"[7] for "giving permanency to the ongoing ceasefire between both the parties—Government of Nepal and the UCPN-Maoist"[8]— but directed senior leaders of the parties to be sincere in "the main policy for long-term peace"[9] as decided in the earlier meetings. It is in fact an output of the several other important efforts made by the SPA and the UCPN-Maoist in different periods of time and contexts, since its preamble acknowledges many of the previous agreements: 12-Point understanding signed on 22 November 2005; 25-Point Code of Conduct agreed on 25 May 2006; 8-Point agreement signed on 16 June 2006; others formal-informal consensuses reached between the SPA led Interim Government of Nepal and the UCPN-Maoist; and the letter sent to the United Nations by both the sides with the similar viewpoints after the successful Mass Movement in 2006[10]. The CPA along with the ongoing peace process of Nepal is a fully indigenous process as there is no formal national/international mediator. It is, as mentioned before, an output of the several confidence building measures that gave the gate pass to the UCPN-Maoist to enter into the mainstream politics. The process of mainstreaming the UCPN-Maoist was initiated and formalized by allowing its members in the reinstated Parliament in 2006 and Interim Government in 2007. The treatment of the state and society to the UCPN-Maoist as to other parliamentarian political parties helped them assimilate with and adopt the culture of the multiparty democracy. It created a well-matured ground for making the interim constitution as per the spirit the historical *Jana Andolan* 2006.

"Declaring the beginning of the new chapter of peaceful collaboration

---

Reconstruction and Peace-Making in Afghanistan, No. 45. Bonn April, 2002.

7 Article 6 "End of Conflict", Comprehensive Peace Accord held between the Government of Nepal and CPN(Maoists), 22 November 2006 as published in Uddhab P. Pyakurel, *Maoists Movement in Nepal: A Sociological Perspective*, New Delhi: Adroit Publishers 2007, p. 184.

8 Article 6.1, *Ibid.*

9 Article 6.2, *Ibid.*

10 Preamble of CPA, Ibid, p.175.

between the parties" the CPA initiates for "forward-looking political resolution", and commands both the parties to go through the spirit of earlier consensuses by internalizing and respecting the respective issues of either side. It orders the UCPN-Maoist to reiterate their commitment "towards democratic value accepting competitive multiparty democratic system of governance, civil liberty, fundamental rights, human rights, full press freedom and concept of rule of law"[11]. It, on the other hand, obliges the SPA "to ensure the sovereignty of people through election of Constituent Assembly (CA), restructuring of the state and socio-economic and cultural transformations"[12]. That is why the CPA is a document that initiates radicalizing the mainstream political parties, and mainstreaming the UCPN-Maoist bringing it in the competitive party politics through a peaceful manner. In fact, the spirit of 12-point understanding between the UCPN-Maoist and the SPA followed by other agreements was for establishing "absolute democracy"[13] in the country. The full-fledged democracy was possible only after "ending autocratic monarchy"[14] and also assuring equality and justice to the people. Thus, the concept of the federal structure of the state was assured by amending the Interim Constitution and the notion of inclusive and participatory democracy was accepted as a major requirement for leading socio-political transformation to a greater extent.

Thus, the peaceful abolition of the 240-year old institution of monarchy and establishment of the Democratic Federal Republic has been seen as the biggest achievement of the Jana Andolan-II. Also, the representation of marginalized communities such as Dalits, Adivasis, Madhesis, women and other minorities in the elected Constituent Assembly (CA) has given a remarkable positive message to the world. The strength distributed in the CA is more than 33% by women, 38% by Janajatis, 33% by Madhesis, and 8% by Dalits, etc. The three major marginalized groups,

---

11 Ibid, and Points 4 of the 12-Point Understanding between the SPA and the Maoists, 22 November 2005.

12 Premble of CPA as published in Uddhab P. Pyakurel, *Maoists Movement in Nepal: A Sociological Perspective*, New Delhi: Adroit Publishers 2007, p.184; Point 3 of 12 Points Understanding between the SPA and the Maoists, 22 November 2005

13 However, the phrase was defined on the basis of their (the SPA and the Maoist) respective understandings and policies. On the one hand, it was defined by SPA as the end of the autocratic nature of monarchy bringing it under the constitution along with the establishment of other universal principles of democracy, and on the other, the Maoist defined it as removal of the institution of monarchy and establishment of republic country, Nepal.

14 Point 1 of 12-Point Understanding between the SPA and the Maoists, 22 November 2005.

irrespective of their party position, have deserved the required critical masses in the CA now. Without their consent, no major decision, while writing the constitution, is possible[15].

Task Opened up by CPA

The CPA talks about the process of democratization of Nepal Army defining it as to bring the NA under the civilian control and the process of professionalization of the Maoist combatants. The restructure of the state is another issue that makes the system more inclusive (by allowing more and more opportunities to the people from the marginalized groups based on caste, ethnicity, gender, region, religion, etc.). The main focus of the CPA is to transform the UCPN-Maoist from an insurgent group into a 'civilian political party'. Thus, it orders the UCPN-Maoist to follow a couple of the measures i.e., to return the property confiscated during the insurgency to the owner; to allow other political parties for political campaign in the country in general, and in the UCPN-Maoist controlled villages in particular. Similarly, the High Level Especial Committee for Army Integration, Truth and Reconciliation Commission, Commission for the Investigation of Disappeared People, State Restructuring Commission, etc., for making federal structure were other important tasks opened up by the CPA. Furthermore,, the election of CA for the making of a new constitution was the major task.. Because at that particular time, the state moves from the divided past to a shared future and requires the capability and feasibility not only to create a just order, but to perform its basic state functions also. That must be the case of provisioning the State Reconciliation Commission in the Interim Constitution of Nepal 2007. But it is yet to be materialized by the governments.

The Agreement on Monitoring of Management of Arms and Armies reached between the Government of Nepal and the UCPN-Maoist on 28 November 2006, is one of the major provisions under the CPA, since the management of Maoist combatants and their arms are most important and difficult issues. To facilitate the work of the arms and armies management, the United Nations Mission in Nepal (UNMIN) was established on January 23, 2007 on the request of the Interim Government and the UCPN Maoist in accordance with the guidance of the CPA. The UNMIN has started working in Nepal as per the United Nations Security Council Resolution number 1740[16] having a limited role, i.e., "monitoring and supervising the

---

15 The constitution says that every decision should be taken either by the consensus or by two-third majority of the Assembly.

16 For more on the UNMIN, log in www.unmin.org.np

peace process".[17] The role is basically to monitor whether the respective parties confine their activities in accordance with the agreements reached between the parties. In fact, the UNMIN has no right of taking the decisive role for the peace process but it can facilitate the respective parties to follow and implement the agreements in letter and spirit. The management process of the combatants of the UCPN-Maoist began on 8 January after a Joint Monitoring Coordination Committee (JMCC) was formed[18] and the UNMIN announced the first result of the verification of Maoist combatants on 27 December 2007[19].

The structure, role and responsibilities of the Army Integration Special Committee, which has been formed "in order to inspect, integrate and rehabilitate the Maoist combatants",[20] are neither effective nor authorized to independently work as required. It was formed for technical purposes and has nothing to do unless there is a political consensus among the major political parties in the CA. The issue of management of Maoist combatants was politicized to that extent that stopped the whole peace and the constitution writing process. The advocacy and counter-advocacy on the issue of the Maoist combatant's management has made the process more complicated. The UCPN-Maoist's demand to make a "national army" by integrating all its combatants in NA, and the position of some politicians along with few in-service and ex-service Nepal Army personnel about none of the Maoist combatants' entry into the Nepal Army have not only helped get the peace process derailed but also helped in politicizing the Nepal Army. It has been reported that both the Nepal army and the Maoist combatants could not resolve their past antagonism after the CPA was singed. But doubt and distrust between the old rebellion groups continued against each other even after the UCPN-Maoist became part and parcel of the government. Ram Bahadur Thapa, the then Defence Minister after the CA election mentioned, referring the Maoist party's

---

17 Letter to the UN by the Government of Nepal, Agreement of the UN with Government of Nepal and the Maoists.

18 Accordingly, the UNMIN recruited a total of 126 monitors including 15 UN monitors, 111 Gurkha ex-servicemen who had served in the Indian and British Armies for the management and verification of the Maoist cantonments and weapons. The monitors were kept under the Joint Monitoring and Coordinating Committee (JMCC) of the Agreement on Management and the Monitoring of Arms and Armies that was constituted by three members representing UNMIN, ex-PLA and NA.

19 The type of weapons registered so far are 91 mortars (of which 55 were locally made), 61 machine guns, 2,403 rifles, 61 automatic weapons, 9 sub-automatic guns, 114 side arms, 212 shot guns, 253 miscellaneous and 244 home-made weapons.

20 Article 4.4, *Comprehensive Peace Accord* held between the Government of Nepal and CPN(Maoists), 22 November 2006.

intelligence report, that the topmost officers of the NA have been mobilized by foreign power[21]. Prime Minister Pushpa Kamal Dahal took an oath for the post in the security arrangement of the Maoist combatants, as it was not recognized as a state security force. The expression of the Minister of Defence and attitudes of PM on NA proved that the Maoist party and its government could rely on neither the information nor security guarding of the NA. The attitude of Maoist leaders in government to promote their own combatants and party intelligence in guarding and spying not only undermine psychologically the institutional role and responsibility of NA, but also humiliate its personnel at individual level. Also, the UNMIN failed to give a right track to the peace process; it was neither able to stop new recruitment of the NA personnel nor could it detach the Maoist combatants from its party rank and file. The mistrust and controversy began while 7,000-8,000 original Maoist combatants[22] reached 30,852 during the entry into the cantonments, and the numbers of Maoist combatants and their register weapons did not match[23]. The JMCC of the UNMIN also declared ineligible some thousands of them as "new recruits" that reduced the strength of the Maoist combatants in cantonments up to 19,603—15,757 men and 3,846 women. The situation further weakened the peace process while the debate was initiated about how to manage the Maoist combatants, how many are genuine combatants and "eligible for possible integration in the security agencies fulfilling standers norm,"[24] and how the rest should be rehabilitated in the society.

The UCPN-Maoist has not been ready to manage its combatants even after the latter were kept in the cantonments. If one follows Kharipati decision of the UCPN-Maoist which came just after the party led the government, there were mainly two strategies of the UCPN-Maoist regarding the management of its combatants; the first one was to try to integrate all verified combatants into the NA, along with the senior combatants into the higher rank of NA so that the NA as an institution will

---

21 Indra Adhikari, *Chisido Sena-Sarkar Sambandha* (Cooling Civil-Military Relation), *Kantipur*, February 1, 2009.

22 Highly controversial tape record of Prachanda's indoctrination programme in the Shaktikhor Cantonment, Chitwan.

23 30,852 PLA members registered at the seven main cantonment sites and 21 satellite cantonment sites. The number includes "522 weapons for perimeter security and 96 weapons registered outside of cantonments" *The Rising Nepal*, 10 March 2007, as given in *Nepal Update*, January-April, 2007, p. 91. *The Rising Nepal*, 10 March 2007, as given in *Nepal Update*, January-April, 2007, p. 91.

24 Agreement on Management and the Monitoring of Arms and Armies reached between the Government of Nepal and the UCPN (Maoist), 28 November 2006.

be either influenced or weakened through infiltration and division. The second was to keep them in the cantonment for long if the UCPN-Maoist could not success in integrating all of them into the NA. By prolonging the life of the temporary cantonment with its combatants, the UCPN-Maoist wanted to benefit financially and politically, as it has been receiving a huge amount of money from the cantonments,[25] and it has been used as a camp for training the people and hiding criminals[26]. The Central Committee of the UCPN-Maoist decided on July 2, 2010 that even if total integration into NA is not possible, its combatants would be under an institution or in a group. It seems that the ultimate motto of the UCPN-Maoist is to keep its combatants under its command forever, if not at least till the next election, so that the psychological strength of its leadership and bargaining capacity of the party remain high.

Prohibited Actions According to the CPA

The agreement prohibits mainly: (1) to hold, carry and display arms, use of violence and armies for creating terror and fear; (2) to intimidate and use any type of violence against people—kidnap, murder, and torture to hurt or render mental pressure against any individual; (3) to recruit additional armed personnel or conduct military activities; (4) to collect cash or goods and services or levy against one's wishes and against the existing law; (5) to restrict free movement of people and goods; (6) to spy on military activities of either sides; (7) to publicize for or against any side and support or protest against any side, (8) damaging and seizing public/private/governmental and non-governmental property, etc. As the CPA was a detailed and comprehensive agreement, it was categorical even in each and every small issue such as leave of the Maoist combatants put inside the cantonment. It has a provision that no more than 12 per cent of the total retained force of the Maoist combatants can be on leave under the deferent cause-medical referrals, visiting families—of a given cantonment.

But in practice, nothing was implemented in a serious manner. In fact, only five out of the nine restricted activities under the CPA, and only seven out of 19 clauses under the Agreement on Monitoring of Management of Arms and Armies reached between the Government and the UCPN-Maoist on 28 November 2006 were implemented by the Maoists; it was the UCPN-Maoist which started recruiting youths to increase the number of the Maoist combatants in cantonments just after it signed the CPA. The

---

25 See Uddhab Pyakurel (2008) "Sociology of the Maoists' Cantonment," *Kantipur*, 23, January 2008.

26 Interview of Subodh Pyakurel on Kantipur TV on June 26, 2010.

UCPN-Maoist called the youth openly by establishing a "recruiting center", cantoned the 'new recruits.' Such recruitment camps were lunched by hanging the banner at many of the district headquarters, with the assurance of a good salary (with a promise of Rs. 7,000 salary per month) and job guarantee in Nepal Army.[27] Then, young students were not only running away from the houses and schools catching the golden opportunity to join the Maoist combatants. And, many of the youths from villages were abducted by the UCPN-Maoist for the purpose..[28] Children-including some as young as 12 years-were taken away from their families to take part in the Maoist combatants and militia activities…[.and] some of them have received military training with weapons since the ceasefire was declared. Even if internationally recognized organizations such as the Office of the High Commissioner for Human Rights (OHCHR) and UNMIN[29] raised question by reporting the similar reports, neither the then government nor the UCPN-Maoist initiated any measure to stop the process. Rather, the UCPN-Maoists' supremo Prachanda, with pride boosted how he and his party fooled domestic counterparts as well as international community saying that his party successfully increased the number of its combatants from 7-8 thousand to 32,250 through new recruitment.[30] Also, the UCPN-Maoist continued its activities of extortion, intimidation, abductions, ill-treatment, violation of rights of internally displaced people[31] and even

---

27 INSEC Online report, "Maoists Running Recruitment Camps," www.inseconline.org browsed on September 3, 2006

28 It has been proved that the seven children of Bhaludhunga Secondary School of Bishnu Paduka School were, in fact, abducted on September 6, 2006 and they were given military training in Motipur VDC of Morang after conscripting them in Ratna Sakunta Brigade Second Battalion. For details, see "Maoists Recruiting Children against Code of Conduct", www.inseconline.org, September 19, 2006. It is reported that some recruitments are voluntary where those who were not physically fit to get jobs in Nepal army and police force, join the PLA with the hope of the merger of the PLA and Nepal Army soon.

29 United Mission in Nepal Press Conference on 8 April, 2008, Kathmandu available at http://www.unmin.org.np/?d=media&p=press accessed by the author on July 6, 2010; see also UNMIN Election Report No 3, 6 April 2008 available at http://www.unmin.org. np/downloads/publications/2008-04-06-UNMIN.Election.Report.3.ENG.pdf accessed by the author on July 6, 2010.

30 The video Tape which was his one and a half hour loan address to the Maoist combatants at Shaktikhor Cantonment. In the address he urged his caders to remain calm till they capture power and establish "people's Republic" as envisaged by Mao and Lenin. Some excerpts of the video is available at http://www.google.com/search?q=Prachanda+Shakt ikhor+Video&hl=en&client=gmail&sa=X&rls=gm&prmd=v&source=univ&tbs=vid:1 &tbo=u&ei=0f8xTPGrG4SYrAfEvrDHBA&oi=video_result_group&ct=title&resnum =1&ved=0CB0QqwQwAA, accessed by the author on July 5, 2010.

31 Of these, most of the deaths in the Maoists custody were because of "extreme beatings and torture" by them after abduction (See "Maoists abduct, kill teenager", *The Kathmandu*

killings after the CPA too, though the numbers of such activities are considerably low. They continued their so-called parallel governments till the completion of CA election, and tried to stop political activities of other political parties till today. According to the OHCHR report[32], the rebels were responsible for the death of at least 16 civilian, mostly innocent villagers and for abduction of at least 184 individuals since the ceasefire declaration of April 26. Though UCPN-Maoist leadership also issued a directive to end human rights abuses in September 2, 2006, no evidence has been found which assures the earlier commitment by the UCPN-Maoist leadership. Here, the question of accountability can be raised before the UCPN-Maoist leadership.

On the other hand, neither the Truth and Reconciliation Commission[33],

---

Post, September 16, 2006. The Maoists issued a statement claiming that the boy died after "accidentally falling off a cliff). Cases of abduction, intimidation, beating of people and extortion are rising by the day (Ameet Dhakal, "Life beyond Communism", *The Kathmandu Post*, September 1, 2006). It was reported that many industries were closed due to Maoist intimidation and "the majority of Nepali entrepreneurs were on the verge of being displaced due to the Maoists' extortions" (See "FNCCI warns of protests if Maoist extortion continues," www.ekantipur.com September 17, 2006) during the ceasefire. Hotels in Nepal faced the threat of closure due to extortion drives and "illogical demands" by the Maoists (See "Nepal: Maoist threats forcing closure of hotels," *The Indian Express*, September 5, 2006). Maoists abducted youth as young as 13 years and have not spared even students studying in grade seven (For details, see "Maoists abduct 3 minors in Bardiya"*Kantipur*, July 11, 2006; "Maoists abduct four, thrash one", *Kantipur*, August 5, 2006; "Maoists keep up abductions, extortion" *Kantipur*, August 18, 2006; "Maoists continue abductions, intimidation, extortions", *The Kathmandu post*, August 2, 200). They detained 15-year-old youngman to 60-year-old man in their "labor detention camp" (see http://www.kantipuronline.com/kolnews.php?&nid=83978).

32   The OHCHR released the previous report on June 27, 2006 which also stated that the rebels were responsible for at least nine deaths since the ceasefire declaration where the UCPN-Maoist leadership expressed the commitment to end such atrocities.

33   Nepali democracy faced ups and downs in the past because the guilty were spared in the name of "reconciliation" after each and every successful movement. The regressive forces had made a comeback and hatched a conspiracy against the democratic system due to failure of the then government to punish the guilty proved in the Mallik Commission Report in 1990. Again, it got repeated in the country as the recommendation of Raymajhi Commission report 2006 got ignored and was not implemented. That was one of the causes of creating mistrust and dissatisfaction over the new government formed right after the successful Janaandolan II. Unnecessary delay in implementing the declaration of the House of Representatives which made very radical announcements as per the mandate of the movement, was another shortcoming of the government. Any excellent declaration having no implementation has no meaning and does not support in the process strengthening and deepening democracy. The Maoists, who played a major role on their part in derailing the democratization process in Nepal from the very beginning, have continued killings, extortion, abductions and recruitment activities after they declared truce and signed various agreements, including the 25-Point Code of Conduct.

nor the Commission for Investigating the Displaced People was formed to manage the peace process and address the victims during the conflict. So, interest of conflict between the rival forces resumed again while the UCPN-Maoist succeeded in making total combatants upto 32,250 without any disturbance of the then government. Later, Nepal Army also initiated the new recruitment[34] process of soldiers advertising on a government owned national daily--Gorkhapatra on November 2, 2008.

Major Movements after the CPA

In fact, the CPA becomes a turning point for various political/social movements in Nepal. The restoration of democratic system after the successful Jana Andolan-II was a context which provided a background for enhancing their movements. Nationwide Janajati Movement had the demands of secular state status and ethnicity based autonomous federal structures. Dalit groups were launching a movement to end caste-based discrimination. Madhes Movement of August 2007 led by the MJF had the demand to declare Nepal as a federal democratic republic and full proportional representation system for the election of CA. Chure Bhawar movement (August-October, 2007) was known as anti-Madhes, because it had opposed the demand of Madhes Movement II led by United Democratic Madhesi Front from December 2007 to February 2008 to declare autonomous 'One Madhes, One Pradesh' and to amend the Election Commission Act in increasing the relaxation for inclusive candidacy (from 20 per cent to 30 per cent). Similarly, the Tharu Movement from March 2-14, 2009 demanded the government to withdrawal its ordinance, which had defined the identity of all communities residing in the flat-land as Madhesi. It had also demanded to replace the terminology "Madhes" by "Tarai-Madhes," and recognize the Tharu as a separate ethnic identity in Madhes and form a federal state for Tharus with their prior-rights on the local natural resources: water resource, jungle and land (*Jal, Jangle ra Jamin*) available in their particular territory. Federal Limbuwan Movement is also an ethnic movement, especially launched in nine districts of the Eastern hills. Their main demand is to form an Autonomous Limbuwan State. These were the major social/political movements witnessed after the CPA was signed and most of these movements have demanded proportional share in each and every government body. The government

---

34 According to the provision of CPA, the Maoists combatant would be managed within six months of CA. When it became impossible, the then government was convinced that the professionalism of the NA should not be captive because of the delay of the management of the Maoist combatants. Then, the process of new recruitment on the vacant posts in technical area of the NA was initiated to fulfil the posts. The recruitment was not additional but fulfilment of the vacancy within the existing strength.

of Nepal tried to be engaged with these movement groups and signed the following agreements to address the problem of respective groups. The major Agreements signed by the Government after CPA are given below:

- With Janajatis (August 7, 2007)

- With Madhesi Janadhikar Forum (August 30, 2007)

- With Chure Bhawar Pradesh Ekta Samaj (September 13, 2007)

- With National Badi (a hill Dalits group) Rights Struggle Committee (October 15, 2007)

- With United Democratic Madhesi Front (February 28, 2008)

- With Federal Republican National Front (March 2, 2008)

- With Federal Limbuwan State Council (March 19, 2008)

Internal Conflict in Nepal Today

Nepal faces multiple conflicts today. However, focus of this section is on such conflicts which are violent in nature. It is reported that some 69 semi-armed groups are active in Nepal (till March 2009) and most of these have mushroomed particularly after the CPA. However, the government of Nepal has recorded that there are 109 armed, semi-armed, and criminal groups intensifying their activities in Nepal and most of these are active in Tarai-Madhes. The number has been increasing day-by-day. Samyukta Jatiya Morcha is the newest organization which was identified for the first time on June 1, 2010 after it took responsibility in planting a bomb in Sindhupalchock district. It had been creating terror in the hilly districts, especially in Kathmandu Valley and its neighboring places and now it is broadening its area of influence and nature of work. Apart from the new one, the following is the list of some of the major armed and criminal groups which are active in recent days in Nepal. It is said that most of the groups have their own military wing and their strength varies from 150 to 2000 in number.

Table 1: Armed/Semi-Armed Forces Born After Peace Accord
(November 22, 2006 – June 30, 2009)

1	Akhil Tarai Mukti Morcha	40	Nepal Mukti Morcha
2	Bahun Chhetri Newar Saamuha	41	OBC Regiment

3	CPN [Maoist (United Bidrohi Morcha)]	42	Nepal Rakshya Dal
4	Chure Bhawar Shanti Sena	43	PalloKirat Limbuwan Rastriya Monch
5	Deshbhakta Army Nepal	44	Paribartan Nepal
6	Gorkha Mukti Morcha	45	Rajan Mukti Samuha
7	Gorkhaland Mukti Sena (Tista Kangada)	46	Rajdhani Army
8	Gorkha-Line Mukti Sena Samaj	47	Ranabir Sena
9	Janabadi Ganatantrik Tarai Mukti Morcha	48	Rastriya Army
10	Jana Samrakshan Sena	49	Rastriya Army Nepal
11	Janabadi Kirant Workers Party	50	Rastriya Samanantar Jwala Mukhi
12	Janatantrik Tarai Mukti Morcha (Goit)	51	Revolutionary Left Wing (National Red Guard)
13	Janatantrik Tarai Mukti Morcha (Himmat Singh)	52	Samyukta Janatantrik Tarai Mukti Morcha
14	Janatantrik Tarai Mukti Morcha (Jwala Singh)	53	Samyukta Mukti Morcha (Ulfa)
15	Janatantrik Tarai Mukti Morcha (Prithvi Samuha)	54	Saghia Limbuwan Rajya Parishad (Lawoti)
16	Janatantrik Tarai Mukti Morcha (Visfot Singh)	55	Sanghia Limbuwan Rajya Parishad (Palung)
17	Karebian Dog	56	Sanghia Limbuwan Rajya Parishad (Lingen)
18	Khambuwan Rastriya Morch	57	Sanghia Lontantric Rastriya Morcha
19	Janatantrik Party Nepal	58	Save the National Army Nepal
20	Kirant Janabadi Workers' Party	59	Shahi Mukti Morcha
21	Liberation Tigers of Tarai Elam	60	Shantikalagi Tarai Kranti
22	Limbuwan Democratic Volunteers Force	61	Shiva Sena
23	Limbuwan Mukti Morcha	62	Sudur Parswim Krantikari Party
24	Madhesi Mukti Force	63	Sup Kranti Dal
25	Madhes Raksha Bahin	64	64 Tarai Army
26	Madhesi Special Force	65	Tarai Bagi
27	Madhes Sena	66	Tarai Camando Lig
28	Madhesi Bises Dasta	67	Tarai Cobra (Naagraja)

29	Madhesi Commando	68	Jarai Janakrantikari Bal
30	Madhesi Janaadhikar Forum	69	Tarai Ganatantric Mukti Morcha
31	Madhesi Mukti Tigers (Raman Singh)	70	Tarai Parishad
32	Madhesi Tigers	71	Tarai Uthan Sangathan
33	Madhesi Virus Cleaners Party	72	Taraibadi Madhesi Mukti Force
34	Mangolian Revenge Group	73	Tharuhat Swatta Rajya Parishad
35	National Terrorist Encounter	74	Trishul Sena Nepal
36	Nepal Ajinger X Samuha	75	Samyukta Jatiya Morcha
37	Nepal Gatantric Sena		
38	Nepal Gorkha Sena		
39	Nepal Janatantric Party		

Source: Bishnu Pathak and Devendra Uprety. Tarai-Madhes: Searching for Identity Based Security. CS Center, Situation Update No. 88, October 14, 2009

Talking about the objectives of different armed and semi-armed groups, some of them are working for the reinstatement of Hindu state; few of them are for the reinstatement of the institution of monarchy. However, most of such groups claim to have a political intension based on ethnic identity. Tarai-Madhes and eastern hill areas are the most affected regions today by the armed and semi-armed groups.

It is also said that there are groups working against other established groups and identities. Almost 60 militant groups in Tarai are working against the Pahadis (living in Taria from hill origin). Out of them, very few are seriously working with the political motto. Others want to intensify their criminal activities under the political cap. Similarly, Limbuwan Volunteers are working against those who oppose Limbuwan as a federal state comprising 27 per cent Limbu population that constitutes 1.6 per cent of the national population. They have a slogan, "Opponents of the Limbuwan can not be alive in this region," ...[if] "No Limbuwan, no Entry." Their claim is that they have already organized 100 fulltime militant cadres in each of the eastern hill districts out of nine. Even

Tharuhat Liberation Army is formed to "revolt against the states', Khas Chauvinism". Other ethnic communities, i.e., Tamang, Gurung, Magar, etc., have a strong possibility to form their military wings, since they have already formed political fronts to fight against the High Caste Hilly Hindu domination.

Causes Behind the Mushrooming Militant Conflicts after the CPA

While dealing with the main causes of the mushrooming violent conflict in specific countries even after introducing the peace process to resolve a conflict, the state power and government policy are the major components whether to intensify more violence or resolve it. Ungar et.al.[35]explain the following as key points:

- Political regime change, including recent transitions to democracy, commonly inflames violence among groups;

- Persistent patterns of violence, along with state rights abuses, exist in every country;

- Large scale economic changes, including programs for economic reform, are associated with rising level of violence, particularly among distinct groups and classes;

- Violent scapegoating of racial, religious, ethnic and sexual minorities persists in many countries; and

- Violence remains a component of many groups' responses to the state, from spontaneous protests to armed rebellion.

Analyzing and contextualizing the cause of mushrooming conflict in Nepal, Kumar mentions the following indicators[36].

- Low level of socio-political cohesion;

- High level of political violence occasioned with state repression;

---

35 Mark Ungar, Sally Avery Bermanzohn and Kentor Worcestor. "Violence and Politics" in Kentor Worcestor, Sally Avery Bermanzohn and Mark Ungar (eds.), *Violence and Politics: Globalizations'* Paradox. New York: Routledge, 2002, p. 2.

36 Dhruba Kumar. "Nepali State and Politics: Inevitable Crisis and Harrowing Transition" a Report submitted to the Center for Nepal and Asian Studies, December 12, 1997. p. 20 cited in Dhruba Kumar. "Proximate Causes of Conflict in Nepal" *Contribution to Nepalese Studies*. Vol. 31 (1). January, 2005 p. 60.

- Political conflict over organizing ideology of the state;

- Major recent change in the structure of political system;

- Existence of proportionally small urban middle class;

- Rampant corruption and government unaccountability;

- Low absorbing capacity of foreign aid and its utilization; and

- High level external penetration.

The existence of any one mentioned above would be sufficient to mark the state as being weak, instable and conflict prone[37]. Several research works suggest that there are several overlapping problems that are directly-indirectly responsible for increasing the numbers of armed and semi-armed groups inside Nepal after the CPA[38]. It can be seen that all these problems came mainly 'due to low regulative capacity[39]' of Nepali state and due to a very limited "presence of the state" that badly affected government-run development and other activities[40]. In fact, the SPA government lost its cohesive power before the UCPN-Maoist even if it tried to implement most of the commitment for making a suitable atmosphere for the peace process. It was reported that the government freed all the UCPN-Maoist cadres from prison, withdrew all the cases filed in the courts, lifted the terrorist tags on the UCPN-Maoist, etc., for making a suitable environment for strengthening the peace process. The situation encouraged the UCPN-Maoist as if it could get more than their expectation and started bargaining further. The tough time not only for the UCPN-Maoist but also the whole process began, when people started counter-action[41]against the UCPN-Maoist

---

37   Dhruba Kumar "Proximate Causes of Conflict in Nepal" *Contribution to Nepalese Studies*. Vol. 31 (1). January, 2005 p. 60.

38   *Ibid.*

39 Ram Kumar Dahal. "Nepal's Neighbourhood Ties During the Interim Government" in *POLSAN Annual Journal on Nepalese Foreign Policy*, Vol. 6 & 7, 1998: 99-115.

40 *The Kathmandu* Post, September 16, 2006.

41 Maoists were beaten and even killed by the villagers when people found the Maoists guilty of killings and beating up innocents. The transport entrepreneurs and hoteliers protested against the Maoists and Federation of Nepalese Chamber of Commerce and Industries (FNCCI), on September 17, 2006, they warned to launch a nationwide protest if the Maoists continued extortion and intimidation. Getting excited by such counter attacks in the village and in city, US Ambassador James A. Moriarty expressed skepticism toward the possibility of holding constituent assembly elections in a free and fair manner. He said, "You can't have peace and violence at the same time contradictorily". He mentioned, "Everybody realizes that the Maoists are engaged in lot of violence right now even here in Kathmandu. There is a lot of

activities by taking law and order on their hands. When the UCPN-Maoist led the government after the CA election in 2008, the situation worsened.

Awareness and expectation were increased by the catchy slogan of the UCPN-Maoist during the insurgency that radicalized the entire society. But these raising expectations remained unfulfilled after the political change. Even if they came in the peace process, participated in the government and parliament, became the single largest party in CA election, and then formed the government under their leadership, the UCPN-Maoist could not make any policy change towards peaceful and democratic ways[42]. In fact, their modus operandi to run the country proved to be more corrupt, irresponsible, unaccountable, incompetent to provide the good governance and less honest to the expressed commitment. As a result, hopelessness and frustration was increasing among the various deprived communities who had no expectation from other parties, and have been helping the UCPN-Maoist with high hope for change. Here, we want to put those main circumstances into different categories of the causes to ease the analysis.

- The first is about the unfulfilled hope of people[43] in general, and ethnic community on the issue of ethnicity based autonomous state in particular. It was the Maoist party which distributed the hopes to the ethnic groups by proposing ethnicity based autonomous states to them even if they comprise less than 30 per cent population in the particular regions. They proposed for a Limbuwan state for

---

extortion, beating, intimidation of people going on, that sort of activities will obviously threaten the peace process (See, *The Kathmandu Post*, 16 September 2006 and also "Sorry if I offended anyone: Moriarty," *The Kathmandu Post*, 16 September 2006). Donors working in the development sector in Nepal have started rolling back their programs from the districts due to strong pressure from the Maoists Department for International Development (DFID) of the United Kingdom working for poverty reduction and development in poor countries, including Nepal (See, *The Kathmandu Post*, September 1, 2006). Concerns shown by United Nations Resident Representative and Humanitarian Coordinator in Nepal, Matthew Kahane acknowledged on September 16, 2006 about the rapidly increasing Maoist influence in the countryside.

42   Indeed, the SPA and the Maoists reached an agreement several times to "reinstate the displaced civilians in their homes and to return all land, houses and property seized unjustly". But till the date, they have neither returned the property nor allowed people to stay in their homes in the village. The Maoist party has played a dual role while talking to implement agreements—the Maoist leadership welcome "displaced people" in the villages by words and circulates secret order to their local cadres not to implement, whatever the leadership said, in action. Then the Maoists' behavior in the village has not changed at all, except the armed activities (For details see http://www.kantipuronline.com/kolnews.php?&nid=83973).

43   Uddhab Pyakurel, *Sambidhan Sabha Ka Lagi Purba Sarta* (Preconditions for the Constituent Assembly), *Nepal Samacharpatha*, 27 March, 2007.

those Limbu (with 1.6 per cent national population) which occupy 27 per cent population in the area. Kochila state was proposed for less than 24 per cent population of such groups. Gurung state was proposed for less than 22 per cent population of Gurungs in the particular region. And Magar state was proposed for 28 per cent Magars in the regions. When the UCPN-Maoist signed the CPA, the communities and its leadership saw less hope of having a state based on the UCPN Maoists' proposal. Later on, when the leaders of such a community came to know that the UCPN-Maoist leadership is not serious about the federal set up as declared during the insurgency, a large numbers of UCPN-Maoist cadres and supporters belonging to Madhesis, Tharu, Newar, Limbu and other communities started going away from the UCPN-Maoist Party to start their own movements. More people from indigenous groups, including Madhesi left[44] the UCPN-Maoist party when the first signed the CPA and agreed to promulgate the Interim Constitution 2007 without mentioning Nepal as a federal democratic republic. Interestingly, they continued replicating the UCPN-Maoists' strategy of selling the emotions of indigenous/ ethnic communities and adopting their mobilization tactics as well even after they left the UCPN-Maoist. Indeed, they have become smarter and intelligent through the knowledge gained by their involvement with the UCPN-Maoist during the insurgency. The cadres indoctrinated by the armed tactics of the UCPN-Maoist has mostly led the armed groups and they are active to attack and weaken the state again for a pressure.

- Secondly, the violent conflict has increased due to the weak and personalized peace process. Conflict management is a the process of concluding a dispute or conflict in which the adversary parties, with or without the assistance of mediators, negotiate or otherwise strive toward a mutually acceptable agreement or understanding, taking into account each other's concerns[45]. Any conflict resolution can be defined as a new formation that is acceptable to all actors and can be made sustainable by them only. The trends of emergence of conflict suggest that mostly the sources of conflict are indigenous

---

44 The series of deserting the Maoist party was started jus after 5 years when Bharat Dahal left the party. Then Jaykrishna Goit along with more than 100 Maoists from Madhes had left the party just before the royal coup followed by Laxman Tharu, Matrika Yaduv and others.

45 Louis Kriesberg. æConflict: Social" in Adam Kuper and Jessica Kuper (eds.) The Social Science Encyclopedia. London: Rutledge; 1999. p. 413.

in nature and means and methods of resolution of such conflict also should be searched at local level where the formation of conflict is rooted. The logic is that the indigenous method can be only a sustainable solution. If some outside parties, as a mediator is called, use the carrot and stick policy to pressure the parties either to accept its measures or to be ready to bear the punishment, then there can be no acceptability or sustainability, unless one assumes that the 'mediator' is a part of the conflict formation.[46] It is neither the outsider nor certainly the above the conflicting parties. Most importantly, the sustainability of violence depends on whether the indigenous resolution method has managed adequate provision for the post-conflict arrangement and addressed maturely the transition and questions of reconciliation[47] or not. If we go through each and every agreement along with the CPA, we can find many good and catchy terminologies put there to move forward the peace process into a logical conclusion. But Nepali transition and peace process could not go smoothly because of lack of effort to institutionalize it. In fact, it was like the personalized issue especially between the two actors—the then PM Koirala and the UCPN-Maoists' Supremo Pushpa Kamal Dahal. Many important decisions taken between them were not documented; people could have no basis to interpret/analyze it. The second person neither in the UCPN-Maoist nor in the NC is fully aware of any consensus between them. To make other leaders of SPA aware of the mutual understanding between them is beyond imagination. As a result, the concerned parties were polarized as per the ideology rather than as per the spirit of several formal agreements, if there was crisis of confidence between two leaders. Why was not the whole peace process documented after the CPA? The simple answer is that the motive of both was to secure their importance permanently in the power and polity of the nation, so that they could change and play the rules of the game in accordance with their respective interests. For them, to establish a stable system, which was expected for fulfilment of people's aspirations—civil liberty, freedom, basic needs and identity, was in second priority.

---

46 Johan Galtung. *Peace by Peaceful Means*. Oslo: PRIO, 1996 p.89 cited in Dev Raj Dahal. "Conflict Resolution: A Note on Some Contending Approach" in Ananda P. Shrestha and Hari Uprety (eds.), *Conflict Resolution & Governance in Nepal*. Kathmandu: NEFAS, 2003 p. 20.

47 Dev Raj Dahal. "Conflict Resolution: A Note on Some Contending Approach" in Ananda P. Shrestha and Hari Uprety (eds.), *Conflict Resolution & Governance in Nepal*. Kathmandu: NEFAS, 2003.

- Thirdly, use of vague, ambiguous and ambivalent terms in each and every agreement is the third cause of the peace process of Nepal which allows the signatories to define the agreements as per their interest.

- Fourthly, the government's modus operandi to deal with the movement groups is the fourth cause which also helped increase the armed and semi-armed groups in the making. When the government had no culture to recognize the opposition and was left listening to the voices raised through peaceful means or protests, many peaceful movements were compelled to harden their movements by adopting violent means. In other words, when government established a precedent giving sense that it gives attention to their demand only if the people opt for one or the other violent means, such groups may increase day-by-day and they start following anti-systemic and extra-constitutional mode of struggle. Similarly, unnecessary excuse and political protection given by the government to the UCPN-Maoist cadre's criminal activities even after they signed the CPA helped weaken the state security mechanism and cohesive capacity. It also ultimately demoralized policy action and gave high hope to the militant groups.

- The fifth, the cause of the increment of such groups, is also the UCPN-Maoist and the government which left their prior agendas-peace, progress and democracy, but started playing double roles with multiple tones. For example, in the case of abolition of Monarchy, the Maoist leadership started saying that they have no problem in accepting the monarchy if the people want, and the SPA leader, then PM Koirala, started talking about baby king, etc. Both positions seemed to be expressed against the people's aspiration during Jana Andolan-II. Similarly, they both had changed their position about the federal issues after they faced a big threat by Madhes assertion. That is why both the SPA and the UCPN-Maoist were reluctant to frame the provision on federal structure in the Interim Constitution, which was promulgated in the consensus of both the forces. It seems that both the forces tried to engage with regressive and traditional forces for balancing them also, after they won their respective battles.

- Sixth, the reluctant role played by civil society and media after the UCPN-Maoist and the then government signed the peace agreement is another cause of promoting and provoking the armed groups. Neither the media nor the civil society groups, which had played a vital role during the Jana Andolan-II, left to be critical to the new regime after the movement was successfully ended and the UCPN-Maoist declared a truce, as if their actual job of civil-society is over. As a result, no critics came for the non-implementation of clauses agreed/signed by the parties, and non-adherence to the code of conduct signed/agreed by the UCPN-Maoist and the interim government. The so-called civil-society was divided as per the party ideologies when parties decided to allocate some seats for the civil society members in the restored parliament. Its division as Maoist and non-Maoist erased the actual role of civil society as watchdog, and issues raised by the members of civil-society were also taken subjectively. Both the parties became free to follow respective paths that automatically encouraged violating the code of conduct and interpreting it in favour of one's own interest. Ultimately, it helped make a more anarchical situation that was never before. Then the situation shifted politics of consensus among the parties to the politics of confrontation.

- Seventh, the UCPN-Maoists' deliberate attempt to create anarchy and instability became instrumental in increasing the number of armed and semi-armed groups in Nepal. The UCPN Maoists' leadership responded to them provocatively, so that an opportunity could come to vitalize the role of their combatants kept in cantonment, and to catch the fish of the power in the turmoil water. They on the one hand said that "Anarchy and instability help the UCPN-Maoist to consolidate power for the further revolution—people's republic" and blamed some genuine movement groups as criminal outfits, imperialist's outfit, etc.,[48] for defaming them. It is proved by the proposal and action of the UCPN-Maoist while the Madhes was uprising. The UCPN-Maoist first provoked the peaceful movement by gunning down a man who participated in the peaceful movement organized by Madhesi groups, proposed for the mobilization of its combatants to control the situation in Madhes, and suggested to the then government not to be engaged with the movement groups through dialogue. Neither the government nor the UCPN-Maoist leaders realized the fact about no military solution was possible to control people's peaceful assertion. Again, the Tharu community was also provoked by the UCPN-Maoist when it was leading the government. When the

---

48 Dr. Baburam Bhattarai said "The naike (derogatory word for leader) of the criminal group [read that as Madhesi People's Rights Forum] must be arrested and the outfit must be outlawed" (Speech of Dr. Bhattarai on March 23, 2007).

government came up with an ordinance to define the identity of all communities residing in the flat-land as Madhesi, the Tharu Movement was witnessed from March 2-14, 2009.

The seven points mentioned above can be considered as general causes which helped in increasing the culture of violence and intimidation all over the country after the CPA was signed. Along with those, there are some specific causes which helped Madhes in becoming the heartland of the armed conflict after the UCPN-Maoist 'renounced' the violence. These are:

1. The first important cause was that the Madhes was not influenced by the UCPN-Maoist during the insurgency, and the SPA, especially the NC and UML, also lost their base after the Madhes Uprising 2007. As a result, there was a vacuum due to lack of existence of the state and the mainstream political parties.

2. The second cause was the strategic geographical area of Tarai. While there was Maoist insurgency, the hilly region became a strategic geographic location for their shelter, the state had less access to the region, and systemic parties were quite strong. But later on, the situation was reversed in Tarai after the Madhes movement when the NC and UML also exited from the region.

3. Third, Madhes used to be a more violent place in comparison to the hilly region with records of killing, kidnapping etc. in the past, especially during the time of elections. When Nepal had a better law and order situation, some of the criminal groups used to take shelter in India especially in different parts of the states of Uttar Pradesh (UP) and Bihar. And now it is said that the situation is reversed; the law and order situation in Bihar and UP states is under control, but has weakened in Nepal. Then many criminals in the border area take shelter in Nepal and commit criminal activities.[49] They even managed to wear the political cap by capitalizing the transitional situation of Nepal and expanding their activities in Tarai.

4. Foreign role is the fourth cause for this. When Madhes became vulnerable, all the international players including China,[50] USA

---

49 Uddhab P. Pyakurel. *Maoist Movement in Nepal: A Sociological Perspective*. New Delhi: Adroit Publishers, 2007.

50 Today China, which used to support establishments, had no access to the people and leaders of any political party, seems to be interested to be engaged in Nepal's internal

and EU[51] tried to engage with it, considering it as one of the strategic locations to influence Nepali politics as well as to weaken Indian influence in internal politics of Nepal.

5. The last but not the least cause is related to the role of Tarai elites. As all we know, the elite from political parties and civil-society of the particular country and society engaged in leading the conflicting sections, dealing with them, and leading the conflict towards the resolution are the vital actors while talking about the conflict management or resolution. That is why, recreating the conflict, resuming the conflict and sustainability of the conflict resolution is dependent on the capacity, responsibility, honesty, accountability and transparency of the respective elites or leadership engaged in the peace process. But misunderstanding and threat to the peace process can be created, while "elite conflict occurs…[and] an elite attempts to undermine another elite's capacity to extract revenue from non-elites"[52]. It is purely implacable to the Madhes in Nepal where Madhes has mainly become the battlefield of the new Madhesi elites and old elites scattered all over Nepal. When one watches the marathon of Madhesi leadership for selling their popular strength, it can be found, to what extent they can compromise the Madhes sentiment with an opportunity for being a Member of Cabinet under different governments formed after 2006; how easily they can sideline their agenda raised during the struggle; and how they can be more divided and competed

matter especially after abolition of Monarchy. It wants an assurance from the Nepali state that Tibetan refugees living in Nepal and their agitation for establishing Tibet as an autonomous state would be in control in Nepal.

51 The EU which used to be active in establishing and strengthening democracy now not only started giving suggestion (rather insisting) to the government, but also invested a huge amount of money in helping ethnic conflicts. For example: (1) EU compelled the government to expel the then Education Minister Ram Chandra Kuswaha charging him of being 'corrupt', (2) A 10-member team of the European Parliament, which arrived in Nepal for a week-long visit in June 2010, had visited the Tibetan Camp on 24th May secretly without taking permission of the Nepal Government. (3) They even had a schedule on 28th May to meet the extra-systemic organization called Limbuwan Rajya Parisad and Khumbuwan. These meets were cancelled after the Nepal Government's strong objection. (4) After the Maoist called off its last month indefinite strike, they kept suggesting to the Prime Minister to resign for reciprocating the Maoist's move and it was good to form a consensus government ruling out the option of majoritarian Government in democracy if there is no consensus.

52 Richard Lachmann. "Class Formation Without Class Struggle: An Elite Conflict Theory of the Transition to Capitalism" *American Sociological Review*. Vol. 55 (3), June, 1990. p. 403.

for their petty interest rather than be united for the interest of the region. Also, the demands[53] put forward by Madhes-based parties before taking part in the election of the CA helped substantiate the argument. They are neither able to show their commitment in the local issue of Madhes nor do they have faith in participatory and inclusive democracy as raised by them for a long time and during the Madhes movement. All causes together help the Madhes to be the heartland of violent conflict.

In brief, it can be said that organizational transformation from armed rebels to peaceful politicians depends on three preconditions—faction, followers and friends. (1)The rebel group's degree of internal cohesion during the peace process, (2) its level of popular support among the population at large at the time of the transition, and (3) the amount of legitimacy that the international community is willing to grant to the rebels through the transition period helps in examining how the rebellion groups are being transferred.[54] But when the UCPN-Maoist opt for playing with their two-line struggle, it seems that they have lost their internal cohesion over the party cadres. In fact, this weakness of the Maoist party ultimately provides a clue not only for its cadres to continue criminal activities along with extortion, intimidation, killing, abduction, etc., but also for other groups who were waiting for a favourable situation to initiate the armed movements to influence the state. That is why we find some commonality in most of the groups today if we follow their movement and demands seriously. In every negotiation talk between the government and the armed groups, they commonly demand eventual integration of their combatants into security forces including the Nepal Army. Militant's integration into security forces has become one of the major hopes of most armed groups. In other words, possible integration in security agencies and rehabilitation in society with handsome amounts of money from the national treasury become a precedence. The violent armed activities become the guiding principle to the unemployed youth. In other words, the agreement between the government and the UCPN-Maoist for the management of the latter's combatants encouraged others to take to arms who are also interested in entering into the security agencies through back-channel negotiations. The trend is likely to be viable for years to come due to the high rate of unemployment of the youth. Today, youth of Nepal can easily join any of such armed group with the motto of just entering into the security

---

53 As per the demand, Madhesi parties were exempted by the provision of inclusive candidacy in the CA. The amendment was not made mandatory for those political parties which fill up less than 30 per cent candidates in the election.

54 Mimmi S. Kovacs. *From Rebellion to Politics*. Sweden: Uppsala University, 2007. p. 8.

forces, which previously used to be very difficult unless one had a political influence. Another cause of possible sustainability of such armed groups in Nepal is due to social respect if one joins in the security forces, especially in Nepal Army.

Internal Conflict and External Consequences

Generally, it is very difficult to term a conflict as an internal problem and its risk spilling over neighboring areas. Indeed, the regional dimension has become "increasingly important in South Asia, if for no other region, having an 'exclusive security complex' and 'security interdependence'"[55] among the countries. That is why regionalism and conflict are related in many different ways and the multiple "aspects of regionalism, security and development are complementary and mutually supportive ways."[56] As General (Retd.) V.R. Raghavan[57] rightly pointed out, even an internal conflict will have external consequences. It is very much applicable to the Nepali context. The reality is that Nepal's internal conflict will have a heavy consequence on India; Due to various factors such as socio-cultural proximity between the two countries (Nepal-India), geographical location through which Nepal is situated in the heart of India and surrounded by it from three sides, India cannot remain unaffected by any kind of internal problem in Nepal. That is why it is called "indo-closed" and "indo-opened" with the sharing of not only open border, but also security problems which emerged in either country. The dual characters— open border[58] and socio-cultural proximity, have "people flow" between the two neighbours and established the good people-to-people relation for centuries.[59] But at the

---

55 Bjorn Hettne "Conflict Dynamics and Conflict Management" in John P. Neelsen and Dipak Malik (eds.) *Crisis of State and Nation: South Asian States Between Nation-Building and Fragmentation*. New Delhi: Manohar, 2007. p. 47.

56 *Ibid.* pp. 48-49.

57 while giving the valedictory lecture in a seminar on Internal Conflict in Nepal: Trends and Consequences Jointly Organized by the Nepal Study Center, BHU; Malaviya Peace Study Center, BHU; and Center for Security Analysis, Chennai held in Banaras Hindu University from June 3-5, 2010.

58   In fact, Indo/Nepal border, which is open, is 1580 kilometers long with 940 KM land boundary and 640 KM river boundary.

59 The political and economic implication of such a relation is worth mentioning. Nepalese prefer to go to India which is an emerging economy in South Asia not only for hunting jobs but also for taking shelter or asylum while there is any kind of political crisis in Nepal. It has been witnessed in the past that the migration from Nepal to India used to increase when there was insecurity in the country due to insurgency and state violence. Similarly, the history says that Nepali leaders and students living in India were in jail with their Indian counterparts who were struggling for independence of India. Also, not

same time, Nepal's internal conflict will be of no consequences, or, it will have negligible impact on on the rest of the countries in the world, including its northern neighbor-China. It is due to not only the open border but also "other natural and practical considerations[60]" which can not be put on equal footing with India and the rest.

However, the responses of the majority of the people, including the government officials, of both the countries (Nepal and India) on the issue of mushrooming internal conflict are disappointing. They neglect other factors and blame the open border as if each and every problem lies on it. As Madhes of Nepal has become the most unstable and deeply troubled region due to today's armed and semi-armed conflicts, many Nepalese perceive that the Indo-Nepal open border helped create such a situation in the bordering area-the Tarai. On the other hand, many Indians especially the bureaucrats also believe in false arguments that the Indo-Nepal porous border has helped increase influx of criminals as well as terrorist activities in India. It meant that both the Nepali and Indian side see an open border through bias eyes; they looked upon open border "as constraint and not as an instrument for developing and enduring and beneficial relationship."[61] In this situation, the centuries long practice of open border followed by India-Nepal Peace and Friendship Treaty 1950 seems to be affected in the near future.

In fact, the 'warm' and 'special' relation between both Nepal and India, by tradition, was realized to legitimatize with the emerging complexities created by the changing times and circumstances. Such relation was formalized by the various provisions including the 1950 treaty. Here, people having anti-Indian sentiment always raise questions against India referring to the 1950 Treaty blaming it as an unequal treaty. Weaknesses identified so far are : (1) position of signatory of the treaty are unequal; (2) it was signed by the oligarchy of Nepal having no popular will and base; and (3) it is a treaty accompanied with letters of exchanges, but the letters were kept secret for several years after signing it. However, both the time and context has changed now; the treaty which was signed from the traditional security perspective to secure the border of either country has now been serving more for the interest of common people of

---

only the working class but also business classes of Indian people are doing their jobs in Nepal.

60 Indra Adhikari, "The 'China Card': Perception and Reality" *Global Nepali* May/June 2009

61 Ram P. Rajbahak. *India-Nepal Border: A Bond of Shared Aspirations*. New Delhi: Lancer Publishers, 1992.

both the countries than that of the state and rulers. In other words, the main thrust of the treaty i.e. defence and security, has become irrelevant today after it was time and again been defied by both the countries. But common people of both the countries, who have no capacity to manage seed money for going abroad for education, work, treatment, etc., are using the open border for their interests. Any change in the provision of open border will neither help India's security concern nor make Nepal's Tarai safe. It is because of the fact that the border, either it is regulated or porous, hardly matters to both the terrorists and criminals as they do not follow rules and regulations of international boundary treaty. Also, neither USA could save Pentagon (from outsider) nor could India avert the Mumbai attack from the Pakistan based terrorists even if they both are very much concerned about the regulated border.

Finally, of the 268 violent conflicts which occurred between 1968 and 2006, 40% were eliminated by police and intelligent agencies, and 43% reached a peaceful political accommodation with their government; 10% of insurgent groups achieved victory and only 7% of the terrorist groups were eliminated by military action[62]. The data mentioned above helps to draw a conclusion that both thoughts--achieving a victory through violent means; and eliminating the groups by military action are either illusions or well accomplished task. So the peaceful political accommodation through dialogue is the only way which ensures peace and makes the internal social transformation easy. For a successful dialogue for reaching a common ground, the process must be as much inclusive, transparent, and institutionalized as possible.

---

62 Seth G. Jones and Martin C.Libicki. *How Terrorist Groups End: Lesson for Countering Al Qu'ida*. Santa Monica, CA: RAND Corporation, 2008.

Chapter XI

Nepal Constituent Assembly Election 2008: An Observer's Account

Uddhab Pd. Pyakurel

Many Nepalese and foreigners who have been carefully watching and following the political developments of Nepal have been surprised by the results of the Constituent Assembly (CA) election which was held on April 10, 2008. There were many pre-poll surveys, guesses etc. regarding the possible election results. There were arguments that voters would again favour the Nepali Congress (NC) and the Communist Party of Nepal-United Marxist-Leninist (CPN-UML) to be the first and second largest political forces as they were after the 1990 polls. There were several forecasts that the Maoists (the former rebels) would get considerable votes and be in the third position after the NC and CPN-UML. However, the election placed the Maoists in the first rank with a huge margin and the poll outcome proved most of the predictions to be wrong. After the election, there are people who argue that the election was not free and fair. They state that the result was the product of intimidation and coercion by the Maoists. Another section of people believe that the victory of the Maoists in the election was obvious as it is quite a popular party in Nepal. Given the background, people around the world are now trying to analyse how almost all the pre-poll presumptions went wrong; and what are the factors which favoured the Maoists at the last moment to win the election.

Pre-election Situation

Being a Nepali citizen, as well as a researcher, I was/am also closely observing Nepal's recent political situation. Though I am in Delhi for my research, I often visit Nepal as well as its rural areas. I visited many parts of the country like Salyan, Surkhet, Dang and Nuwakot during the time of the nominations filed by candidates; I also visited about a dozen constituencies of different districts just before the election. Again, I travelled at least 20 km by road and on foot and visited nine polling booths on the day of the election, to observe the election related activities. On the basis of my field study and observations, I want to share some points about the poll which surprised the whole world.

Till April 7, that is, three days before the Election Day, I also thought that the Maoists will emerge as the third largest political force with 17-25 per cent of the total votes. However, I was compelled to change my view when I entered the rural areas, started talking to the voters and observing the pre-poll situation in the different villages. The change came about due to the reluctance of the voters to talk about the election. Those who could frankly involve themselves in the political discussion and argue for and against the parties in the past were silent just before the election. I got an indication that there was something wrong. I tried to find out the cause behind the silence or reluctance of the voters, but could not fathom it immediately.

Rasuwa was the district which I visited just one day prior to the election. As it is my neighbouring district and quite close to my polling booth, I visited the polling booth and went to Laharepauwa Village Development Committee (VDC) of Rasuwa. Again, I was interested in visiting that VDC because of the fact that both the NC and CPN-UML candidates of Rasuwa were from there. While I started talking about the election, a teacher from one of the primary schools argued:

Since the state is not able to provide security to the leaders and candidates, how will it give us security? In this situation, it is better not to be so active. If the election takes place, we hope that we will be able to enter the polling centres and cast our vote. However, there is no situation by which we can mobilise ourselves in the election.

Another person, who seemed to be an NC sympathiser, added: Our candidate is in hospital. The NC led government could not give security to him. If we go for the election campaign, we have to convince the people that NC will take the responsibility for peace and security as it is our slogan in the election. How will people believe us? That is why we are feeling hesitant to go for the election campaign.

These arguments reflected the reality of Rasuwa where the NC candidate, Bal Chandra Paudel, was hospitalised after being physically beaten by the Maoists during his election campaign. Though it was one day before the election, people were not very enthusiastic about the election; and I have not seen the people who were mobilised in preparing for the election the next day.

After Rasuwa, my destination was Nuwakot constituency Number Three in which one of the senior Maoists leaders, Post Bahadur Bogati, along with others, was the candidate for the CA. From Laharepauwa of Rasuwa, I crossed the Trisuli River and entered Bogati's own village named Tupche to observe the pre-election situation. When I crossed the Trisuli River, I met one of my relatives on the way. She enquired about my destination and my well-being. When I told her about my intention of visiting Tupche, she tried to stop me on the way and said: "Many Maoists are mobilised in the village. They may manhandle you, as you are new for them. It is better not to go there this time." I tried to convince her. However, she argued: "The Maoists need only some pretext and they want to terrorise the people anyway before the election. If they find some money in your pocket, they may take it and argue that they were stopping someone who was trying to buy votes from the people." Finally, I was compelled to disclose my identity as an election observer to convince her.

As mentioned earlier, it was just one day before the Election Day when I visited Tupche. The villagers did not appear very enthusiastic. Very few people were moving around. Most of them were confined to their respective homes. She was right that there were some young Maoist supporters mobilised in the village. I could locate plenty of NC and CPN-UML flags put up in the houses but no groups of the NC and CPN-UML were seen on the way. I took two-three breaks on the way during the visit and tried to initiate the election debate. However, I found that people were trying to avoid the debate. They were praying that nothing would happen till the next day, that is, the Day of the Election.

Finally I returned to my own home which is in Nuwakot constituency Number Two in the evening. As it is a common practice in the village to have discussions with neighbours in evening time, some of the members of our village assembled at my house and started discussing about the contemporary situation. In between, my mother came and told us that this is not right time to assemble and discuss about politics. She further argued: "The incidents of beating, manhandling and defaming the opponents have increased due to the Maoists' in recent days. It is not the election as it was before. If you continue this discussion, someone may come and something may happen here too. Therefore, it is better to stop such a discussion now.

It is advisable to go to the polling booths early in the morning and come back as soon as possible after casting the vote. This is not the right time to be in the polling booths the whole the day. All are scared that something may happen." After her repeated requests, we stopped the discussion and went to bed early. Before going to bed, she again requested us to close the room properly before sleeping.

Whether the Intimidation was the Wish of the Maoist Leadership

When I recall the whole narrative mentioned above, I remember a telephonic conversation with a friend who was close to the Maoists. The conversation took place a couple of days prior to my visit, while I was still in Delhi. When several intimidating activities of the Maoists were being exposed, I had discussed with the friend about the Maoist leadership's reluctance to stop these activities. I had thought that perhaps the Maoists were losing more at the national and international level by such activities. However, his understanding was just the opposite of my understanding. He tried to convince me that those activities were the last weapons which the Maoists would use and that they would get considerable votes only if they continue these activities. According to him, such intimidations were the deliberate attempt by the Maoists to terrorise the people. He also told me that Prachanda, while addressing a meeting of his cadres, instructed them not to stop, but to continue these activities. I wondered and asked him about the rationale behind such activities. He just replied: "You will see their implication during the election."

What I saw on Election Day

Keeping all the above mentioned narratives in mind, I went to the polling booth early in the morning, as I had to cast the vote first and then visit as many polling booths as possible to observe the election. However, I could not cast the vote in the beginning, as there was already a long queue before I reached. After spending an hour in the queue, I ultimately cast my vote and started the other job, that is, to visit more polling booths as an election observer. That day, I was able to visit 11 different polling booths of Nuwakot.

Observing the election was not a new assignment for me. I had observed the two last parliamentary elections in 1994 and 1999. The location also was not different. However, the scenario differed in this election from those of the earlier elections. The difference was seen not only around the polling booths, but also on the way to the booths and in the village itself. Some of my observations are as follow:

1. Earlier, people used to think of the Election Day as a day of festival. Most of the voters used to stay in the booth premises the whole the day, even after they had cast their vote. They used to utilise the day to meet friends, share their feelings etc. Each and every party used to set up at least a stall close to the polling booth to serve food and snacks to their sympathisers. The objective behind such a management was to win their votes and get the support of the voters, and to stop others if they wanted to disturb the poll with a common effort. Such a gathering would also back the polling agents to perform their roles if there was something wrong. However, this time many people went back to their respective homes immediately after casting their vote. There were no stalls set up by parties, except by the Maoists. When I visited some Maoist stalls I came to know that those who left the polling booths were mostly the voters of other parties like the NC, CPN-UML, RPP etc. I talked to some of them on the way while they were going back to their homes and asked them about the reason behind their leaving the polling booth immediately after casting their note. The common answer was: "Due to security reasons." "We think that something will happen during the election. Therefore, we came early to cast our votes and are going back soon. If something happens here, who will save us? You know the fact that there is no government to provide security to us. Police do nothing to those Maoists who create an uproar," one middle-aged woman from a group of people replied.

2. In the past, people used to hang around whenever there was a dispute between the polling agents of different candidates if they suspected that someone was trying to cast a proxy vote. If one agent favoured the casting of such a proxy vote, all others would resort to hangama to prevent such an exercise. However, this time the presence of all agents, except the Maoists' agents, was just a mere formality. In the presence of all agents, an 11-year old girl child, who was there as a guest, cast a vote in the Bageswari polling booth without any obstacle. One of the agents who belonged to an NC candidate mentioned, after the polling was over, that when he tried to stop proxy voters, the Maoists' agent threatened him with dire consequences. According to him, he himself also allowed some proxy voters to vote. However, he found no one from the NC side who dared to cast the vote. "Our

supporters were afraid and did not come to counter the Maoists even if they attempt unfair activities. For our voters what mattered was only the holding of peaceful election. We did not bother if someone cast proxy votes," he said.

3. Talking about confidentiality of the polling booths, it was also unique this time. All the ballot boxes were placed outside near the queue of voters, even if there was sufficient space available inside the booth. This situation helped those who thought that the Maoists have such instruments which would let them know about who casts the vote and from where. Since the ballot box was in the open, it was obvious that people were scared about the confidentiality of their votes.

4. There were security personnel employed in the booths. As the government had helped to reduce their morale, there was no expectation that the security forces would perform their job. In the given situation, they were looking more like mute witnesses, than an authority employed to provide security.

After the election was over, I found the reality that people were passive and frightened only because of a sense of insecurity. When the Maoists started spreading the activities of beating/manhandling the opponent candidates of the CA, disturbing the meetings of others, stopping voters from entering the constituencies, and when the people saw the incompetent role of the government to stop such activities, most of the NC and CPN-UML sympathisers were compelled to be passive in the villages. Apart from observing the situation, I talked to the people about the styles and strategies applied by different parties during the election campaign. According to the voters, most of the candidates were seen in the village for the campaign. However, there was a fundamental difference between the Maoists and others: the Maoists tried to convince the voters first; if the voters were not convinced, they resorted to threatening the people. Similarly, voters were told by the Maoists either to vote for them or be ready to face the situation as it was during the "people's war".

Though there are reports that the Maoists in the different parts of the country threatened a large number of the people and compelled them to favour the CPN-Maoist, I met very few people in my area who complained about the Maoists personally threatening them. However, the repeated media reports about the Maoists' activities in the different parts of the country forced the people to be subjected to a sort of psychological terror. As each and every household has access to the electronic media, the voters were kept fully informed about the day-to-day coercive activities and electoral violence of the Maoists. The objective of the media was not to terrorise the people, but to put pressure on the Maoists to refrain from activities by letting the people know about the realities. However, I found that the people took the media reports rather differently, that is, as security failure posing a common threat to them. All the accounts mentioned above—the arguments of two gentlemen of Rasuwa, my relative of Tupche, my mother, and the voters who were on their way to go back home immediately after they voted—reflected a kind of sense of terror, or feeling of insecurity.

In the evening of the Election Day, after the polling was over, I again dialled the number of my friend and told him that I had come to know about the implication of the repeated terrorising activities of the Maoists even after heavy national and international criticism. He laughed loudly and asked me about the facts and findings of my observation. I shared the fact that the Maoists succeeded in leaving a trail of physiological terror on its opponents, which helped them to control the villages without adequate manpower. He said as earlier: "It was a deliberate and strategically decided attempt by the Maoists. If they did not repeat such activities before the election, the cadres of the NC and CPN-UML would be so active that they would be able to push the Maoists into the corner. The Maoists really succeeded in this regard. They are champions in adopting a strategy to face any adverse condition."

After the conversation, I suddenly recalled an incident of such terror: though there was no activity of the Maoists during the "people's war", people from the Maoist free zone were frightened on just hearing the name of the Maoists. It was around 1998, when the "people's war" was in a preliminary stage, that a poster of the "people's war" was stuck outside the club for the first time in our village. After knowing about the poster, a nine-year old boy came to me and in an excited tone said: "Uncle, uncle, I saw a Maoist in our club. Don't go there." I asked him to show me the Maoist. But he said: "I saw the Maoist pasted on the wall of our club. Please, don't go there." The boy had seen several such posters before. But, the poster distressed him as he listened more about the Maoists' activities in negative terms. During the "people's war", people would easily lose their heart when they encountered Maoists. There were many incidents where people were cheated by dacoits and others in the name of the Maoists. They used to carry dummy guns and ask for money in the name of donation for the Maoists. All these things happened due to the fact that the people who were not in touch with the Maoists conceived the "people's war" as an instrument of terror.

Here, I can't blame the Maoists alone for being responsible for such a fear psyohosis among the voters. The government and its security agencies were also equally responsible, as they could not ensure a feeling of security to the people. As we are in the transition from the warfare situation to that of peace, it was the responsibility of the government to assess the situation and develop a mechanism to overcome the weaknesses. Just a couple of weeks before the Election Day, the United Nations Mission in Nepal (UNMIN) issued a press release concerning the repeated warnings, threats and intimidations by the Maoists, which resulted in a state of fear in the community at large. It also pointed out that a number of commanders and members of the Maoists' army were involved in the election activities which, according to the Comprehensive Peace Accord (CPA), was a serious violation of the agreements and accords signed by the government and the Maoists. However, the government did not feel it necessary to take note of these accounts even if a responsible partner of the CPA raised it. Ultimately, such terror **toctics** created a vacuum with the absence of other parties in the political field in the villages, polling booths etc., and helped the Maoists to play their role there.

Outside Observers and their Limitations

When I came back to Kathmandu the day after the election, I had an opportunity to share my experiences with some international election observers. The peaceful environment of the polling booths surprised most of them. As most of the voters came in the morning and left the booths immediately after the vote, there was no doubt that there was a peaceful situation prevailing during the entire day.

Some of them were anticipating violence during the poll. Those who were in Kathmandu and Pokhara to observe the election were arguing that they never saw such a peaceful environment in the election. They were more impressed by the long queues of voters much before the poll started. When I shared my experiences with them, they endorsed their limitations as outside observers and said: "Without observing the background and without going out of the booths, no one could understand why the peace prevailed and why they came early in the morning to the polling stations before the poll started."

I met a team of the international observers from the European Union (EU) in the Betrawtai polling station in the Pasang Lyamhu highway in the morning. I tried to discuss with them but they were busy capturing the scenes of the booth in their cameras. Before I left the booth, I as an observer asked one of the members of the EU team about their next destination. However, she said that it would be decided after they discussed with the team. But she disclosed that they had no plan to visit the polling booths which are in remote areas and with poor accessibility. Except the EU team in the Betrawati pooling booth, I saw no other international observer in booths where there was no road access. After I talked to the international observers in Kathmandu, it was more than clear that that they hardly travelled on foot to observe the election in the polling booths situated in the remote areas.

Conclusion

Before concluding, I want to make it clear that it is not my intention to say that the Maoists won the election only by coercion and intimidation. As the Maoists were popular in the urban areas, especially among the urban labourers, obviously they got votes from many of them. They also got a considerable number of votes from the people of the different marginalised communities. We have to respect the people who cast their votes in favour of the Maoists of their own volition. At the same time it is our duty to disclose the reality to the world about the reasons behind the unexpected results of the CA election, and what were the factors which helped to change the result at the last minute.

Before I decided to write my experiences, I talked to the people from different parts of the country, read different reports and checked whether my experience was exceptional. When I came to know that the scenario was mostly similar, I decided to write this account. Apart from the instances of intimidations and coercion, the inclusive character of the candidates, fresh and attractive slogans, radical agenda, spirit of the cadres, dynamic strategy etc. were the strengths of the Maoists to deftly manoeuvre the pre-election situation to reap benefits. On the other hand, old candidates, old slogans, old agenda, internal rivalries etc. were the bane of the NC and CPN-UML, which also helped the Maoists to attract the voters. Likewise, the government's failure to provide security to the candidates and sympathisers of different parties, and the coercion of the Maoists were equally responsible in terrifying the people, which suddenly helped to change the election results.

However, those who lost the election need not feel hopeless by the outcome because there will be more elections if we are able to reinforce democracy in the country. As the Maoists have repeatedly made their commitments to democracy and adult franchise, we should take these to watch their modus operandi under their own leadership in the CA and the government as well. Simultaneously, the other parties should take a lesson from these experiences and think of how to strengthen the security of the public in future elections.

Chapter XII

Relevance of Lohia in Nepali Political Crisis Today

Uddhab Pd. Pyakurel

As the political situation in Nepal has been in turmoil for a long time, some scholars used to say that Nepal is in a permanent transition[1]. Even 60 years after the end of the Rana hereditary prime ministerial system in 1951, the political situation neither has been stable nor has improved. In fact, the Nepali democracy struggle gathered momentum from the 1940s, especially after four Nepali youths were sentenced to death by hanging, by the government in 1942, as they were involved in protesting against the Ranas. It can be said that the movement in Nepal was inspired by the anti-British movement already going on in India. The Nepalese, especially those who were in India as students, were the key factors which led the anti-Rana movement. Formation of Nepali Congress (NC) and adoption of a strategy of the armed revolution to overthrow the Rana regime at its Bairgania (India) Conference of September 26-27, 1950 were two bold decisions which helped and inspired the Nepalese to strengthen the movement. Later, the revolution was supported not only by the then King Tribhuvan, but also by Indian and Burmese socialists, as the former put the throne to risk and went into exile in India; and the latter fought as comrades-in-arms physically too.

The anti-Rana revolution successfully ended on February 18, 1951. It was followed by a tripartite agreement that led Nepal on the path to democratization. But after two years of the successful movement, the then king Tribhuvan started violating the mandate of the movement, agreements and constitutional provisions. Later in 1959, the King agreed to hold general

---

1 Uddhab Pd. Pyakurel, "The Vision of the Jana Andolan II for a future of Nepal" in B.C. Upreti (ed.), *State and Democracy in Nepal*. (Delhi: Kalinga Publications, 2011).

elections for parliament only after strong pressure by the political parties. The election had paved the way for formation of the first elected government in the country. The king, however, dismissed the government on December 15, 1960 after one-and-a-half years of its formation, and imposed party less political system — *Panchayat* - claiming that he (the king) is the source of the constitution, and sovereignty also belonged to him. Nepali people once again threw out the authoritarian *Panchayat* regime through their continued struggle followed by the successful Jana Andolan II in 1990, and restored the democratic set-up. However, this struggle could not be sustained for long as it was challenged by both extremists - the extreme left (the Maoist), and the extreme right (the royalists). Again, people came out on the streets to protest against the violent and authoritarian activities of both the extremists in 2006; and succeeded in a democracy struggle by winning over all the threats - the institution of monarchy, the political parties, the Maoists, and the international community[2]. However, though Nepal witnessed a historical political transformation after 2006, it is yet to overcome the political crisis. In fact, there are still challenges ahead before ending the ongoing political transit by drafting a new constitution. Why? What were the major deficits in Nepal and Nepali leadership on account of which the democracy struggle did not succeed? It failed to institutionalize the achievements of the various successful and historical movements. Weak, vision-less and inefficient delivery systems of the subsequent governments formed after the revolutions, "unnecessary" dependency over external powers, especially India, and lack of clarity of political parties about how to deal with the issues of minorities and deprivations, are the major fault lines of Nepali political parties which directly and indirectly weakened them at local level. Lohia was the one who sensed the likely failure of Nepali leadership in consolidating democracy. The following section discusses some of Lohia's thoughts which are not only directly related to the crisis that has been facing by Nepal, but are also very relevant to deepening democracy in the country.

Political Transition and Delivery System with People-Oriented Program

In fact, Lohia was the one who engaged himself with the struggle of Nepali democracy since Lohia met B. Koirala for the first time in 1946. According to Lohia, they (B.P. Koirala and Lohia himslef) had a very close relationship, as if they were two colleagues of the same party, or

---

2   for details, see *ibid.*

two brothers of the same family[3]. He was one of few Indians who was imprisoned in Nepal during Nepal's democracy struggle. Along with his close association, he had given a couple of suggestions to his colleague B.P. Koirala, which according to Lohia, could help in consolidating democracy in a society like Nepal. In fact, the three major suggestions given by Lohia to Koriala were : distribution of land, start campaigns to hold the election of the constituent assembly, and fight against nepotism. Lohia was of the view that socio-economic reforms, such as land distribution or land reform, would be possible only if undertaken immediately. He said these could not be achieved if the issues were delayed after the revolution. With this objective, Lohia kept suggesting to Koirala to start land distribution and campaigns for constituent assembly election right after the NC controlled Biratnagar, and came into power in 1950-51. But Lohia was disappointed with the Nepali leadership, especially B.P. Koirala when NC joined the interim government in 1951 just after the revolution against Rana oligarchy, and Lohia saw no indication of implementing the programs suggested by him. Perhaps Lohia mistakenly read the tripartite agreement of 1951 and blamed B.P. Koirala only for not taking initiative for implementing the progressive programs such as land reforms, etc. This is because NC, though it mobilized Nepali people and defeated the autocratic Rana regime, it did not have more say in the interim government since it was one of the three coalition partners of the cabinet without the prime ministership. And, it time and again witnessed that the other two coalition partners - the royalists and Ranas - jointly opposed it, once the NC proposed to go for people-oriented programs . And when the NC came into power with two-thirds majority in the firstly elected parliament in 1960, it introduced various people-oriented socio-economic reforms, including land reforms. However, the NC government led by Koirala was thrown out.

In fact, Lohia should be recalled for aptly saying that every program would be possible if it is introduced just after the revolution is over. And, that has been the missing link of Nepali democracy struggle time and again. One could easily argue that if the interim governments - in 1990 and in 2006 - formed just after the revolutions (people's movement) were over, introduced pro-people socio-economic policies and programs, it would have been a different situation than at present. In fact, such a program could have helped the common people to own the system, and thus it was the best way in deepeening democracy at local level. It was fortunate that the same NC party could lead two major mass movements

---

3 Ram Manohar Lohia, Samajbadi Andolan Ka Itihash (History of Socialist Struggle), Hyderabad: Ram Manohar Lohia Samata Nyas. 1993. p. 38 (in Hindi).

in Nepal after 1960 – led by the NC leaders K.P. Bhattarai in 1990, and G.P. Koirala in 2006, and the interim governments after the movements. And it was unfortunate that both the governments could not come up with the programs which could encourage commoners to support the changed situation, and weaken anti-democracy elements in the country. Rather, it eventually led to instability and misgovernance as the democratic set-up after the revolution was comparable to 'old wine in a new bottle'. The country has time and again faced difficulty in saving even the essential democratic rights, i.e., non-implementation of socio-ecomonic programs, which created frustration among people. And, today's anxiety over whether the country can complete the institutionalisation process of democracy, has also been completely related to the failure of the interim government to introduce and implement the people-centric programs suggested by Lohia.

Nepal-India Relations and Nepali Democracy

It was Lohia who could sense the real tendency of Nepali leadership in terms of Indo-Nepal relations. He once stated that leaders of India's neighbouring countries often visit people like him if they are not in power. When they are in power, they stop being in touch with Indian people who helped them in their democracy struggles, and they confine their contacts only to the Indian government. What Lohia said about the behaviour leadership in neighborhood in the past, is still valid after 60 years. Also, it is witnessed in the later days that Nepal's relations with India have been somehow confined to the level of bureaucracy in India. And, unfortunately, it is not due to India but due to Nepali political leadership's choice to avoid having a dialogue with their Indian counterparts[4].

Even today, Indian civil society blames the Nepali political parties and leaders for using their Indian counterparts merely as a ladder to capture power in Kathmandu. Once they are in power, they prefer not to maintain such relations. The trend has created severe problems in respect of Nepal-India relations also, as it results in misunderstandings among the political forces, including civil society of two countries . Nepal should understand that it is the political parties which could help in consolidating the achievements of democratic struggles. They also need to understand the limitations of bureaucracy; unlike political parties and their leaders, it has nothing to do with any radical/progressive agenda. It is the institution only to run the system. Here, we Nepalese should learn from Lohia that Nepal

---

4 For details, see Uddhab Pyakurel " Some Reflections of Nepal-India Relations in the Context of Nepali Nationalism," *Think India Quarterly*, Volume 13, Number 4, October-December 2010. pp.305-318.

should be able to differentiate people-to-people relations and government-to-government relations, and should not think of using one against the other, but engage with both on the issue of deepening democracy in the country and region – the South Asia.

On Minorities and Caste-Based Discrimination

Nepal's major problem today is how to handle the issues that have been raised by minorities and socially excluded groups. Lohia's ideas on minorities and caste should be useful to Nepal today. He not only talked about the issues of religious minorities, but also strove for the cause of social equality for women. Regarding women's oppression, Lohia not only touches upon their issue of representation and participation, but also discusses about how to compensate them for the work they perform in the kitchen. He states:

> *The women's problem is undoubtedly difficult. Her slavery to the kitchen is an abomination, and the stove that smokes horribly. She must be given a reasonable time-table for food and also a chimney that spirals the smoke away. She must indeed take part in the agitations against under-feeding and unemployment*[5].

Lohia was of the view that affirmative action programs were essential to bring the excluded communities in the mainstream. However, he was aware of the various limitations of affirmative action for the emancipation of Dalits from caste-based social order. That is why he came up with a conclusion that no reform is possible unless the problem of caste is tackled. "It is certain that without first tackling this problem [caste], no reconstruction of the country is possible, not to say anything about the advent of socialism", Lohia mentions in a letter to a Sudra, in March 1953[6].

In fact, both Ambedkar and Lohia shared a common approach to dealing with caste related issues. They were both very keen to eradicate the evils of caste system so that caste-based prejudice could be eliminated and other social reform programs could be implemented systematically. On the one hand, they both were together in regard to advocating one or other model of the reservation policy. At the same time, they were convinced that such a policy, in a long-rum, would not be helpful for the depressed classes to overcome caste-based atrocities and prejudices.

---

5 Ram Manohar Lohia, *The Caste System*. Hyderabad: Navahind, 1964. p. 5.

6 Ram Manohar Lohia, *The Caste System*. Hyderabad: Navahind, 1964.

With this objective, Ambedkar published the essay titled 'Annihilation of Caste[7]', in which he defined caste similar to a monster, and said that you "turn in any direction you like, caste is the monster that crosses your path. You cannot have political reform; you cannot have economic reform; unless you kill this monster[8]".

On the other hand, Lohia repeatedly advocated a proposal to enhance the trend of inter-caste marriages. He was of the view that the government should provide jobs only to those who marry out of caste. He states:

> *On the day that marriage between Sudra and Dvija is designated as a qualification, among others, for recruitment to the administration and the armed forces and refusal to interdine as a positive disqualification, the war on caste will begin in earliest[9].*

His other proposal was *Jati-Todo* (break caste barriers) campaign, which included not wearing the sacred thread and dropping caste names. According to him, inter-caste marriages and inter-dinning would be the first and foremost step for the purpose of annihilating the caste system.
To conclude, Nepal has to first handle its disparities with comprehensive packages, and a "strong political will" to strengthen the democracy in the country. Since there are different marginalized groups with different scales of marginalities, Nepal has to come up with policies and programs to tackle all the problems on priority basis . Dalits, as the most marginalized groups, should be given priority to bring them in the mainstream by removing all hurdles. For that, Lohia's thought to introduce parallel programs such as *Jati-Todo* to annihilate the caste from the society, and affirmative action programs to bring the marginalized section in the mainstream, would be a path-breaking step for Nepal. Then only the caste-based prejudices and caste-based marginalization could be wiped out. Secondly, pro-people policies and programs such as land reform should be immediately introduced to stop frustration of people towards new but democratic regime.

---

7 "Annihilation of Caste" is the speech prepared by Ambedkar for the Annual Conference of the Jat-Pat-Todak Mandal of Lahore but not delivered owing to the cancellation of the Conference by the Reception Committee on the ground that the views expressed in the Speech – linking caste to the Hindu religious tenets and calling for their destruction if caste is to be eradicated - would be unbearable to the Conference.

8 B.R. Ambedkar, *Annihilation of Caste.* New Delhi: Critical Quest, 2007. p. 14.

9 Ram Manohar Lohia, *The Caste System.* Hyderabad: Navahind, 1964. p. 4.

Index

Party 63

O

Office of the High Commissioner
for Human Rights 235

P

Panchayat Regime (1960-1990)
155
People's Front of Nepal 69
Political Transition in Nepal v, 4,
13
Prithvi Narayan Shah 6, 144, 145,
146, 147, 156, 175
Pseudo-Democratic Period (1951-
60) 153
Pushpa Kamal Dahal 18, 25, 30,
44, 56, 120, 165, 193, 233,
245

R

Ram Bahadur Thapa 25, 44, 120,
193, 232, 273
Rana Oligarchy 5
Rana Regime, 1846-1951 149
Rastriya Janamorcha Nepal 19
Rastriya Prajatantra Party 19, 63,
90

S

Samyukta Rastriya Janaandolan
78
Seven Party Alliance 2, 5, 15, 41,
69, 162, 203, 229
Shaktikhor Cantonment 47
Sher Bahadhur Deuba 2
Small Farmers Development Pro-
gramme 115

State Restructuring Commission
5, 16, 23, 48, 163, 165, 231
Stree Shakti Sangathana 207

T

Tarai-Madhesh 10
Telangana People's Struggle 197
Terai Madhes Loktantrik Party 21,
49
Terrorist and Disruptive Activities
(Control and Punishment)
Act 66
Thematic committees 18, 19
Tiwari, Bishwa Nath. 12

U

United Communist Party of Nepal-
Maoist 41, 229
United Nations Mission in Nepal
43
United People's Front 63, 78, 108
Upreti, B.C. 12

V

Village Development Committee
115

W

Women in Armed Conflict v, 8,
197
Women in Conflict v, 7, 170

Y

Youth Communist League 24

Copyright Acknowledgements

The chapters collected in this book have appeared in similar manner or slightly different form in the following publications and the authors acknowledge the same:-

1.   Pyakurel, Uddhab Pd., "Political Transition in Nepal: An Overview," in BC Upreti and Uddhab Pd. Pyakurel (eds.) Contemporary Nepal: Reflections on Emerging Political and Social Issues and Trends, Delhi: Kalinga Publications. 2012.

2.   Adhikari, Indra, "Conflict Transformation: A Nepali Perspective," in Moonish Ahmar (ed.), Conflict Transformation and the Challanges of Peace. Karachi: University of Karachi. 2011.

3.   Adhikari, Indra, "Democracy and Problems of Democratization in Nepal," in V.A. Pai Panandiker and Rahul Tripathi (eds.), Towards Freedom in South Asia: Democratization, Peace and Regional Cooperation. New Delhi: Konark Publishers Pvt Ltd. 2008. pp.65-80.

4.   Pyakurel, Uddhab Pd., "Genesis and Growth of the Maoist Movement in Nepal," in his own book Maoist Movement in Nepal: A Sociological Perspective. New Delhi: Adroit Publishes.2007.

5.   Pyakurel, Uddhab Pd., "Changing Patterns of Nepali Ethnic Movement and Consequences," in V.R. Raghavan (ed.) Internal Conflicts: A Four State Analysis (India, Nepal, Sri Lanka, Myanmar). New Delhi: Vij Books India Pvt.Ltd. 2013.

6.   Adhikari, Indra, "Women in Conflict: The Gender Perspective in Maoist Insurgency," in Lok Raj Baral (ed.) Nepal: Facets of Maoist Insurgency. New Delhi: Adroit Publishers. 2006.

7.   Pyakurel, Uddhab Pd., "Women in Armed Conflict: Lessons to Be Learnt From Telangana People's Struggle," Contributions to Nepalese Studies, Vol. 33 (2) July, 2006. pp.237-248.

8.   Pyakurel, Uddhab Pd., "The Vision of the Jana Andolan-II for the

Future of Nepal," in B.C. Upreti (ed.), State and Democracy in Nepal. Delhi: Kalinga Publications. 2011.

9.   Adhikari, Indra and Pyakurel, Uddhab Pd., "Internal Conflict in Nepal after the Comprehensive Peace Agreement (CPA)," in V.R. Raghavan (ed.) Internal Conflict in Nepal: Transnational Consequences. New Delhi: Vij Books India Pvt. Ltd. 2011.

10.   Pyakurel, Uddhab Pd., "Nepal Constituent Assembly Election 2008: An Observer's Account," Mainstream Weekly, Vol. XLVI. No 29. 2008.

11.   Pyakurel, Uddhab Pd., "Relevance of Lohia in Nepali Political Crisis Today," Janata (Remembering Lohia in the Birth Contrary Year), April 24, 2011.pp.22-25.

www.ingramcontent.com/pod-product-compliance
Lightning Source LLC
Chambersburg PA
CBHW051735250726
48659CB00001B/69